A GLIMMERING IN DARKNESS

A collection from the principal records in the "archives" of
Graham Balcombe on the events leading to the foundation of

THE CAVE DIVING GROUP

and notebook records of the early "ops." in which he took part.

Edited by Duncan Price & Dave Irwin

Published by The Cave Diving Group

www.cavedivinggroup.org.uk

ISBN 978-0-901031-03-7 (HB)
ISBN 978-0-901031-09-9 (SB)

Titled in appreciation of Martyn Farr's history of cave diving; "The Darkness Beckons"

Quantities are shown in the units of the day, generally imperial but occasionally metric.

Font cover photograph: Operation Buxton's Choice, 1 October 1955, with the divers John Buxton, Graham Balcombe, Oliver Wells and Luke Devenish. Controller, Dan Hassell is between Buxton and Balcombe. Audrey Buxton and Cybil Bowden-Lyle are keeping the divers' logs (Phil Davies).

Rear cover photograph: Graham Balcombe at the Historical Diving Society conference, Whitstable, 30 May 1998, with the "bicycle respirator" used in Swildon's Hole during 1934-36 (Clive Gardener).

Contents

Contents

Preface

Graham Balcombe arguably "invented" cave diving in Britain.   Balcombe and his friends – most notably Jack Sheppard – were keen cave explorers who adopted diving as a means of finding new territory.   At the time, there were no training courses, no manuals, nor even readily available equipment. These they had to devise for themselves - a happy tradition that persists amongst the Cave Diving Group today.

Francis Graham Balcombe was born on 8th March 1907 in Manchester, later moving to Southport. Scouting activities took him to the Lake District whereupon he developed an interest in rock climbing. A job with the Radio Branch of the Post Office Engineering Department brought him into contact with John Arthur 'Jack' Sheppard, two years his junior. Balcombe introduced Sheppard to climbing and the pair soon found themselves at the sharp end of the sport. A chance encounter with a group of cavers diverted their attention to the underworld and, when the pair were transferred to work on the Portishead radio station near to Bristol - the scene was set for events told in this book.

Balcombe's retirement from active cave diving in 1957 did not diminish his interest in the activity and he remained an inspiration to younger generations of cave divers - contributing materially to their activities by the gift of battery powered drill for use beyond Far Sump in Peak Cavern. Eczema on his legs led to the adoption of the inimitable Balcombe kilt. Balcombe survived his wife, Mavis (née Dickenson, they were married in 1941) and after her death cared for his sister until she died. In later life he re-established contact with a former fiancée, Ann Turner, and the two became engaged again.   After a spell in care, he returned home to help clear out his belongings but was taken ill and rushed into hospital where he died, aged 93 on 19th March 2000[1].

Jack Sheppard's contribution to the genesis of cave diving is often overlooked. University studies and overseas service in the Royal Signals during World War 2 limited his involvement, but Sheppard was instrumental making contact with Sir Robert Davis to understand diving theory and arranging the equipment for the early Wookey Hole dives. Sheppard survived Balcombe by 16 months, passing away on 14th July 2001[2]. His implacability made a good foil to Balcombe's doggedness and organising skills.

Balcombe originally penned his memoirs in 1987, but the manuscript received only a modest circulation at the time, acquiring an almost legendary status. In the centenary of the author's birth it is appropriate to make this document available to a wider audience. The source electronic copy of this book was kindly provided by Dave Irwin along with photographs from Balcombe's personal collection and that of the late Bob Davies which have been used to illustrate the text. The latter are reproduced with permission of the trustees of the Wells & Mendip Museum. Other photographs were kindly provided by Phil Davies, Clive Gardener and Chris Howes. The contents of this manuscript were corrected by reference to one of the few hard copy "editions" of Balcome's original text belonging to the late Bob Drake. Sadly, Dave Irwin died in March 2007 and I would like to express my sincere gratitude to him for his advice and encouragement in publishing this work.

Duncan Price

---

[1] CDG NL 136:1, Caves & Caving 88:9 / 89:28 and Descent 154:20
[2] CDG NL 141:1, Caves & Caving 91:6 and Descent 162:30

Introduction

The techniques of cave diving have grown so rapidly and the following become so widespread and important in speleology that my own early experiences have had forced upon them a significance hardly dreamt of at the time. I feel compelled therefore to collect and set them down as the original records would be likely on my demise to be consigned to the rubbish dump of history and be lost for ever.

In raking through those early records I make no pretence of achieving a best seller, merely to present what is available should any later investigator wish to use it as a quarry Quite a bit of quarrying has already been done and a good account of the early days of cave diving made by Martyn Farr in "The Darkness Beckons"[3], the intriguing title of which gives the suggestion for this collection. However, although drawn mainly from the same sources, Martyn's record is necessarily drastically abbreviated and in any case an alternative covering of the same material could well provide useful comparison as well as a detail fill-in.

I take a rather narrow definition of "cave diving": I take it as the application of diving equipment to further the aims of the cave explorer and to exclude the cave operations of those who are primarily interested in diving whether as hobby or profession. Hence the bold divers of the Fontaine de Vaucluse I exclude. Likewise the magnificent passing by Casteret of the sump of Montespan is excluded for he did not use any equipment to permit breathing underwater.

Thus, by deliberation or otherwise, this account is restricted to my own early efforts and later to those of my immediate associates in The Cave Diving Group. By

---

[3] M J Farr, "The Darkness Beckons", Diadem Books Ltd., London (1980)

deliberation, evidently, but in any case I am not qualified to write on any other aspect of the movement.

At first there was but an impoverished record: cryptic jottings of the briefest form in diaries, supplemented by the occasional article for a caving club "log" or magazine. It has always been my regret at every stage that the records and technical prowess of the earlier stages were always below what could have easily been achieved. The short-comings were partly due to lack of time and money - at times it seemed I must have been spending well over twenty-four hours a day, and my job must have suffered correspondingly, also I was perpetually hard up - but I must admit to a lack of professional approach to the problems and to an excited over-eagerness to "have a go". Be that as it may, in the event the efforts were just adequate to start the unstoppable boulder of cave diving to roll down the slopes of historical development.

Luck had its part to play. It was sheer good fortune that the first sump that lured me on, and which my companion Jack Sheppard passed in 1936, led after a short submersion to a very worthy dry part of the cave. The Cave Diving Group probably owes its particular form of birth to the great excitement of that discovery. Needless to say, it was only the particular form for, had we not founded the group, others soon would have done so, for the time was ripe or rapidly ripening; it was again a matter of chance where and in what form a Diving Group would begin, for history had already settled the "when".

From the early fumblings - I refer to my own; Sheppard's equipment was well thought out - came the next phase, the development or acquisition of improved equipment. That the acquisition aspect led to the first diving at Wookey Hole was also quite inadvertent. We flexed our muscles there; the recording was still abysmal but at least a slight improvement. That "The Log of the Wookey Hole Divers" now commands such a considerable price in the market is no recognition of intrinsic merit but of the tremendous success of those who followed in our footsteps and then broke out to do much greater things; "The Log" basks now in their glory[4].

The development of suitable cave-diving equipment - for that used at Wookey was almost the least suitable imaginable, but it was available thanks to the generous interest of Sir Robert Davis of Siebe Gorman - led gradually to much more detailed recording of, well, of everything, often to the point of being unintelligible. The notes piled up in school exercise books; forty-three of them lie on the shelf; I hope to decode them with the aid of an octogenarian's memory.

After the birth of The Cave Diving Group a distillation of these more voluminous notes, inter alia, was circulated to members and a number of cave clubs as Letters to Members so the Letters should be available for the searching. My own file is not quite complete for I must have committed the folly of lending one of the folders. Fortunately, most have been replaced, largely from my late wife May's collection; May, the self-styled President of the Anti-CDG. Happily for the CDG as it was then evolving, her protests were but token and the work continued. The records, too, continued until 1957 when my enthusiasm had almost died and better men had taken over. They have told, are telling, or will tell, the story thereafter.

Happy caving

Graham Balcombe

Graham Balcombe
(F.G. Balcombe) 13-3-87
Goffs Oak, Waltham Cross, Herts.

---

[4] Reprinted in 2009 by the Cave Diving Group

The Caves

In order of the diving records.

Swildon's Hole, National Grid Reference ST 531 513, is a swallet, or swallow-hole, in the central area of the Mendip Hills close to the village of Priddy, Wells, Somerset, and at approximately 790 feet OD. It engulfs a small stream draining the western slopes of North Hill. At the time of the early diving there the stream was thought to have its resurgence in Cheddar Gorge, but that has been shown to be incorrect; the water reappears at Wookey Hole, in the River Axe of which it is the major of several tributaries. The earliest explorations began about 1901 when H.E.Balch and his parties made their way, eventually, to the first sump which halted further progress.

Wookey Hole, ST 532 480, collects the drainage from the south-western slopes of The Mendips just north of Wells; it is an open cave of debouchre and was occupied as a dwelling from the Early iron Age until the end of the Roman Occupation. Access to its first five chambers was possible until about 1850 when a dam was constructed at the resurgence. The subsequent water level prevented access to the Fourth and Fifth Chambers, but a tunnel has since been driven from the Third Chamber to give visitors access to some of the inner chambers including the Ninth, discovered by divers.

Keld Head, SD 696 766, is a major rising, the debouchre of much of the drainage of the fells around Kingsdale above Ingleton, Yorkshire. Before our diving there had been no really serious attempt to enter the upstream system. Reg Hainsworth of Ingleton had bravely attempted entry by "naked" diving after lowering the level of the beck but the attempt was doomed to failure, as we soon found and later diving has shown, since the cave continues submerged for over 6,000 ft.

Alum Pot, SD 775 756, is an open pothole on the hillside west of Selside in Ribblesdale, Yorks., giving access to a considerable stream which carried the drainage from the slopes of Park Fells and Fell Close. It was first descended in 1848 and it ends, until now at least, in a pool or sump; the water reappears at Footnaws Hole west of the River Ribble, it then flows under the river and reappears again at Turn Dub on the east bank.

Goyden Pot, SE 100 762, is a large cave-mouth in the upper Nidd valley, above Lofthouse, Yorks, it is a point of intermediate access to the river in its subterranean passage from Manchester Hole, 300 yards higher up the valley, to the Nidd Heads Risings below Lofthouse whereafter the river runs its course above ground.

Ffynnon Ddu, The Black Well, SN 848 153, in Higher Ystradgynlais, Swansea Valley, is the resurgence of a considerable stream draining the hills on the left flank of the valley. The presence of a large cave system, thought perhaps complementatry to the show-cave, Dan-yr-Ogof, on the other side of the valley, had long been suspected. Shortly after the diving team had left the scene an entry was found and there was evidence (a skeleton) that in past times the cave had been accessible though all record and recollection of it had been lost.

Llygad Llwchwr, or The Eye of Loughor, SN 669 178, near Trapp, Camarthen, and about 700 feet above sea level, is the visible source of the River Loughor; it has long been known but water prevented deep penetration and even now it resists the diver's efforts to discover "the big one".

Stoke Lane Swallet, or **Slocker**, ST 669 474, at Stoke St. Michael, Somerset. The diving record includes a general description.

Peak Cavern, SK 149 825, is the great open cave to the south of Castleton, Derbyshire. Geologically it is far older than the maze of streamways it now accommodates; it has an industrial history for the damp atmosphere and its great size made it a very suitable place for rope-making. It was the scene of the big discoveries in the early days of cave-diving with Don Caose and Bob Davies as the leaders of the exploration.

Black Keld, SD 974 710, near Kettlewell in Wharfedale, is the rising from the Mossdale Cave System, a three-mile system of difficult and very dangerous cave (it is liable to sudden flooding). The now walled-up entrance to the system is at Mossdale Scar on Conistone Moor. As a "dry" cave it was graded as the Super Severe cave of the district.

Key to Operations

DS .. Derbyshire Section; L .. London-based members; SS .. Somerset Section; SWS .. South Wales Section. (L-ops. were assisted by members from all Sections.)

ACHERON	Llygad Llwchwr, source of River Loughor	SWS
ALPHA	Rising in Ogof Ffynnon Ddu	SS
ALUM POT	Alum Pot Sump	L
AVANTI	A. Wookey Hole, Ninth to Eleventh Chambers	L
AVERNUS	Clapham Cave	DS
BETA	Buxton Water and Swine Hole, Peak Cavern	SS & DS
BLACK KELD	Black Keld, Kettlewell	DS
BUNG	B. Wookey Hole, Resurgence to First Chamber	L
BUXTON'S CHOICE	Wookey Hole, diving with O. C.Wells	DS
F	F. See Photography	
FFYNON DDU	Ffynnon Ddu debouchre (The Black Well)	L
"FIFTY" (F1-FT1)	Wookey Hole, Ninth Chamber, survey and photography	L
FLASHLIGHT	FT. Wookey hole, photography	DS
FOOTRULE	F. Wookey Hole, surveying	DS
GOYDEN POT	Goyden Pot, main River Passage tc Lower river Passage	L
INNOMINATE	I. Wookey Hole, Ninth to Eleventh Chambers	L
INTO THE LIMESTONE	ITTL. Wookey Hole, Ninth to Eleventh Chambers	L
JANUS	J. Wookey Hole, environs of Seventh Chamber	L

15

KELD HEAD	Keld Head Rising	L
LINLAY	L. Wookey Hole, line laying	L
LOOPWAY	LP. Wookey Hole, below mudslope of Ninth Chamber	L
MUCKMENT	M. Wookey Hole, The Scullery (First to Third Chambers)	L
NITRATE	N. Wookey Hole, filming	DS
PREHISTORY	Wookey Hole, First Chamber and environs	L
REARGUARD	RG. Wookey Hole, construction of platform in Sixth Chamber	L
SANDBLAST	SB. Wookey Hole, archeological work using water jet	SS
SCRATCH	Wookey Hole, Sixth and Seventh Chambers (purpose uncertain but for BBC)	L
STOCKPILE	SP. Wookey Hole, Ninth Chamber, equipping forward base	L
SWANSONG	Wookey Hole, Balcombe's last dive	DS
VERNON	Training	All

Chapter 1

Streamlets

Jack Sheppard, T. G. "Jumbo" Baker, Graham Balcombe, C. W. "Digger" Harris, Bill Offer, F. R. "Mac" Brown and Bill Tucknott, Swildon's Hole, 17 February 1934 (Frank Frost).

SWILDON'S HOLE

I was born in Manchester and spent the early formative years in that area and at Southport. All not very far from the great caving, or should I call it "pot-holing", region, but not until my twenties did I know anything about caves and caving. At Southport as a Scout, I occasionally visited The Lake District then found O.G. Jones's classic in the Library and became enthralled with rock-climbing. Schooldays ended and I timidly started to work for a living, first in Liverpool, zig-zagging to Manchester again, then south to Reading, Ascot and finally London where I spent the rest of my working days in the quite pleasant service of the Radio Branch of the Post Office Engineering Department.

One Christmas, on a climbing holiday with members of the Cooperative Holidays Association (later Tricouni) Mountaineering Club, we fell in with a small party of campers. They were members of the Northern Cavern & Fell Club and "You should try pot-holing" they said. On their invitation we did. Actually whether Jack Sheppard was with me at the time I really cannot remember; that was probably just before we struck up a climbing partnership, but no matter he certainly participated in the upshot. Jack was an office colleague, working on erecting radio masts and aerials while I had a rather more hum-drum job indoors installing the equipment. We often had a real breath of fresh air eating our packet lunch at the top of one of his tall masts and dreaming of Scafell Crag or some such. At weekends we would dash up to Yorkshire and with Cliff Downham and his lads, as tough a crowd as one could wish to meet (the "Tavern & Hell Club"!, The Northern Cavern and Fell Club), we would push this or that nasty passage, often as the victim "volunteers". Now it is one thing to be a bit scared of a venture but quite another to duck it and often, when the effort is made, the result is success and one's repute is enhanced. Next time it is "He's tough, put him in!" and it becomes a spiral. When thus sufficiently trained, our jobs happened to take us to Somerset for re-constructions at the then Portishead Radio Station and we looked for new worlds to conquer. Again I am not quite sure whether Jack was in on my first Mendip cave trips: I think he followed shortly afterwards.

Balch's book was my introduction: enthusiasm bubbled. I met Balch and was introduced to "Digger" Harris of Wells. "Digger" was a solicitor, having taken over from his father and among much else he handled the financial affairs of the Cathedral; in private he life was a volunteer fireman in the Wells Brigade and a leading caveman with especial interest for the care of aspiring novices, and, moreover, he was a delightful and exceedingly tactful person. He got me out of many a minor scrape with landowners and the like and ably shielded us from the unwelcome attention of the press. He showed me down

Swildon's Hole among other caves and initiated me into what was known of the drainage systems from the hilltop to Cheddar and Wookey Hole in particular. Swildon's Hole at that time was thought to drain to Cheddar Gorge. By now Speleococcus sp. had got a good bite on me and eventually I came to look on the terminal pool of Swildon's Hole, terminal since 1921, as a must in any caving development. Diving was an obvious possibility but even more obvious was the need to keep any equipment down to minuscule bulk and weight and, anyhow, we had no equipment.

In my misguided enthusiasm I chose to believe the encouraging stories of my acquaintances about how easy it was to breathe underwater through the common garden hose. My father had spent quite a lot on my education including elementary physics. I should have applied a little of it before rushing in. Maybe it was as well I did not, for in the event we blundered forward to eventual success whereas, had I stopped to think, the project would have floundered before it ever got under way. So it was that an old bicycle frame from a dump at Broadstairs was carved up, fitted with the minimum to permit breathing-in from a garden hose and out to water. Why Broadstairs? Well, a radio station is there, and radio stations have girded or walled in my activities for most of my life. Doubtless there were many other bicycle frames lying around the country but that one and I met and it directed much of the rest of my life. Preliminary testing was in the sink at the radio station, the more "advanced" testing in the bath at home, after improving the makeshift assembly in my bedroom-workshop. The bath was a real "advance": there was quite six or nine inches of water! Clot never took it to a river, lake or swimming pool, just barged ahead with the inevitable outcome.

The diving party was summoned up by Digger from the Wells Natural History and Archaeological Society which had a Mendip Nature Research Committee, (MNRC), - how we loved to acquire a scientific mantle in those days! - it was the active local group of cavemen in southern Mendip, and Jack was there too. The effort failed to make any advance into unknown territory, a dismal and deserved failure in that respect but it welded together a strong group of stalwart enthusiasts determined to do better next time.

The diving attempt having failed, new tactics came into play; we had gained a suspicion - little more than that - that the sump was short and shallow. I could have and should have devised means of testing the idea but instead rushed in with the hope of chipping a lump off the roof to make a through airway. The chipping tool in vogue was gelignite and the orthodox way would be to drill a shot-hole. So I collected the simple hole-making tools of the day (drilling bar and hammer), sent out a circular to the boys announcing the intent and invited co-operation but timed the trip for a week-day. I turned up at the hour, found myself alone so began a long porterage to the pool. I cannot recollect the number of trips to the bottom, probably four possibly five, and, without help to untie the packages when lowered to the bottom, the pitches presented special problems. In those days the upper pitch was quite a wet one.

The jumpering did not go well either; there was little room to swing the hammer and hours of work produced a hole a mere few inches deep. Eventually I pitched camp, if that is what it might be called, on a gravelly patch not far from the sump, ate and turned in. It was weird to waken during the "night" to the loneliness of the cave with only the ripple and murmur of the stream and occasionally voices,(so it seemed but presumably) it was only the sound of pebbles being rolled down a nearby water-chute. Next day Jack arrived and we decided to fire a small shot in the hole and to hope for the best. My ancient memory seems to be a little at fault here for the diary notes show a slightly different version, but of little importance. The shot or shots had little effect. The effort had been another failure but maybe it produced the then record for the longest-duration trip down Swildon's Hole. I suppose that was something to build on.

We certainly had no intention of abandoning the project and elected to try contact-blasting with more generous charges. Jack took over here and constructed a cane support to carry the bomb. The support could be erected against the passage roof by pulling cords; the bomb was an old oil-can stuffed full of "jelly" and electrically detonated by an alarm clock to enable us to get out of the cave, for we could not be sure what might be the consequence of firing about ten pounds of explosive. Actually, on one occasion, a side-effect was to loosen a huge block wedged up near the roof for at some time later it fell and its fragments obliterated the gravel patch where I had slept.

Again the result was less than hoped for; a few shots like this brought down big lumps of rock locally and the tidal waves washed away Balch's terminal cairn but made no real progress at water level. We returned to diving. It was Jack's turn and he constructed an elegant and amusing outfit from waterproof sheeting, totally enclosing the diver; it had a cemented-in perspex (or similar) visor and a built-in headlamp and he called it "Jimmy". It was fed by a football inflator as an air pump (remember the extreme restrictions on size and weight) and it necessitated a rigorous breathing drill on the part of the diver and regularity of pumping to suit; breathing and pumping had to be exactly synchronised. In due course the party gathered and Jack in "Jimmy" went through to the other side. He would have gone further had not some clot left a dying acetylene lamp by the pump intake (touché, I wonder?). The lamp died and we pumped the poisonous fumes to the diver who not long after began to feel the effects and had to retreat. Indeed, he had a very bad night back at the club hut. Such things pass and may be forgotten but that day, 4-10-36, will ever be remembered for the first successful sump crossing with diving equipment.

The fine passage which then greeted the explorers made hopes and expectations for the new era soar to great heights: a sump had been passed with every promise of future success. Indeed, the actual success has far surpassed our then expectations, but that was achieved by others who in due course followed on with better and better equipment. Swildon's II, as we then dubbed it, ended eventually in a second sump; it was my turn and to take it on I simply added a bottle of oxygen to the original respirator; no reducing valve, the gas was controlled, on-off in time with the breathing, by the cylinder valve. A crude and dangerous device but with it I did manage to pass the next sump only to be stopped by a third - or rather by the fortunately short length of line connecting me to the base party.

As an exploratory gain it was quite insignificant, as an experience it was one of a lifetime. It could have been a short lifetime, too, for after the exposure - and nervous tension - of the event I had a real taste of hypothermia; there was no protection against the cold water. Fortunately, I was fighting fit and recovered when back in the main cave, scared but a little wiser.

EARLY DOCUMENTS

(These have been lightly edited but only in irrelevant respects.) From the Swildon's Hole and Waldegrave Swallet file.

"FURTHER NOTES ON SWILDON'S HOLE, SOMERSET, 1934"

(No record is held of any previous notes save a reference to their loss)

Unfortunately, the report of the very earliest episode when Sheppard and I stayed below for 37 hours is not among them. ...." Balcombe to Balch, 9-9-35; nevertheless, note the uncertainty,the reference here is to a "report" not an article. The present article comes from The Northern Cavern & Fell Club Log. 1936-1937.)

"After the disappointment of the earlier attack with jumpers and gelignite hope was never really given up. A sneaking idea that something could be done still lurked in our minds eventually forming into a plan.

"There must be a way on big enough to crawl through - or almost "must be" - so if by any means we could crawl through it perhaps an obstruction would be found easier of removal than the barrier massif. Hence, after a long time toying with the idea, the risks of diving seemed to grow less and less until quite justifiable and a Heath Robinson respirator with 40' of garden hose was finally constructed and tested in the domestic bath.

"For the benefit of those who may consider rubber hose as a means of air supply for human consumption it may well be mentioned that half an hour of breathing through this foul-smelling medium is enough to turn the strongest rather green.

"The respirator itself was of very simple construction, the seat-tube of a lady's bicycle forming the principal member. This was cut down to suitable dimensions, 'raspberry' valves fitted at either end, and the curved member hacked off to take the mouth-tube. Connection to the hose-pipe, a face-strap to hold the mouthpiece in place, a nose-clip, swim-goggles, a headlight and a rope round one ankle completed the equipment - save for about as much 'guts' as the average man can summon up to his assistance.

"The ghastly noises emanating from the devilish gear have to be heard down in the bowels of the earth, in misty dim-lit surroundings, to be appreciated to full extent.

"But to the history of the job. Three attempts were made to locate the exit and when found the respirator failed to respond at the depth necessary, and it was impossible to pass through without inviting serious consequences. An attempt was then made by Jack Sheppard but, alas, the hose had been badly fixed on re-assembly and came adrift at the farthest point reached - about 20' under the rockshelf - it is thanks to his exceptional under-water experience that I am not writing these notes in the 'In Memoriam' column.

"Now two things have been learnt from this escapade; first that the respirator must be pressure-fed and second that waterproof clothing is needed as the low temperature of the water (coupled with a blood circulation impaired by the inevitable nervous apprehension) is more than ordinary mortal can stand.

"So, with a record dash for the surface of the earth to try to restore our dangerously chilled bodies to normal warmth, the second phase of the attack closed. But no: there was an aftermath. The excited tongues of visitor-members of the party wagged too rapidly and too loudly and the wily pressmen pricked up their ears and foul calumnies appeared in the Western press over which we had better draw the veil.

"The third phase opened with assault and battery. A charge of 10 lb. of gelignite was laid against the roof of the newly-found arch and fired on time-delay. At 1 a.m. a dull rumble as of distant thunder disturbed the countryside and the slumbering village shook and trembled.

"A party went down next day" i.e. later in the day "with ill-concealed excitement to view the wreckage. But there was none. Or only a flake looked a bit loose and the mud of a tidal wave was plainly evident. Jack Sheppard, the most intrepid of the advance trio, attacked the flake with a crowbar and suddenly - woof! splosh! The lights" (candles?) "went out and time stood still, or nearly so, as something that seemed like the whole roof fell down before us almost scraping our knees then drenching us with the splash.

"A deathly silence followed, no one dared to speak until, the spell broken at last, we assured each other that we were untouched and then lit up. About twenty tons of rock had peeled off the roof and now lay half-buried in the mud of the pool. Thus was our objective brought a little nearer.

"Another trip was arranged and, loaded with 30 lb. of 'jelly', we wormed our way down to the pool and planted a shot in the mud in the hope it might dislodge the supposed obstruction. Only a tidal wave resulted.

"Another and larger shot was then fixed under the archway and shot off. It was evident from previous experience that it was quite safe to stay below during the fireworks and really it seemed that more disturbance was caused at the surface than below. We even managed to keep one of the many candles alight when the shot went off though the air surged violently up and down the passage in which we were ensconced. It appeared later that this shot went off during evensong" (owing to a mis-setting of the clock) "in the village church above our heads. Rumour had it that the hassocks jumped six inches off the floor. The congregation probably thought the Day of Judgement had indeed come and afterwards, according to our information, the vicar was heard to exceed his allotted vocabulary of 'Dear me! Tut, tut!'

"But we are straying. When the fumes had suosided a little the damage was inspected. The object of our attack was untouched, solid and immovable, but the adjacent rib of rock had shed an enormous pile of blocks and had utterly changed the configuration of the final chamber.

"Alas! thus doomed to this another disappointment we retreated once more to think it over. The project was announced at the time as 'officially abandoned' but 'hope springs eternal' as the poet has said and we hope to have another look at it some time later in the year.

"Better that we leave it awhile and let the spirit of peace once more settle on Mendip, let the press reports of earthquakes in the West be forgotten and let the inhabitants replace their broken crockery before we venture forth again to the attack. ...

F.G. Balcombe 25.6.34"

REPORT

(these "Reports" were issued to Mendip Nature Research Committee and a few interested clubs).

"Swildon's Hole Further work at the pool."

Saturday, Mar. 10, 1934

Present: Baker, Sheppard, Ingram, Balcombe.

"Descended 6 p.m. approx., laid charge of 10 lb. gelignite on cane frame... [gelignite] packed in ½ gallon oil tin....Given 2 hour delay on clockwork exploder. Exit from cave approx. midnight. Charge exploded 1 a.m. Ingram reports a sound as of distant thunder and that barn (Priddy) shook unmistakably for several seconds. "

Sunday, Mar. 11 Inspection party.

Present: Harris, Baker and friend, Palmer, Duck, Bufton, Sheppard and Balcombe.

"Descent about 11 a.m. Apparent damage limited to upheaval of mud and fragments of previous shot onto the bank below the cairn, to a depth of 9" approx. and slight cracking of rock face. Preliminary work on apparently unimportant fragment brought down the whole front...

"Observations on this point are not certain; it is now thought possible that some of this rock had fallen with the charge. No more material could be brought off, even with a small shot so the remaining explosive, 3½ lb. Abelite, plus 4 oz. Gelignite, was floated under the arch on a cane raft.... This charge... had no apparent effect. (Fired by exploder at 15 min. delay.) The sound observed at a distance of approx. 300' was not appreciable but a pronounced oscillatory air-wave was observed, blowing out candles and lasting for 1 to 2 seconds.

"Exit from cave at 6 p.m. approx.

"Sunday Mar 18.

Present: Sheppard,   Stone,   Bufton,   Tucknott   and Balcombe.

"Descent at about 12 midday. Pool rodded with jointed broomsticks...A 9 lb gelignite charge was then exploded at...furthest point to which the charge could be pushed....It was observed after this shot that an almost imperceptible crack had opened along a joint on the cairn side of the rift over the edge of the pool.

"The pool commenced to rise steadily, doubtless owing to mud thrown up on the other side which will be cut away immediately the water surmounts it. If this proves to be so it would be evidence that an air-space exists within easy distance of the point of the explosion.

"An 11 lb shot was next fired on a raft...did no damage in the immediate vicinity but dropped off a mass from the joint just mentioned. It was not possible to inspect closely owing to the fumes but the mass is thought to be similar to that brought off on Mar 11/12, namely 10-20 tons, and further the contour at the far end... of the pool is probably much altered. This can be decided by the next party to descend. Both shots were felt and/or heard at the surface the second causing considerable disturbance. Exit 10 p.m. approx."

Conclusion.

"Drilling the rock to take explosives has failed owing to the extremely arduous nature of the work.   "Diving   with elementary apparatus failed to give satisfaction and further attempts are liable to be dangerous owing to...loosened rock at or beyond the arch, the effect of blasting.

"Contact explosions using large quantities have been found of little use and, moreover, the continued use...would cause serious inconvenience, if not danger, to the inhabitants of the neighbourhood.

"The project was therefore abandoned at the time but subsequent ex-perience suggests that the further attack might be profitably pursued, employing 'sledgehammer' blasting tactics by which is meant the continual firing of small shots against a particular spot after the nature of sledgehammer blows.

"Further, the risks of diving seem to be justified and after long consideration the construction of suitable equipment is in hand. It is proposed that J.A. Sheppard, who is designing and constructing the suit, should lead the next expedition.

F.G. Balcombe 21-3-34 revised 7-9-35."

Letter from Sheppard, 30 Oct 1935

"Dear Graham,

Swildon's Hole, 1935

"Diving suit is now practically complete. I spent 20 minutes in a pond at Borough Green on Sunday and am still alive. The suit is not quite according to theory as, even when deflated as far as possible, there is still too much buoyancy. Hope to make a further test next Sunday but it will probably be necessary to use weights of some sort.

"Provisional programme is as follows. Am arranging for ladders, &c., to be left in the cave on 10 Nov. (W/E with the Camping Club.) The diving trip to take place the following W/E, Sunday 17 Nov., meeting Priddy 9:00a.m. I shall spend the night at the Grange.

"Weight of gear has been kept to a minimum but a party of 9 will be required....

Cheerio, Jack"

REPORT

"Somerset, Swildon's Hole

"Since the last attempt to force a way through the barrier at the bottom of this hole J.A. Sheppard has spent much time in constructing a diving outfit suitable for the passage of this hole.

"The apparatus having been proved, it was arranged to make an attempt on Sunday the 17th Nov.

"Owing to the heavy rains the stream was considerably swollen and the 40' pitch was re-rigged in consequence. This was done by pitoning the nose on the left, about 10' out and down from the lip of the fall, and drawing the ladder over to this point whence it hung clear of the main fall. In using this rig it will be necessary to run the life-line via an auxiliary karabiner attached to one of the ladder karabiner.

"Exceptionally heavy rain fell during the night and, on visiting the hole on the Sunday, the grating was found to be impassable; the pond water was approximately a foot above it.

"On Monday, in spite of almost continuous rain and drizzle, the water was down to passable level again. A further attempt will be arranged in the new year.

F.G. Balcombe 22-11-35."

EXTRACT FROM LATER SUMMARY

"No.6 by J.A. Sheppard October 4th, 1936.

"Complete (home-constructed) diving gear and party of twelve: tunnel located at third dive and passed. Suit removed and 100' of cave explored.

"No,7 by J.A. Sheppard October 18th, 1936.

"Sump swum and rope fixed: Balcombe through on rope: 800' of cave explored: rope left in position.

ARTICLE FROM NORTHERN CAVERN & FELL CLUB LOG. 1936-1937.

SWILDON'S HOLE AGAIN

"Following the visit to Swildon's Hole II when an attempt to pass Sump II was made but proved unsuccessful the original diving respirator used at Sump I was re-conditioned and adapted for use with compressed gas supply, thus becoming a crude self-contained unit. Oxygen was used since it was readily available in the small cylinder sizes, beneficial if there were a deficiency of oxygen in the cave air, and simultaneously would relieve the distressed breathing presumed to be due to carbon dioxide and finally it could not be harmful.

"....

"Samples of air were taken at the bottom of Swildon's I and again at Duck II" (near Sump II) "by T.A.J. Braithwa te ....

"The barometric pressure at one atmosphere); here again these pressures would have no noticeable effect on lung ventilation and such effect as would exist would be beneficial. Hence we must look elsewhere for the cause of the distress experienced when below.
    "....
    "A... description of the reactions to exposure might not be amiss: 'We arrived at the bottom and my companions unpacked the bottles and took air samples while I assembled the respirator. As this task neared completion a sense of the irrevocable nature of Time began to make itself felt; two more screws to tighten up and then I was bound to start off on a voyage pregnant with possibilities and involving no small risk. As the seconds passed, snatched away one by one as if by some unseen hand, the possibilities of catastrophe rose up and called for a revision of the situation but another quieting response told me they had all been considered and dismissed as justifiable risks. Forward then, and on with the job. Right up to the moment of submersion these apprehensions fought for place. Once underwater they had gone and the sensation of cold had flown and in its place was just an absurd amusement at the oddity of the situation, one hand holding my nose for the clip proved none too good, the other working the gas valve; my feet were on a fairly hard bottom and I assisted in propelling my body by my head working against the roof. This desire to laugh proved too much with the result that the mouth-piece was blown out from between my teeth. Somewhat sobered by this experience I followed the rising roof until, behold, an air space! Taking a breath, 'just to see what it smelt like', then, refitting the mouthpiece, I found the way led on through a muddy orifice into a second air space, a really worthy chamber this time. The water was just about chest deep and, wading towards the end of it, I longed that the lifeline would run out before I got there. The wish was fulfilled so, after a few seconds gazing at this virgin dome, I dived anew, making speedy progress guided by the line, completely missing the tight section and finding a roomy corridor instead. Still there was no sense of cold but once out of the water this began to show. In a matter of a few

yards it had asserted itself to cause a strong disinclination to move and the prospect of passing the Duck" (which separated the Sump from the base party) "was scaring. With an effort I plunged through the water and at the other side started to dismantle the gear when suddenly the reaction set in in full force; my hands trembled and my arms lost their power the lights seemed to be going out and I slipped back into the water. My companions had meantime arrived and had taken over the re-packing of the apparatus. I felt I must keep moving. I started back and soon the command over consciousness returned. Higher up the cave I traversed the sandbank a dozen times on hands and knees but still that terrible depression, desiring only to lie down and go to sleep but too scared to do it. At the bend I climbed seemingly interminably up and down the steep bank, waiting for my companions to follow, but there was no sign, no sound. I went on, and in a desperate wrench plunged under the next duck to find the welcome companionship of a few dimly-burning stumps of candle. To pass the barrier to the old cave was less of an effort; the sump becomes more friendly on acquaintance, the ducks more aggressive. Back in the old cavern I paced wearily up and down the stalagmite bank below the Priddy Water but gained no relief. A vicious attack of cramp had come and passed away then I sat down, huddled over my little acetylene lamp, jealously guarding every ray of heat. The rock did not seem so cold then I remember nothing until hearing a subdued splash in the pool. My companion? Yes, but he had been there some time not aware of my presence and was busily engaged in hauling through the tackle. Had I slept or had I been unconscious? It is impossible to say now but I awoke a new man; all the chill and feeling of oppression had gone and gone was also that lack of energy; what had passed was like a dream made real only by the sinister packages and, finally, the appearance of the last man's head through the water of that evil-looking pool.

"So it is Swildon's turn to laugh again; we have battled and lost, we have reached the outer limit of endurance, it is folly to press further with present methods.....

F.G. Balcombe 11-12-36"

DIARY EXTRACTS

(Being primary documents there has been no editing save as indicated by omission dots)

"1934, January. MEMORANDA (an undated space following SUNDAY 21).

'The Swildon's Blast' 1

"hole cave limestone (Carbon) with calcite 7 hrs. 18
"
.....

"MONDAY 22 Swildon's lone descent with 60 lb. of clutter 3:30-12:00 midnight Tough work"

"TUESDAY 23 Swildon's fair night in the dry passage Chipped 18" hole at the pool and blew ½ ton off Two shots. Joined by Shepp.

"WEDNESDAY 24 Exit 11:30 to 4:00 a.m. Gear left head of the 1st pitch"

(I prefer the diary statements to the later rendering.)

"THURSDAY 25 Recovering gear. Jumbo Stone & Phyl" (Phyllis Balcombe)

Jumbo (T.G.) Baker was one of the greater guys of the Wells contingent, apart from cheering us from time to time with "Smoke gets in your eyes" he would regale us with tales of how they made processed cheese at his factory. He had an accident or became ill, went to hospital, married his nurse and lived happily ever after or until death took her. Utterly trustworthy, a splendid supporter.

My sister, Phyllis, was no mean caver and had had many exploits on Mendip; I think she was one of the first to do Swildon's without ladders. Stone I fear I cannot remember; it was a long time ago.

"February

"MONDAY 5... Broadstairs ....

"TUESDAY 6 Experiment on respirator for

"WEDNESDAY 7 Swildon attack

"SATURDAY 17 Swildon meet Shep BTY" (i.e. Burnham Radio Station)

"8:00 p.m. ..Collected blasting licence 10 lb. of Abelite & 100 dets.

"Continues in SUNDAY & MEMORANDA, MONDAY and TUESDAY spaces as a linked entry, i.e. no exact correlation of dates and entries, thus:

"SUNDAY 18 diving at Swill not 100% success but good information gathered Apparatus limited by pressure on lungs &

"MEMORANDA temperature of water. Made three short efforts & then sped to exit. Jack made an attempt

"MONDAY 19 but hose came adrift due to faulty fitting by willing but misguided assistant

"TUESDAY 20 no harm done. Exit 4 am. Kipped in hay loft. Jack exits 5 am. main party 7 am.

"March

"SATURDAY 10... Planted the charge - 10 lb. - on cane frame. Jack taken bad, returned from 40'. Left bottom approx 11:00 out approx 12. Bomb at 1 am.

"SUNDAY 11 said to have shaken Priddy Barn!! Return trip 11 am. Fumes almost imperceptible little apparent damage, 9" mud and stones (old blast debris) thrown on bank, but about 15-20 tons peeled off under crowbar – quite.

"MEMORANDA unexpected - ask Jack!! Swill big blast. Laid new bomb of 3 lb. Abelite and fired it by clock while in stalac. passage higher up. Practically no sound .

"MONDAY 12 or percussion but oscillatory air wave gave about five 'beats' putting out the candles. Unable to inspect owing to fumes. Air wave also.

"TUESDAY 13 felt in White Way. Out 6:30.... Sat:- Jack Jumbo Ingram and self.

"WEDNESDAY 14 Sun: Digger, Jumbo, Palmer, Duck, Jack, Wilf Bufton,friend of ??? and self.

"SATURDAY 17... 10 jelly from... Shepton Mallet

"SUNDAY 18... Pick's Sat. party failed to ladder for us. Descent approx. 11:30 Wilf" (Bufton) "Tucknott, Jack, Les Stone. Stone" (infra)

(Bufton, son of a Taunton telephone Engineer and companion on our earliest adventures in Somerset caves, I met through office links. We were jointly unjustly, maybe slanderously, accused of having wreaked havoc among the stalactites of Holwell Cavern on Quantock. It still rankles. Bill Tucknott was another of the MNRC greats: he also had a lorry, which later plied in the service of the hard-hat divers of Wookey which made him a "double-great".)

"MEMORANDA not well returned from 20'. Shots at 5:1 5 & 6:30 approx 9 & 11 Stone heard 5:1 5 at surface." (9 & 11 presumably means lb. of explosive.)

"MONDAY 19 ...second knocked saucer off Maine's dresser. Time not conclusively verified however ...

"TUESDAY 20 ...Reports of earth tremors. Telegraph quotes Sat. others 'weekend' apparently coincidence.

"1935, November

"SATURDAY 16 Jack Sheppard executed" - not our Jack, but the highwayman,1724!

"Swildon's. Boss at 40' awash. Stalagmite nose drilled & two pitons driven with hemp packing" (hardly a worthy substitute for the modern bolt!) "Ladder re-hung clear of water....

"1936 October

"SUNDAY 4 Swildon's Pool. Good turn-out (12 men) Fairly dry, grand trip Shep got through reports 30' pool & 100/150' extension of cave.

"MEMORANDA Harris Murrell Balcombe Sheppard Braithwaite Morley Tucknott Jumbo" (Baker) "Shepp bad, complained of C_2H_2. Out with Harris ....

"SUNDAY 18 Swildon's....Platten down at 40'. Used his gear....Sheppard 3 attempts to locate hole, rodded and found Followed through. Quite pleasant.

"MEMORANDA Next 'trap' proved to have airspace Duck and under. Repeated at second Duck. Crawl. Bend Final Sump (Sump II)

"November

"SUNDAY 1 With Shep & Harris Swill II: everybody else had important engagements. Tried to pass Sump II with broomstick - no luck."

(no rope handy, broomstick merely lengthened Digger's arm as the link with base.)

"SUNDAY 22 Swill, Shep & Bracers" (Braithwaite) "Water almost awash. Air samples at end of Swill I and by Duck II ...Reached" (infra)

(T.A.J. Braithwaite was for a long time a staunch supporter at the arduous excavations at Waldegrave Swallet; he was studying mining at University College of South Wales and Monmouthshire and he brought with him the refreshing aura of a rational thinker. There were indeed others who rendered most valuable assistance but of the more transitory nature.)

"MEMORANDA Little Bell on 1st dip at Trap II & Great Bell on 2nd trip. 40' out. Limit of endurance reached. Recovered in Swill I waiting for Shep and Bracers"

Chapter 2

Hard Hats at Wookey Hole

Penelope "Mossy" Powell and Graham Balcombe, Wookey Hole, July 1935.

With our eyes set firmly still on the scene of our recent defeats, we found events took an unexpected twist. We sought self-contained light-weight equipment for Swildon's Hole and suddenly found we were offered the loan of standard gear, with tuition to boot, for Sir Robert Davis of Siebe Gorman, the submarine and safety engineers, took interest in our adventures but I fear we completely failed to convey to him the true character of the scene of work and the difficulties of access to it.

What should we do? Clearly, if the gear did not suit the cave then we should choose a cave that suited the gear. So eyes turned to Wookey Hole. Wookey Hole Cave is the resurgence of much of the water that falls on Mendip and churns out 40 million gallons a day in flood-time; its passages are fairly spacious and there is an excellent base for operations less than a couple of hundred yards from the entrance. Our links with Balch and the excavators who had done so much for the cave in the past proved to be the golden key for access. The owner, Wing-Commander (then Captain) Hodgkinson, surely did not see the possibilities for his cave any more than we did although his lady did in one respect, admitting that no publicity could be bad publicity, however sorry one might be for any unfortunate divers. So we moved in, on sufferance we felt, and on the strict condition of good behaviour, which condition, we being what we were, inevitably would sometimes be honoured in the breach.

This was still the period of scanty recording but gradually there came changes. First there was the need for training, Siebe's strict condition, and their diving instructor, Charlie Burwood, arrived, soon after the ton (more or less) of gear, to teach us in the nearest safe open water, Mineries Pond on the uplands near Priddy. He was a delightful character, steeped in the traditions of the naval diver. The first essential was a massive wooden diving stage from which to operate and every dive had to be recorded in detail on a logsheet. Each one of the team of six was dipped and logged until reasonably proficient whereon the party moved on to the Cave. Getting the stage and the pump in particular to the diving base in the Third Chamber was a process of the greatest exacerbation and physical exhaustion then, on top of that, the ballast as foundation for the stage had to be brought in from outside; although there were hundreds of tons of the stuff under our feet, nothing would be permitted which disturbed the sanctity of that inner chamber.

At last diving began. Initially six divers were put in one by one into the exciting green water in the region already explored in years gone by, by lowering the water level to get access for a boat. It was soon clear that sharing the diving among the six was quite impractical in time expenditure alone and the number of divers was reduced to two. Choice was difficult; the lot of one diver fairly naturally fell to me and by general agreement impartiality would best be served if the second diver should be the one woman of the party. She, 'Mossy' Powell ex-employee of Gough's Cave (Cheddar), an archeological excavavator on Mendip, tea-planter's ex-wife, a courageous and tough caver, acquitted herself well indeed despite the handicap of a diving-dress designed for near-giants.

The story of our successes and setbacks was later written up and given a limited circulation, 'made to order', typed, cyclostyled, stitched and glued in the back-room but blocked and covered commercially. The rather high price it now fetches is far more the recognition of the vast development in cave-diving which Wookey Hole and its parallel adventure in Swildon's Hole triggered off than of any intrinsic merit.

Hitherto what little diving we had done was aimed solely at getting to dry land beyond the sump but here the scene changed radically; the sump was huge and to cavers' eyes exceptionally beautiful so there arose a different attitude; diving for diving's sake became a reality and finding dry land at the end would be perhaps just an exciting climax to a dive. The water was occasionally entrancingly clear and green until disturbed so a leading diver would enter an entirely new world, intimidating yet enthralling. Progress was very, very slow and in those days our activities interfered both with the Cave Management's prime interest in getting tourists through the cave and that of the Paper Mill which depended on the river for its supply of clean water; the situation was not improved by the strained relations between the two managements nor by my own somewhat abrasive manner, as Mossy Powell's mildly satirical and delightful story of Matthew Walker recorded in The Log. Access was limited and finally withdrawn. Asssuredly no-one foresaw how the cave and mill would eventually come under common ownership, 'The Cave of the Witch' become 'The Cave of the Divers' and the occasional sight of the divers would be an added attraction for the visitors.

THE LOG OF THE WOOKEY HOLE DIVERS

The following extracts are mainly the work of Mossy, (Penelope, or P.M., Powell). They tell pleasingly the general story of the undertaking: the sketches, logsheets and other items interspersed between Mossy's records, will be of little interest now but, if reference needs to be made, there should be no insuperable difficulty in getting access to the original work.

"THE WOOKEY HOLE EXPLORATION EXPEDITION"

(Such were our hopes at the time but not to materialise.)

"The work of the 1935 Expedition has been brought to a close. The possibility of exploration at Wookey Hole has for a long time been evident but work elsewhere, lack of experience and a certain diffidence about working in a commercially-operated cavern have all contributed to defer until 1934 the decision to start an expedition. By a magnificent offer from Sir Robert H. Davis, Managing Director of Siebe Gorman & Co.,Ltd.,submarine and safety engineers of world-wide repute, the major obstacle, that of equipment, was removed from the path.

"By late June this present year our equipment was ready and diving lessons began. Here again we are indebted to Sir Robert Davis for we had his firm's technical representative, Mr C.H.Burwood, to give us our instruction. Burwood is past-master in diving and the allied arts and his diving, anti-gas and anti-smoke proselytes number thousands.

"It was some weeks before we essayed the first dip in the grim surroundings of the River Axe. Diving is no easy art to acquire and it is only now, on concluding this year's work, that we begin to feel really capable and masters of our job. Our technique for progress under the unusual diving conditions has been almost perfected and our mentalities properly modelled to the new surroundings: we are ready now to challenge the unknown.

"Our first dip in The Axe on July 13th was not expected to produce any exploratory results, only to give us some idea of the conditions awaiting us, but since then until September 1st every week-end has been spent in the serious work of fixing underwater plant, pushing forward into the unknown, examining every possible outlet and inlet, mapping and recording.

"From week-end to week-end the magnitude of the undertaking has been further pressed home to us but so far we have been able to rise to the occasion and find the solution to the problem.

"The first trip up the bed of the River Axe is a revelation of the beauties of this underwater world. It is almost impossible to describe the feelings as, leaving the surface and the dazzling glare of the powerful lights and slipping down from the enveloping brown atmosphere, one suddenly enters an utterly different world, a world of green, where the waters are clear as crystal.

"Imagine now a green jelly where even the shadows cast by the pale green boulders are of the same hue only deeper; as one advances light green mud rises knee-high and falls in deady silence softly and gently into the profound greenness behind. So still, so silent, the floor unmarked by the foot of man since the river was brought into being, awe-inspiring, though not terrifying, it is like being in some mighty and invisible Presence whose only indication is this saturating greenness.

"Travelling along a gully about twelve feet deep, against a rock wall on the farther side of the river, passing beneath the archway into the fourth chamber, we see the rock above appears to be a warm pinkish brown while every depression in its surface contains a silver bubble created by the slowly escaping air. The archway passed, we enter the Fourth Chamber. Overhead the surface of the water is moving away with the rising air and a myriad silver flakes dance with it.

"Here the floor becomes steeper and slopes down to the right. In front is a climbable bank of sand reaching to the surface where it is suddenly cut across by a line of inky blackness. Over the descent, pale and mighty, looms a huge projection of rock like the opened lid of some great mysterious casket hiding in its interior secrets too deep for human eyes to see.

"Ahead is an interminable green distance, becoming more and more intense as it increases, broken occasionally by some ghostly shape as the boulders insinuate themselves into the channel.

"Turning round and facing the archway whence we came we see the water is lit up with a fairy-like sunshine, the attenuated rays of the immensely powerful lamps on shore, and, on the floor, a series of great footprints ever changing shape with the current of the river until, as if dissolving, they become round dimples in the mud and then gently, oh! so gently, they disappear.

"Four pulls on the lifeline, the signal to come up, and the diver leaves those majestic depths to be unceremoniously hauled ashore by a couple of cut-throats who wrest his belongings from him in a very few minutes and, with his wits still in fairyland, he is sent to take his spell on the pump.

"That first was a most edifying night's work and we returned to our stronghold on the Mendips with a great feeling of exhilaration, having at last got our teeth into the job and made acquaintance with the outskirts of this great field for adventure.

"It was intended that all six divers of the party should go down, for then in our inexperience we thought that in one or two bids we would walk right through to our destination, open unsubmerged cave, or alternatively would have run out our full four hundred feet of pipes and have realised the impossibility of reaching our goal.

"Conditions soon proved the task was no child's-play and the original intention stood condemned by the time required to send down relays of relatively inexperienced men. Continuous concentration on one man and a competent assistant was obviously demanded but in a party of volumteers such discrimination is a difficult problem. The choice of No.1 Diver was easy; it was Balcombe's job, as inaugurator of the expedition; it was with No.2 that the difficulty would arise since all the divers were about equally competent.

"It was finally decided that the best way was to give the place to the woman of the party and royally has the choice been justified. Cool, collected, showing no fear, she has carried out her every task with an assurance that none could better. There is only one criticism which can be levelled at the choice; much time has been lost owing to her physiological handicap of small wrists.

"Relatively small that is. The diving suit was made to fit a seaman's wrists and stoppage of the circulation from the amount of tight packing required almost always ensued. This is a difficulty which should have been removed by the substitution of more suitable cuffs or bands and the trouble not allowed to persist. Various experiments were in fact made but up to the closing of the present work no satisfactory solution to the problem obtained. Before the opening of the next attack this will certainly have been remedied.

"The particular obstacles to progress, of which we had been warned in no uncertain terms, was a hole in the floor of the Fifth Chamber whence Glencot Spring a little farther down the valley was suspected to draw its water and which, owing to the volume flowing, would present a danger indeed, and a second consideration that the river had been said to rise up into the same Fifth Chamber (the farthest point previously reached) with such force as to rock a boat."

(The boat-rocking could well be so in high-flow conditions; although we found no sink to Glencott, Balch's judgment was to be vindicated later by the discovery of just such a sink in the Ninth Chamber.)

"The point of exit for Glencot Spring has not yet been met," (in 1935 that was) "wherever the spring has its source, it is not in the Fifth Chamber and the hole in the floor is now buried by a long sandbank presumably silted up in the last thirty years, that is since the original observations were made; the water from the presumed, but certainly not legendary, Sixth Chamber flowed up so slowly that the drift of the disturbed sediment could scarcely be detected.

"This was encouraging although a faster current would be of tremendous assistance to the divers for the greatest handicap is the persistence of disturbed sediment. The onward march progressed with unsuppressed excitement. Deep down under the overhanging wall, at the far end of the Fifth Chamber, and a full twenty feet below the surface, a narrow squeeze was discovered which seemed to lead up beyond into a further chamber.

"Wyndham Harris was the first man through this tight hole and returned to tell of his discovery, of a great water-filled space similar in appearance to the underwater portion of the Third Chamber in which we have our diving base. Later another way through was found, to the left of the tight part of the entrance, which gave comfortable access to the cave beyond. A surface was discovered; here indeed was the Sixth Chamber, the first milestone in our progress.

"Meanwhile, as there was some doubt about our point of exit from the Fifth Chamber, a boating party was arranged and, with the water lowered to its minimum by means of the mill sluice-gates below the cave mouth, the leaking boat was propelled under the two low arches into the far chamber and behold! there was the guiding shot-rope streaming away in the jade-green water below, down under the overhang in the south-east corner, away into the green infinity!

"This shot-rope is the diver's best friend; anchored firmly at the diving base and, at intervals along its length, to heavy concrete and iron weights it serves both a means of progress and a guide when the water has been disturbed by his passage.

"The task of the first man is difficult and arduous for he has to carry the shot-weights, over half a hundredweight each, and drag along the rope, besides having to haul his own air hose and telephone cable behind him. Under these conditions the ascent of a steep bank taxes his ability to the uttermost. Indeed, one problematic pitch at first seemed unsurmountable. Across the entrance to the Sixth Chamber, a yard or so from The Squeeze, lay a huge fallen block many yards in extent, half buried in the sandy floor and blocking the path ahead; the top of the block was smooth and slippery with fine silt.

"Three times the diver lost his hold and fell back into the pit at its foot. The next effort was crowned with success; his cragsman's training stood him in good stead, even in those clumsy lead-soled boots, and a hand grasped the incut back of the rock and the task was accomplished. A weight was attached to the shot-rope and dropped over the back of the block and now its ascent and descent is a mere bagatelle.

"All these efforts after the first were in total darkness for lights are unavailing once the diver's passage has sent up those beautiful, yet fatally handicapping, clouds of that red and white silt which covers floors and ledges and clings thinly to the walls and roof; it is better to save the batteries than to clamour for a useless but undeniably comforting glow.

"Forward is the order and forward they go, through the Sixth Chamber to a point where the low roof shoots suddenly upwards and the diver's discharged air can be seen sending out great radiating waves which lose themselves in the darkness beyond. Yet another chamber, the Seventh, and this time of great magnitude. Excitement runs high as the components of a floating shot-rope are dragged through from the base and assembled.

"The need for this device will be evident when it is remembered that, although a diver can float himself up to the surface and then sink again, he has little or no control over this manoeuvre. Imagine our diver, rushing up to the surface, out of control, the air in his suit expanding faster than he can get rid of it, shooting out of the water like a porpoise with a spike or solid roof an inch or two above waiting to greet him! Not a pleasant meeting.

"Or again imagine the diver sinking out of control and call to mind that a fall from the surface to a depth of some 30 feet or so is sufficient to kill him, or at least he will be the victim of severe internal injuries from the sqeeze to which he is subjected. The depth at this point is some twenty feet and a yard or so away yawns a pit of unknown depth waiting like a death-trap to catch the unwary.

"Therefore a rope to control the speed of ascent and descent is needed. The device used here is probably unique in the annals of diving history," (!) "and consists in its elements of a float attached to which is a rope with an anchor at the lower end. In practice two oil drums were used, filled with air from the diver's helmet, connected by an iron bar, and with a thick Y-spliced tail rope tied down to two heavy weights. The diver ascends as slowly, or fast, as he pleases, rises between the drums and there leans across the bar to view the surface."

(Little wonder if it really were unique; the inflation technique was thoroughly corny. Think it out; in a different situation the outcome could be quite hilarious.)

"The point had been reached where the diver could no longer pull his trailing ropes and pipe and the assistance of the second diver to help him do this was found essential. Here, at the point where the roof rises so steeply, was found a flake of parent rock handily offering its security as a tie-on point. In optimism it was christened Belay 1 and here Diver No.2 was belayed with a loop of rope and a karabiner, that handy device used by mountaineers abroad and probably having for ancestor the little spring hook on the dog's leash, and from here No.2 sees to it that the pioneer has no more trouble.

"Tense with anticipation, the divers went aloft in turn, the first ever to set eyes upon this vast and gloomy recess of Pluto's Kingdom.

"Well may they have risen in the River Styx itself and be looking towards the gloom of Hades. Above, the vertical walls shot upwards towards the surface of the hills and the feeble lights were unable to penetrate their immense height; away upstream they ran, still parallel, till swallowed in the darkness. No more than a stone's throw could be discerned, though this makes it the greatest chamber yet, and within this compass the red-brown walls revealed no beauty of draping stalagmite; they are too steep, no drip of water from the roof would ever strike them; just at one spot is a patch of this white substance, dribbled over a ledge where perhaps a stream once flowed.

"It is a world detached where, were it not for the steady hahrrh hahrrh of the pump and the occasional call on the telephone, which keep the lone pilgrim tethered to the real world now far behind, the spirit would wish to obey the command and slip quietly out and over the still river into the darkness where Charon would await to speed its journey into the land of the lost.

"Thus, in a series of seven efforts, extending over a period of more than two months of week-end work, this point has been reached, some 170 feet from the base and with a great chamber overhead.

"This is but the threshold of the realms which will now be accessible to us: the work has been stopped for the moment but 1936 should see another expedition launched, this time knowing what has to be faced and prepared for it in consequence. In comparison the 1935 Expedition will be classed as little more than a preliminary investigation to learn what might be expected.

"The River Axe is the source of drinking water for part of Wookey Hole village as well as being the supply to the old-established paper mill in the valley below the cave mouth. The operations cannot, therefore, be over-welcome to these parties. The repeated disturbances cannot be allowed to continue; greatly indeed do we appreciate the tolerance on the part of the water-users which has permitted work in the river each weekend for over two months. Next time arrangements must be made to overcome this difficulty.

"... [This done,]... greater progress is expected. The divers will be experienced and competent in this unusual type of work; every forethought will be concentrated on having available at a moment's notice all equipment likely to be needed. A sectioned raft will be built, ready to be taken through and assembled underwater where required, and with it a searchlight and universal camera for both under- and above-water photography.

"The size of the party necessary will be reduced considerably by introducing a motor-driven pump. This is an important factor with a volunteer party; it is very difficult to find a couple of dozen enthusiasts who are in a position to spend night after night at the arduous tasks of the diving base.

"On reaching that part of the cave where the floor again rises above water the type of diving equipment must be changed. Having proved by exploration with a pipe-fed suit that the passage can safely be made without great delay, self-contained apparatus must be employed and on reaching the far bank the amphibian divers will crawl out of the water, like some lesser saurians of ancient days, to continue the exploration upwards towards the source of The Axe. Maybe they will be cut off from the world for days at a time, examining, measuring, sketching and photographing.

"This then is the ambition; its successful execution is a mighty task, in which many factors play their part. We, the divers, feel confident that we can carry it through but finance will present one of the most serious problems. ....

"Preparations are already well in hand and the zero hour creeps slowly on. The day when we next venture into the green and chilly waters of the Axe is awaited with unsuppressible keenness.

"What will it reveal of the hidden wonders in the Great Cave of Wookey Hole? This mighty cavern, which throughout history has drawn men from all parts of the world to view its present-known magnificent vaults and chambers and has been the dread of many as the home of old Pen-Palach, the Witch of Wookey, is about to reveal some more secrets which would otherwise lie hidden until countless ages hence when cracking frosts and ceaseless dripping of water will have laid open the cave as a yawning gorge giving access for the casual glance of a race of future creatures.

"Or will the Witch of Wookey, whose spirit still seems to haunt the cave, decree otherwise?

F.G.Balcombe & P.M.Powell, 16-9-35"

"Digger" Harris, Graham Balcombe, Charles Burwood and Penelope Powell, Mineries, 7/8 July (Frank Frost).

"FIRST DIPS

"It is closed season at Waldegrave Swallet as The Gang has temporarily abandoned its frantic effort to reach Australia via that tantalising and sweat-making shaft.

"On the arrival of two large chests and one doughty diving instructor from Siebe Gorman it downed tools and trekked a little farther across Mendip and is now found to be playing havoc with the nervous systems of thousands of helpless tadpoles which up to now have dwelt in peace in Mineries Pool. There is of course a more serious objective in view and later it will be interesting to observe the reactions of Witches and other denizens of the Secret City of Wookey Hole!

"So far, Mineries Pool is the only spot where the gang is able to keep its activities fairly private and where there is sufficient water in which to learn the gentle art of diving; and, believe me, there is more to it than meets the eye!

"The first week-end gave us a magnificent start; a stage was completed and in place by ten-thirty on the Saturday and medical certificates were duly inspected. Under the excellent tuition of that great lad, Burwood, we were all able to take our first dip (as he so lightly put it!) and become more or less familiar with the art of dressing a diver and, moreover, to experience the extraordinary sensation of sitting at the bottom of the diving ladder blowing bubbles.

"Rumour hath it that one member had two certificates, one to prove him fit to dive the other to prove him too ill to work. 'Nuff said!

"The heat of the sun made the diver's lot a hot one indeed; clad in thick woollen sweater, stockings and cap, with the sweat running down his face, patiently sitting on an upturned box while his assistant, assistant's assistant and assistant's assistant's assistant fumbled about with their nuts and fittings and gradually bowed him down with 180 lb of brass and lead accoutrements! It was a relief to feel the rush of cool, if somewhat effluvian, air (we discovered later that all feet should be kept clear of the air intake!) rushing into the helmet as the pump started, dispelling immediately the sensation of being trapped as the helmet was screwed down.

"The walk round the stage was a bit of a trial but once the weights were on, bull's eye in place, and helmet duly tapped upon the dome, there was no further hope of salvation and with one last despairing look at The Beaming Burwood the diver slid down the shot-rope, every hair stiffened with anticipation.

"But we loved it! Once the raspberry machine by your ear was adjusted to satisfaction, with the cool murkiness of the water was coupled a feeling of absolute security. In fact, after the first few minutes of awful suspense, it became quite evident that life below Mineries Pond is 'just the mossy'.

"Sunday morning dawned fine and bright and we had been at practice some time before Burwood arrived from Bristol for the gang had camped on the spot of course.

"The diving order was as follows: Balcombe, Harris, Powell, Frost, Bufton and Tucknott. The latter, by the way, was unable to turn up on the Saturday so took his first dip on the Sunday for all first dips had to be made under the direct supervision of the Instructor.

"We spent a most profitable day and, sunburnt to the bone, weary but contented, we loaded up the lorry to disband, another milestone of our life's journey set behind us.

Mossy, 1-8-35"

"AT PRACTICE Week-end 6/7 July

"Again the Hand of the Lord was with us; the day was fine and bright and a lot cooler than the previous week. Tents were pitched and, many hands making light work, the stage was soon in position at the water's edge in readiness for the 'morrow.

"Ten o'clock found us preparing to send the first man down. With this heaven-sent coolness even the dressing was a pleasure so that soon Mendip was alive with ecstatic divers leaping and skipping down the sunny slopes to the pool. Even the Martyrs at the Pump were heard to change their long-continued blasphemy for something lighter and more spring-like; the man on the lifeline stayed at his post to enjoy the breeze instead of the usual practice of tying the unfortunate diver to some convenient post and returning to camp for a pull at the cider bottle.

"The tadpoles had tired of their gloomy black skins and had gone away to change into frogs so even that wriggling impediment had been removed.

"We all found that we had gained a lot of confidence but Saturday night showed us that three divers in the nude were even more at home in the water than we (especially when they found to their dismay that their towels had vanished!).

"We each got our half hour in comfortably and came up showing no signs of distress whatever; the constant changing of the water in the pump had a lot to do with this as there was now a nice cool flow of air; in fact so cool that Mossy, getting an extra fierce blast, thought that the bull's-eye must have come off! A first impression Mossy would get; she is like that. A frightful moment for all that!

"We all came bubbling and beaming to the surface with little souvenirs of the trip. The worst thing about our practice pond is the mud we have to contend with. Our seventeen-pound boots sink into it with merciless regularity and it makes the going extremely arduous also it gets so churned up that all chance of seeing where we are going is completely lost.

"In spite of these difficulties Graham managed to travel out some 26 feet and to return with some souvenirs which he laid upon the feet of his attendant. Then he proceeded out across the pond for 45 feet to the full extent of the life-line and amused us with various aquatic antics including an attempt to squirt his attendant via the spit-cock. In fact, he became such a trial that it was decided to cut off his air supply for ten minutes or so but, as his full hour was nearly spent, we agreed to bear with him until the alarm went.

"He emerged as fresh as paint, leapt lightly onto the dressing box, and was soon dismantled and into the thick of packing up.

"No-one else has done the full hour as time invariably presses on these occasions and dressing and undressing plus the time below is a long act of many scenes. Also it is a long job packing up the gear at the end of the day. A few hours will be saved next week-end as Mossy, in the teeth of fierce competition from all parts of the globe, has, with her pocket watchdog Ting, succeeded in obtaining full-time custody of the whole paraphernalia.

"So far Balcombe and Bufton are the stars. The arrival of a Diving Manual for each member of the gang caused great delight and next week-end should show definite improvement.

Mossy 2-8-35"

"GENTLEMEN, THE WITCH!

"Saturday, the 13th, found the gang making ready to pay a visit to the Witch. With their usual nonchalance they managed to arrive three hours late but what odds to people who calculate by millions of years and to whom the period between the cretaceous and the jurassic is but the turning of a page!

"As a matter of fact, it took those extra few minutes to load up the ever-obliging lorry with Mossy's bags of 'corn-plaster' from Waldegrave" (sorry, I was not in on that one, but it refers to the sacks of ballast she had filled to make a base for the diving stage) "and weren't the trippers disappointed to learn that it was 'dump'" (spoil from the excavation near the pond) "and not bodies which lay so heavily on the stretcher used for transport!

"Darkness fell as the Paramount Cave of Mendip hove in sight and, after much anxiety and waiting, the Gallant Captain steamed into view, not in too good a humour, as becomes one who has let all the water out of his cave and then had to let it all in again!

"Three eager wheelbarrows were commandeered from the paper-mill and agonies of sweat were the order of the night. Did those bags get heavier and did they multiply? I reckon! How we staggered and groaned but how willingly we slaved and again how willingly we rifled the guides' bottles of sweets to ease our parched innards. Alas! They had taken their milk home with them!

"Bag after bag was laid beside its fellows in the inky blackness of the cave floor, inky indeed until someone, siezed with an experimental recklessness born of desperation, switched the light on .... the skies fell not neither did an alcoholic conscript although ready he was and about due for an unpremeditated fall down the precipice and would have done so had we continued to study economy!

"Now this cave and its surroundings is, as the posters have it, Unparalleled in England and of all the Caves of Mendip, Paramount; so it must be kept clean at all costs and so with mop and broom, like the seven Maids in the Walrus and the Carpenter we went along the paths and most carefully wiped up any spots of sweat or grease and brushed away all the crumbs of alien soil that fell from our feet and, incidentally, any odd half hundredweights that sploshed out of the bags in transport.

"Then as pilgrims of old, bearing caskets of treasure to the Witch, we proceeded through the cave with that apparatus of resource, the stretcher, coming to the fore again. Three men in front and three behind was the obvious way to tackle the burden, the four outside men falling away in the narrow places then darting back immediately the passage was wide enough to let them take hold again. The whole squad, attired, of course, in their usual Saville Row suitings, striding along, every muscle taut and their shoulders squared, made the picture of physical fitness and cheery determination which we in the gang describe in the one short word 'Tuff.'

"The burdens were dumped on a little causeway in the third chamber and as each was dumped a grin of relief went round then, pausing only to hitch up their falling slacks, they 'bout turned and begorrah! they were gone to fetch another one!

"At last sufficient bags had been deposited on the causeway and a foundation-building party was held on the mud to the tune of 'Smoke gets in your eyes' so soulfully rendered by Jumbo Baker that even the Witch was seen to wince a little!

"The sweeping and mopping was finished to the last degree of purity and the debris pushed down a rat-hole just as the clocks struck four and dawn began to tinge the sky. Sagging at the knees, glazed of eye and feeble of gait, we made off to our various destinations, the Wells contingent to their orderly beds (tho' ask not what happened when wives saw sheets later in the day!), the Mendippers to their stronghold on the weald to proceed with the night's poaching, gutting and ham-stringing, before the well-earned repose in some grassy hollow, tucked away in the bosom of that old rascal Mother Mendip."

(What a wasted effort: we immediately discovered that Naval practice was quite unsuited to our purpose and, no sooner had old Charlie disappeared, we abandoned the crazy diving stage.)

"By Sunday lunchtime most of the gang had recovered sufficiently to arise and stagger drunkenly to the tadpole-infested water to lave themselves into some degree of wakefulness then, after lowering a colossal meal, proceeded to arrange the diving gear at the water's edge. The effects of the previous night's effort soon wore off and the diving stage was promised a nice weekend on sandbags at Wookey Hole.

"The wife problem is beginning to look very black indeed but by hitting on the magnificent idea of bringing the wives along too, decanting them at a reasonable distance from operations, two more members of the gang were able to put in an appearance just about tea time and so get in their usual Sunday dips. There were no incidents of any great interest; the signals were still on the weak side, oh! those signals! swot them as you may and as full of confidence as you may leave the surface, the moment you touch bottom all recollections of them seem to fly out of your head with the air bubbles! In fact as you wrack your muddled mind and, while in the throes receive the simple "O.K.?" signal from your attendant, you become so desperate you could almost cut through your life-line to frustrate the blighter!

"Again, how the feverish attendant prays 'I hope the mutt is alright', or 'I hope he won't remember a signal or try out anything rough on me', 'I wish he'd be quick and come up before he thinks of something', 'I wish he'd jolly well drown himself', etc. until it is obvious that the time has come for a series of signal classes.

Mossy"

"JADE GREEN WATER

"Once again Saturday evening. Great loadings of lorry, this time with the diving gear and the famous stage in sections on the floor. And so awa' to Wookey Hole.

"There was a feeling of suppressed excitement for were we not on the threshold of a real adventure?

"The sweat of hard labour, however, soon calmed everyone down to normal as item by item the whole outfit was hauled out of the lorry and carried into the cave. The gang will dream about Pump for many days to come, I reckon!

"Two of the more wife-bitten members knocked off at ten o'clock and left a diving team of four, namely, Balcombe, Powell, Frost and Perry. Fortunately, F.R.Brown of The Caves was on late duty and jumped into the breach right nobly sparing neither breath nor perspiration the whole night and to him we send a hearty vote of thanks for without him it would have been impossible to carry on.

"After some investigations it was found possible to dispense with the stage, which would save hours of hard labour, and accordingly the pump was mounted on the causeway," (at this stage the pump used was a 'lightweight' lever type; the really big brute came later.) "bolting it down to two long planks so that it could not rock, and by carrying the air pipe and lifeline across to the other end of the chamber the diver had a place to dress upon a low stone wall.

"The iron ladder was lowered from the latter point and lashed to pitons driven between the stones of the floor while, nearby, all the odds and ends were kept together on the stretcher. As Graham tapped those pitons home there was a far-away look in his eyes... was it Central Buttress straight up from Lords Rake?

"When everything was ready we had a quick meal of bread and cheese and tea. When we had finished we felt considerably better and Balcombe, donning his diving costume, was the first man to walk into The Beyond.

"He had some difficulty negotiating the ladder but once he touched bottom he was away as fast as his attendant, Powell, could travel across the mud with the air pipe and the lifeline; at the pump the lines were coiled down and operations carried on from that point as it allowed the diver a considerable amount more latitude.

"As he passed under the archway into the fourth chamber his bubbles ceased to be apparent but for a moment or two occasional flashes of his torch told us he was not far away then they too ceased to show. Signals were difficult to get through and it is quite obvious that a telephone is an immediate necessity. He carried the shot-rope with him to its fullest extent and after half an hour returned by the same route.

"His progress up the rocks, which he considered less difficult to negotiate than the awkwardly lying ladder, was an exhibition of skill and endurance not often seen and, in the intense gloom of the echoing brown cavern with its illuminated jade-green water scintillating behind, it made a truly weird picture as this awesome monster came blundering up over the slippery brown rocks. In fact a diaphanously clad spectator was so enthralled with the sight that she stood glued to the ground and clutched her skirts so frequently in her excitement that by the time he drew alongside they were well above the waistline... it was noticed on removing the diver's helmet that he had broken into a violent perspiration; was it all his woollens?

"The next diver down was Powell whose dressing was interupted by an amusing entr'acte in the far end of the chamber when a member of the party fell overboard with a resounding splash!

"Powell had a good trip below though the wrists of the suit sprang a leak and a return trip had to be made and readjustments done during which time the back weight managed to get trapped in the ladder and caused some amusement before the victim got free. Powell was not amused.

"The experiment of hauling the diver up the mudbank below the pump was tried on the return journey and proved so successful that the next man, Frost, both departed and returned that way and it has been agreed to operate from there in future.

"It was perhaps fortunate that our tether prevented further progress; from the end of the fourth chamber the way on looked ominous in the extreme; a huge black wedge-shaped rock with no apparent support hung across the path and the floor dipped rapidly downwards. Whether an experienced diver would feel at home in this place we know not but we are not yet sufficiently Germanised 'to do and, if possible, die also.' Our leader freely admits it was a relief to feel the ropes pull taut and happily excuse the necessity for that next dread step.

"How different the reactions at this same point when the whole chamber had been lit with fairy sunshine, a product of this blessed age, and familiarity had wiped away this fear.

"We still have the dangers of Holus Balchi to consider and are seriously entertaining the idea of using a Yo-Yo or something of that nature as a suction detector. Holus Balchi, familiar for Spelunca Balchi, is the supposed source of the water that feeds Glencot Spring and, as this debouches some 350,000 gallons a day, H.B. would be a spot to be respected.

"Thus, advancing along the river bed, merrily toying with his Yo-Yo and the said instrument being suddenly or rudely snatched from his hand, any diver of average intelligence would be led to suspect something amiss whether it be his own carelessness in letting go of the string or intentional suction on the part of Holus Balchi. Our diver's natural reaction to such an occurence would be to return immediately to the surface and report, among other things, that he'd been and gorn and lorst his little Yo-Yo thereby accidentally saving his own life. Also we avoid the contamination of Glencot Spring by divers.

"There was a small collection of sight-seers in the cave who were duly thrilled by the performance, judging by the continual tittering and facetious remarks. A newspaper reporter was there who spent the greater part of his time upside-down with his hands in the water, fully under the impression that he was a diver too - we longed to realise his ambition for him. We do not expect any unwanted publicity from that direction for, as you may have gathered, his powers of observation were dimmed by the absorption of excessive C_2H_5OH.

Mossy, 26-8-35."

"DISCOVERY

"Saturday, July 20th, and a lorry flying the colours of the House of Tucknott thundered into camp. Signal practice was willingly abandoned, the gear hurled aboard, then off again it went at such a speed that a whole Midgetful of forgotten odds and ends was forced to follow in the rear.

"Signal practice, or The Attendant's Revenge, is a great game: the victim wears helmet, corselet, breast-rope and air hose, and in some cases the bull's-eye, since no-one can spit and swear through half an inch of plate glass. He is then guided into every possible obstacle by his attendant and forced to climb, top-heavy and sweating, piles of loosely-stacked timber and tripped up on heaps of ropes and, finally, if the attendant is skilful, he can be caused to blunder into his own tent, completely wrecking that structure, and drag the remains after him all tangled up with his various 'blowpipes' as they were heard to be called on one occasion.

"The diver, in his turn, can retaliate by sending constant demands for ropes, slates, and more air; he can too, should he be cunning enough, get possession of the full length of rope and hose by dint of ringing a continuous series of 'four bells' and then, squatting out of sight behind a bush or pile of tarpaulins, with one well-timed jerk throw his tormentor to the ground.

"But to return to the night's activities. We arrived about 9-o'clock at our destination, the Third Chamber of the Home of the Witch; where the B.B.C. was in attendance with coils and coils and coils of wire everywhere, myriads of microphones, wreaths of cigar smoke, a wealth of gents' natty suitings, fortunes in cuff-links; in fact the only thing missing was adhesive tape, which Mossy provided off an Oxo tin, and a sock to put in the loud-speaker. The Western Electric were well represented by an amply-cut motoring coat containing a not so amply-cut Engineer who provided the public address system for the benefit of the general mob."

(This occasion was a trial run for a broadcast; no actual transmission was made.)

"Through the smoke one caught occasional glimpses of the ample starn-pieces of the B.B.C., more coils of wire, pipe and rope, sometimes even a diver, and, on rare occasions, the River Axe itself.

"There was trouble with the telephones at first but the experts soon settled that and after sitting fully-dresssed, barring the weights, for quite half an hour Balcombe, the man of the moment, was allowed to enter the water where the stress of that last half hour was forgotten in those serene depths.

"At short intervals he reported his progress and what he saw as one by one he lugged his colossal monuments, the concrete weights, along with him and attached them to the shot-rope, there to remain until dissolved by the etching waters.

"The loudspeaker, as has been mentioned before, had forgotten its sock and the result was terrible; one long and awful blare of voice and occasionally an intelligible word. The cave guides will have us believe the acoustical properties of this chamber are perfect; if acoustical perfection includes a ten-second echo, they are probably right!

"Signalling has been dificult for the lines catch on the rocks and it is next to impossible to get a signal through by them but the new telephone was perfect.

"It had been raining during the week and the water was not so clear as on the last occasion. After Balcombe came up Harris made a trip on which he descended to the low archway, the limit of Balcombe's forward march, and crawled through to the space beyond where he discovered a chamber of large dimensions. Still holding on to the distance line, he stood peering round in this newly-found wonder-world until the clouds of billowing sediment arose to obscure the view.

"On his return a third diver went below for the gang was still fit and, this time, myself. The divers had agreed to record their impressions separately but it is doubtlful if those lazy blighters Balcombe and Harris will ever submit theirs. Here at any rate is my story:'I did not think I was going to have a chance that night; it was getting awfully late, well after four, but the gang said they were O.K. and, in spite of the fact that the remaining woollens were being used as a bed for someone, they succeeded in dressing me in record time. 'My wrists are an awful nuisance; they are so puny I have to have rings, and rings, and rings'" (Rubber rings used as packing or as contracting bands) "'and they are not too comfortable then but, after fixing them in a new way and testing them in a bucket, everything seemed alright and I was soon slithering down into the water. That way over the mud is an absolute gift. 'The river was not so clear as the first time I went down; it was a sort of thundery brownish foggy colour, if you know what I mean, and instead of enticing you like the fairy green of the week before it kind of hated you and said 'Get out!' as if it could not tolerate a third diver that night. Anyway, I went on, wallowing in the colossal boots like a slow-motion footballer, holding on to the shot-line with one hand and flashing the torch about with the other; everywhere was this baffling fog, the rocks only came into view when the torch nearly touched them and they glowed back with a sort of reddish-brown. 'I travelled along the rocky and muddy terrace to Harris's low archway, secured the distance-line round my right wrist, and waited a few moments for the water to clear before I inserted my cumbersome bulk into that depressing little orifice. It was the first one I had navigated and I dared not lie right down and wriggle like a lobster for fear of blowing up so I proceeded very carefully, as some of the stones seemed a bit loose, on one hip and shoulder with my helmet bumping and scraping at intervals on the roof. 'Flat slabs of a sort of tufa stuff kept on falling past the bull's-eye, slabs ringed with little silver bubbles, and finally I came into the new chamber. I saw a huge boss of stalagmite on the floor and went across to it to rest; the mud I'd kicked up rose above me, curling down again round my helmet like heavy smoke clouds, and finally dispersed.' On the far side of the chamber, opposite the place by which I had come in, I could see what looked like a long dark archway, low but very tempting; unfortunately, the distance-line wasn't long enough for me to get close to it and examine it so I sat a bit longer, hitting one or two edges off the boss with the torch in true tripper style, then I rang up the shore and announced my intention of returning. 'Again that beastly squeeze but much less difficult the second time as it slopes up and you don't have the feeling that you might suddenly go up faster than you want to. The mud was very thick by this time; my hands were getting cold and the rubber rings making them numb but, once I'd let go the distance line and got a grip of the shot-rope, progress was easy despite the thick fog all round me. Suddenly I found myself pulled up tight and to take another step, however hard I tugged, was impossible. It requires a good steady pull to lug the lines along but this was no ordinary resistance; it then dawned on me that, the quintessence of bad diver-craft, I WAS NOT ON THE SHOT-ROPE AT ALL; I was gaily using my own breast-rope which had somehow become hitched up good and hearty behind me and I had doubled back on it. The telephone was just the limit; I could hear nothing they said and apparently they were deafened by my silvery voice and could get very little of what I said. It was lovely to hear the steady hahrrh-hahrrh-hahrrh of the pump and to know that, never mind how long you stayed there, or what predicament you were in, it would continue; the good old gang breathing for you! So I sat there, with a huge bank of mud looming beside me in the thick still water, waiting for it to clear a bit. After a while my hands got too numb to use my fingers and I could only do my useless best with my two wrists and one knee, lifting and gently jerking, I dared not do it too hard in case something got loose and fell on me, then waiting for the water to clear a bit to see if it had been any good. Gradually the air pipe became more tractable and, by dint of first my pulling a yard and then the crew on shore pulling a yard, it got loose; oh! The joy as it slowly but surely floated past my bull's-eye! 'With a little encouragement, the breast-rope came too and I shall never know what they were hooked by owing to that fearful mud. Then I 'bout turned and slunk home; I felt simply awful, for I knew I'd been a fool again and had broken one of the most vital rules by letting go the shot-rope and I crept out of the water wishing I'd never been born. If only I'd discovered something wonderful, or got an awful cut, or anything, but no, they didn't even rate me, which was awful; my teeth chattered though I wasn't cold, and I was afraid they'd hear them. My rings were taken off, my hands chafed, and I was undressed in stony silence broken only by a curt 'stand up!' or 'sit down!' as the occasion arose. 'Still, I've learnt something; I've learnt the consequences of not ascertaining that it is the shot-rope, before letting go the distance line; I've gained an enormous amount of confidence underwater and further I've learnt to sit down quietly and to think a thing like that out instead of getting a vertical breeze so, in the face of the fact that I always shall be a fool, I do feel that in one direction at least I'm a wiser fool.'

Mossy"

DISCOVERY (continued)

"On Sunday morning, having partially recovered from the return to camp at 8 o'clock that morning, we unearthed semi-respectable clothes and a small expedition set off to Wookey Hole to report progress, return utensils borrowed from various departments the night before, and incidentally to gather any news likely to be useful to us of the gang. We were greeted with such kind words and so many promises that we are beginning to feel quite popular in spite of the fact that we have been certified mad, but delightfully so, by the B.B.C.!

"We were informed that we had entered the sixth chamber but told to keep it under our hats.

Mossy. 12-9-35"

(There follows Mossy's story of Matthew Walker and the record of the overwater survey of the Fourth and Fifth Chambers and, of course, the usual Diver's Observations and the logsheets; not being directly relative to the present purpose they have been omitted but the story continues.)

Chapter 3

From Sixth to Seventh Chamber

Graham Balcombe and Penelope Powell setting off with trapeze, Wookey Hole, August 1935.

"THE HAND OF THE WITCH

"Saturday 3rd of August, Bank Holiday Week-End. The promise of the week before held good and the Wookey Hole van tootled down the track and through the rushes at precisely nine fifteen pip emma. The paraphernalia was quickly slung aboard and away she went, while the Balcombian and Sheppardian Midgets loaded up the odds and ends and followed in her wake."

(Just to keep the record straight, Sheppard's transport was a Wolseley Hornet.)

"Sheppard has now finished his period of C.B. and is now back with us as a B.Sc.

"Consternation reigned at Wookey Hole as everyone of any importance had already arrived and it only required the presence of the increasingly unnecessary diver to complete the evening's publicity. In fact, two reporters and Fox Pictures told us that Captain Hodgkinson had himself gone to see what had happened to us." (Recollection eludes me but the occasion must have been another trial run for B.B.C.)

"The usual procession of pilgrims, each bearing a nautical burden, filed past the Witch and, in spite of various little tableaux for which Fox Pictures kept on stopping us, everything was soon in readiness and the begrudged meal of tea and bully beef set upon with gusto.

"The B.B.C., the very cream of mortals, hung up their dignity on the Witch, ate and drank with the worst of us, and later took a spell on the pump right manfully. An hour or two at the base camp earlier in the week seems to have worked this wonder for there, in the centre of all Mendip Madness, even on the briefest visits, one is doomed to carry away the germ.

"An excellent spot of microphone craft was done by the B.B.C.; Diver Balcombe, fitted with headphones instead of the usual doings in the top of the helmet, then went down to explore the 'legendary sixth chamber' as the newspapers so romantically put it.

"The water was of its pristine greenness and he had a good trip, found 'The Boss' or said he did, discovered that Mossy's archway had no through route, and described the chamber as a long tunnel with little or no air space above.

"He took a shot as far as the squeeze and planted it there then turned his attention to the shot-rope the idle end of which had been coiled down but now was in a fearful mess; he spent much valuable time below in an endeavour to unravel the mad tangle and then finally gave up the attempt, detached all the weights, and had it hauled up. It was tremendously twisted owing to shrinkage underwater, hard as iron, and when the loops which had wound round and round themselves, like an octopus crossed with a super garden creeper, were cleared there were still convulsions down the whole length to be dealt with. Kink by kink they were freed until the whole beast lay still and passive from the diving base to within a few yards of the Witch who, though she kept a stony silence, no doubt had something to do with it.

"Three quarters of an hour later the shot-rope was ready to be relaid and our Graham departed with it at such a rate that Jack Sheppard, who is not fitted with roller-bearing armpits, was jolly nearly towed in after him. Fortunately Graham had to brake a bit to attach the rope to the shots again and as he approached the thirty miles-an-hour speed limit in the fifth chamber there was time for Jack to breathe again and free himself ready for the next mad rush.

"The whole business of relaying the rope and returning to the surface took just under half an hour, an absolute record." I have a vivid memory of a pump jam. The air flow ceased completely but there was enough air in helmet and suit to see me out, especially as the route was upslope. Oddly, there is no log record at the time of occurrence.

"The time underwater was some five hours after which we tidied up and left everything carefully covered for the day on the shores of the River Axe.

"Sunday's diving was more a matter of gang than anything else but a neighbouring Scout Camp provided the necessary Armstrong Crew and again we found ourselves assembled in the third chamber. The kit was assigned to its proper places and the pump then tested. Much to our consternation and the disappointment of the ring of scouts we discovered during this operation that one cylinder had packed up and the discharge valve of the other had had its washer-retaining screws chewed off. The Witch knows something about this. There was a wailing and gnashing of teeth for there could be no more diving that night though we sent up a silent prayer of thanks for the defeat and failure of the Witch's real base designs and the safe return of the diver the night before.

"Again chartering the Wookey Hole van, we set out for home. An encounter with a bottle party by the roadside made a pleasant interlude; free drinks were pressed upon us and rejoicing was on every hand. Thence to camp where a large feast was ordained ending with a competitive bombardment of cherry stones. In this great test of spitting skill, Brown was an easy winner both on range and placing.

"The van then started back on its way home and the rest of the gang prepared for bed. The nightly wrangle over blankets, pyjamas etcetera, was soon over and the sun rose upon the various corpse-like forms sleeping off the night's activities in their nests in the long grass.

Mossy, 12-9-35"

"THE BIRTH OF THE FLYING TRAPEZE

"Of the week-end of August the 11th and 12th little is to be said. Pump had been taken to Bridgwater, dealt with, and brought back to the base camp in working order on Saturday night. On Sunday afternoon Digger and Jumbo turned up, also Fred Frost, making enough gang to allow Digger and Graham to try an experiment with a drum.

"The idea was to fill a drum with air while under water, float it up to the surface, then climb up its anchor rope and so view the surface-scape. This was Graham's cunning idea for use in Wookey's 'legendary chambers'. Digger found it more satisfactory to fill the drum from his sleeve than from the spit-cock and performed the experiment successfully, then Graham followed suit.

"Both agreed it was far from ideal and a scheme was devised using two drums connected by an iron bar and employing a thicker tail rope.

"Graham blew himself up very effectively and, what is more, succeeded in deflating himself again. This procedure is normally a forbidden fruit but under the conditions of the work in cave-land, if a diver should blow up, he has only himself to rely on for extrication from his predicament and therefore such practice must be considered part of the routine. The ability to handle such an emergency is an accomplishment necessary to those who wish to wander alone in the watery labyrinths of the Axe.

Mossy, 12-9-35."

Considerable difficulty was experienced in trailing behind each diver the separate air-hose and life-line, which eventually circum- scribed the divers' range and they always held the risk of snagging, so trapping the diver. Divers' Observations, Saturday, 17-8-35, have this note:

"Each diver's hose and cable were seized together at six-inch intervals and this effected a great improvement. A diver can now pass unaided farther that the point where previously he was brought to a standstill by the drag."

The discovery of a seventh chamber was at first hardly recognised; we had seen its surface from Six, and, indeed, Seven is probably best recognised as just a part of that same chamber but, having been named, the name will stick. The first mention comes on 16-8-35 as the divers were preparing to surface there:-

From the chapter "*ON BEHALF OF THE BBC*"

"...Wishes for each other's health were exchanged through the medium of the air valves and Mossy was given the iron trapeze with the drums to look after while Graham returned to base for shot-weights. The murkiness began to clear and the water became steadily greener; Six became visible, away down at the bottom of the sandbank, and Seven breathed with an intense and pregnant greenness from the opposite direction. It looked a rather steep drop down over to Seven and Mossy, holding tightly to the shot-rope, lay on her tummy as far over the pit as she could and had a good dangle in it but, having learned the diver's most bitter lesson, she refrained from letting go the shot-rope and nosing about on her own as the Witch whispered her to do.

"It was a long wait, then a wrist began to leak but a bit of manipulation against the rock put that right. Then three noises like faint thunder were heard, then some fiddling with the torch put it out and slight panic was felt until it was discerned that it was merely switched off. Then more faint thunder; careful examination of the surrounding rocks revealed nothing out of the ordinary and peace descended once more." (Mossy.)

Mossy was at Belay 1: from there the depth of Seven could not have been seen; one has to climb to Charybdis for that delightful spectacle. I think she must have been looking down the Giant's Staircase, the route to Eight. We had no explanation for the noises. The next night was taken up by a broadcast: there were no discoveries so the record is skipped, bringing the story to 24-8-35 which illustrates how progress gets bogged down by the details of housekeeping and more or less how we got our notice to quit.

"SHORT TIME

"August the 24th, a wet autumnal evening with much apprehension, we wondered whether the rain would have made the River Axe angry and once again produce that horrible brown colour that seems to put our divers so completely off their stroke though Graham is seldom off his; even if the water were like tar he would go down to find out why. Our Mossy likes it green and if it is not so there is trouble; she gets caught up in things and becomes an absolute menace. Anyway, only Graham went down that night to do a lot tidying up and altering things.

"The gang was lucky because the cave had been brooding on the pipes and cables all week; seized together they were too unwieldy to take back to camp also the joy of our lives, that ruddy pump, had been left so the gang was on easy shift and so able to watch Diver No.1 do all the work.

"Clad as usual in an armour of concrete blocks, he waded into the water and soon the week-end's choicest diction floated merrily from the telephone. The water was reported to be clear but flowing a bit faster; the mud he kicked up disappeared faster than it usually did so all was roses. He tidied up the electric light cable and arranged the lamps to his liking then turned round to discover two holes between Five and Six, which caused him some consternation. It transpired a long time afterwards that on making exit he managed to become wedged, head downwards, and there blew up but managed to extricate himself. He was too cunning, however, to report his bad divercraft for record on the log sheet.

"There was no time to do anything further as the inhabitants of Wookey Hole, the village of Wookey Hole, don't like the state in which their water supply arrives on Sunday mornings so, after wrestling with a shot and breaking off the wire ring, he substituted another weight and proceeded to shore.

"To his attendant's great delight he got foul in the process and had to be flipped clear. It has been discovered that a diver who fouls between The Squeeze and the Third can generally be freed if the attendant runs with the pipe and line in the direction of the Hall of Wookey and gives a few flips when the lines float away from whatever is obstructing them. This tip should be useful for next season.

"The usual clearing up took place, with the customary lack of gang, and so to camp to talk over the night's work and of the hope of a possible extension to do some more during the following week-end.

"Curiously enough, the order to cease diving was occasioned by nothing more or less than a worm! What little things can alter the course of great undertakings!"

(Is that not a trifle arrogant, Mossy? Doubtless unintentional)

"This little blitherer did; it appeared in an old lady's sink way down the village on a Sunday morning and instead of asking it where it had come from and whether it had been making a night out and was cooling its head prior to returning home, or if it had merely fallen out of her own Sunday cabbages, she blamed its sudden appearance on the wretched divers and seizing it by the scruff of its neck (where is this, please?) she madly waved it in the air making the welkin ring with her outcry against befouled drinking water.

'Beastly improvident little worm!
'The Good Book hath it, you may turn,
'Turn all you like, but next time think,
'And don't turn up in someone's sink!'

Mossy, 22-10-35."

DIVERS' OBSERVATIONS Week-end 31st August - 1st September

"Permission for a final effort had been obtained, thanks to the splendid efforts of Brown, secretary to the cave management and now a firmly established and prominent member of the Expedition. This permission had been given in order that the underwater tackle might be recovered.
"It was felt that the opportunity would be much more profitably used for a final bid at exploration at cost of abandoning the gear. ...."

"FINALE

"August the 31st, our very last trip; it was raining and cold; most of the rushes by the pool had been cut and the grass hung wet and rank about our ankles; the tents looked pale and squalid in the chill autumn light and flapped as though they shivered when a wintry breeze passed among the boughs above and showered down raindrops from them. Time to strike camp thought everybody.
"In one tent lay a tiny canine mother beginning to enjoy again the life which Mossy had fought so hard to keep within her. Ting had borne a son and that son's name was Matthew Walker."
(An earlier contribution from Mossy's pen was a light-hearted story of Matthew Walker, 'An irritating sort of a diver', prompted by the gang's preoccupation with that delightful

70

stopper knot, the Double Matthew Walker, but aimed, I think, mildly satirically at the somewhat strained relations between the Captain and Diver No.1.)

"A fine lusty pup he was; too lusty to be allowed to beat about his frail mother so he had to become one of the gang at the age of three days and, complete with milk and fountain pen filler, rolled in flannel and safely packed in a tomato basket, he set off, as all good gangsters do, to pay his weekly visit to the Witch.

"Lots of shopping had to be done in Wells for the week-end and the sawdust on the shop floors felt most unpleasant to bare feet. but the business was soon over and, having washed off the dust of Wells in the flooded gutter, we shot away to Wookey Hole. ...

"A large meal of stew, tea, bread and methylated spirit (this last by accident and not design), was gladly eaten after the gear had been lugged in and then came the rigging of the telephone and dressing of divers. Someone accidentally bunged the telephone connector in the wrong way then gave it a hearty wrench with the spanner, just for luck, after which we spent an hour putting it right again."

(Trying to, it seemed.)

"When at last the time came for testing it, everyone was suprised to hear a little whimpering noise going on; again and again did Mac demand absolute silence but always that little noise. Sudddenly Matthew Walker was called to mind and he was discovered parked in his basket beside the receiver and on being unrolled the full brunt of his din was borne upon us, for it was just on feeding time. He was quickly removed and fed by Mossy, whose jobs are many and varied, and he soon fell again into blissful slumber.

"The divers were dressed and descended for the last time into their limpid wonderland. It was curious but on this their last trip they felt a sudden and complete confidence. They moved about as easily with the drums, coils of rope and weights, as if they were on dry land; the new pump is largely responsible for this, of course.

"Diver No.2 was securely lashed to Belay 1; it was no time before the trapeze was rigged, inflated, and wobbling about on the surface in Seven, its tail neatly coiled and tied to a concrete weight below. Then, of course, the wretched No.2's wrists leaked so both divers had to return to base as No.2 had outgoing communication only, having nobly volunteered to carry on without the disabled receiver, and therefore needed an escort to translate the instructions into rope signals.

"Hot tea was poured into their mouths and soon they were off again. Going through from chamber to chamber in meditative manner you cannot help being struck by the strangely different atmosphere in each. Four is rather a scrambling place, all big untidy stones with very little beauty, except it be contrast to Three. Then Five where you have the illusion that you are a giant standing miles above the earth and looking down onto a vast expanse of desert where no sign of man is visible, not a mark disfigures the even ripples of the sandbank, and where the light fades a little in the distance" (we had a light fixed in Five) "the deep shadows cast by the overhanging rocks creep together to make dark mysterious forests, silent on the desert's edge. There is not the slightest sensation of being under water and the whole illusion must be caused by the position of the lamp, high up like a sun, above the fleecy clouds of surface.

"Having passed through The Squeeze into Six, where there is no lamp, you suddenly find yourself, a tiny awestricken creature, standing in a colossal world, half dark and rising around you like the sides of a bowl; pale clouds billow and fall away on either side; the floor is tumbled rocks again, like that of Four, and in front an enormous sandbank looms. Away into the distance the shot-rope trails over its ridge and out of sight so that you know that it is not new country but it is somehow new to you. It is the charm, the spell the Witch had cast upon us, which makes us wander, for ever seeing anew the things with which we are already familiar, as did the spell-bound folk of old, who wandered in an enchanted forest which was really their own orchard, planted by their own hands.

"Above the sandbank is an aperture, a window shaped like two stars, a large one and a small one holding hands. And far above is a crazy moon, expanding and contracting and with each movement shaking off great flakes of itself which writhe and turn, travelling for ever away from their parent, disappearing as suddenly as they came. It is the air space in Six. The moon is the light of your torch shining on the escaping bubbles from your helmet.

"As you begin to ascend the sandbank, and navigate the rock in the middle travelling towards the stars in front, reality again descends and before many minutes have passed an ordinary human being has arrived at Belay 1, between Scylla and Charybdis, and contemplated a trip up the trapeze.

"There was a lot of hand tapping and signalling on bull's-eye; the receiverless No.2 was again belayed to the rockside and No.1 went on his way to the surface. His suit began to swell, he waved his hand, grasped the rope, and up he went, slowly and in the most dignified manner possible; the last that Diver No.2 saw were those fearful brass toecaps disappearing in a sulphur cloud, like a person going up to Heaven. Diver No.2 is earthbound so was more or less prepared when, with a sudden crash, down came No.1 on her helmet! Diver 1 then did some curious antics, whether from pleasure or from rage it was difficult to tell. Diver 2 promptly put through a request to go up also, granted by No.1, who proceeded to de-karabine - or should it be entkarabinen? - the coil of rope, spare shot-rope, so that the ascent would be less encumbered. Then up, up, went Diver No.2 and, when her head popped out and she saw Seven in all its glory, the telephone in Three echoed and re-echoed with squeals of delight as she hung, swinging and wobbling, on the iron bar of the trapeze, bathed in the orange, red, brown and gold reflections on the water.

"Here was Seven, winding away as far as the light could reach, towering above as far as the eye could see, two gigantic walls of clean rosy conglomerate; how could it be so many million years old? It looked as fresh and new as the day it left the Hand of its Maker. This cathedral of peace is guarded not by an angel with a flaming sword but by a huge and pointed boulder ready to destroy all who are not fit to enter and for whom it is waiting, so keen and sharp, so watchful; La Guillotine!

"Along one side, the river's left, is a huge overhanging square-cut ridge, like the one in Five; the opposite wall is practically vertical though high above is a smaller ridge that has at some time caught a drip of water and made a tiny cascade of white stalagmite; it gleams with a pearly radiance and in that lofty place it is as a sleeping soul, perhaps the little keeper of the cavern resting, head on arms, against the rosy grandeur of the wall. On return it was described as a place like a shag's nest.

"When the divers were reunited on the riverbed below they executed a regular war dance, hand in hand, until their helmets crashed together and finally Diver 1 pushed his companion over which ended the performance and, sorrowful but triumphant, they wended their way home, stooping, climbing, crawling and at times shooting along face downwards as the attendants and coilers waxed more and more and more energetic and tugged with all their might.

"Carrying out the gear was a long and sad task; even Pump had to go; seizings were ruthlessy cut, cables and piping separated and loaded onto some pack conscript. We thought we were tough but Mac and his brother, the former having first removed Mr.Matthew Walker from his shirt, showed us how to carry weights. Having stuck planks behind their ears as easily as they would cigarettes and filled their pockets with half-hundredweight concrete blocks, these Devonshire giants began in an amiable way to carry loaded sea-chests out of the cave at such a speed that the slave-driving Mossy took it for granted that they were empty and handed them a few helmets and boots to take out in them! Thereafter Mossy, shame to her eyebrows, did some carting herself for a change.

"We were all superhuman that night and huge loads of piping ran out of the cave, apparently under their own power, until somebody accused that power of having pinched Graham's boots and then discovered him in the middle of the coil.

"It was a fairly full camp and would have been almost overcrowded had Captain Ford and friend" (conscripts) "accepted the invitation to join us; they took advantage of our nonchalently proffered haystack as a dormitory but it seems to have proved too much for them for they did not appear at camp for breakfast.

"The Witch, who let us ourselves return so many times unscathed from her terrible domain, had taken her toll at the precise hour at which we emerged triumphantly in the Seventh Chamber. Ting, the little faithful heart, the tiny guardian of our camp, had died surrounded by every canine luxury. Think a moment! Who can escape the Witch? Laugh, snap your fingers at her, but surely, surely she will break you...

"Rain fell all day and the gang, never to be beaten, made a wonderful house among the sea-chests, carpeted with hay, thatched with a bicycle, with a good covering of canvas overall forming a large warm waterproof canteen. The alleyway to the entrance made an excellent kitchen and the rain for once became tractable and did the washing-up.

"Gang departed and Mossy, feeling rather as Mrs.Noah must have done as the floods began to rise, hired an old white horse and an older four-wheeled waggon, loaded up the camp, lock, stock and barrel, and disappeared. Various ingenious methods were used and an assistant, who arrived for the second journey, was surprised to find sea-chests already up at the clubhouse, unloaded and neatly stowed although weighing tons. Mossy thinks he can keep his amazement if he could not think of emptying a chest first, heaving into the waggon, then re-loading!!

"The last trip was an amusing sight. Piled high with odds and ends and crowned with a tin of ever-escaping eggs, with paraffin cans, bicycle, and bottles of sauce swinging gaily at the back, the waggon squealed and lumbered on through the lead mines to The Grange where a frantic last wash and pack took place before the beloved diving gear was dispatched to London, back into the safe keeping of our valuable friends Siebe Gorman, until next we pit our skill and fortune against the guardians of the Unknown Land.

Mossy and Graham, 22-10-35"

Chapter 4

With Wookey Hole in the Sights

The evolution of WHODD-WHODBA

(The Wookey Hole Diver's Dress-The Wookey Hole Diver's Breathing Apparatus.)

The hard-hat diving ended with no clear solution to the basic problem, but events had their own momentum. The euphoria of the achievements at Wookey gradually died and were replaced by the starker realism; hard-hat diving there had no future save for cleaning-up the outstanding work in the near chambers. We had no detail knowledge of these; no real survey, no photographs. While good results in each of these fields could be achieved with hard hats, so little ground had been gained that the urge to snatch a bit more from the unknown before tackling the protracted detail work was very strong. Time slipped by, the world grew ever more disturbed and war broke out. I was in a reserved occupation, based on Harrogate on the fringe of the Yorkshire pot-holing area. Gradually my attention drifted towards a d.i.y. solution, the manufacture of a self-contained diving outfit. I had taken a small lathe and sundry workshop needs with me on leaving London and now got them out of storage and into the loft in our temporary home; a patch of the rafters was boarded over with material filched from a derelict hen-house not far away, and a base of operations established. This was the period when the series of Diver's Notebooks began, at first mere doodlings and da Vinci-type sketches (pardon, Leonardo!) but gradually becoming an almost intelligible record. Let these notes insinuate themselves and later tell their own story.

Extracts from the Diver's Notebooks:

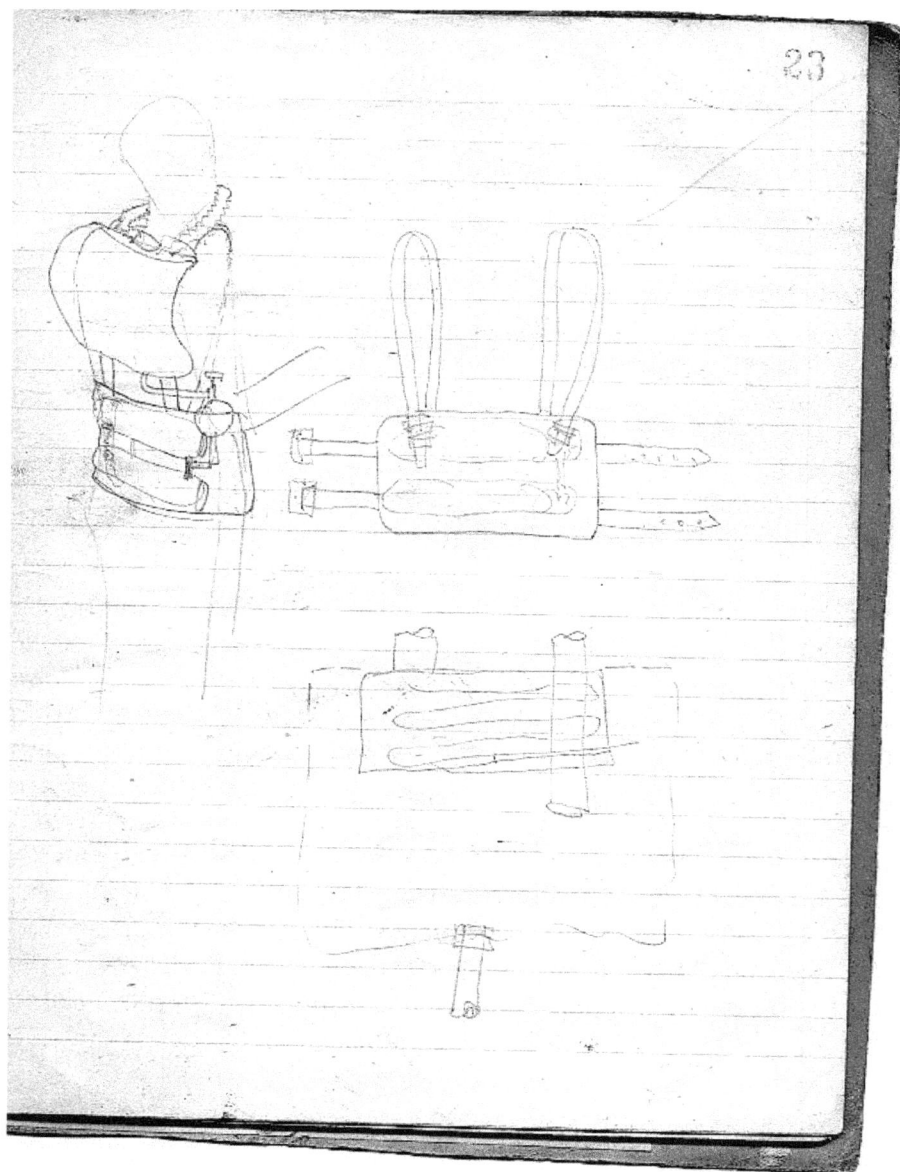

From Notebook No. 1.

Notebook No.1.

The germ of what was to become Whodd-Whodba, a dry-suit and self-contained breathing apparatus (scuba), and of our interest in Keld Head, to become the scene of the first cave-dives with them, become discernable in scribbles started on 25-8-44. The sketches are crude in the extreme but improve just perceptibly towards the end of the book. The note on Keld Head is a sketch giving rough record of the water depths along the line of the cliff. My attention was directed to Keld Head by Raymond Nunwick, enthusiastic younger-generation pot-holer from a neighbouring village. He figures largely in these early ventures, not least to ensure the diver did not chicken out. Nothing in the notes is worthy of recall, beyond maybe that date.

Notebook No.2.

As yet, bar the date just quoted, the scribblings are undated. The nucleus of the design was a little ambitious: it was for a re-breather using oxygen from a pair of cylinders and carbon dioxide removal was to be by sodalime. Nothing unusual so far but the breathing circuit was to be a one-way system with a rather complicated system of cocks and valves. This would ensure the best possible scrubbing of the respired gas, but the penalties did not become quantitatively apparent until most of the work was done.

Notebook No.3.

Still undated. The crude sketches now include scratchings of the dry-suit. Here and there are signs that a straight-edge had been used! A little practical work had been done to gauge the sodalime requirement. There is a tick-record of a 30 minute breathing run, so poorly recorded as to be meaningless now, but it indicates that construction work had begun, if only of a simple character, on the basis of the earlier scribblings. The elements of the breathing bag appear with its eventually rather elegant entry port, which shows that the decision to house the sodalime within the bag had been taken. That did prove good but restricted the sodalime load to less than desirable. A date appears towards the end of the book, a wee scribble "E.E.Roberts, 29-12-44." Also script appears among the graphic scribblings. Then another breathing test, slightly more clearly but still inadequately defined. It was for symptoms of oxygen lack, and I happened to survive.

Notebook No.4.

Yet again undated. Rough sketches and bits of script continue but are still mostly unintelligible, as were they prompts for something being worked out on the bench.

Notebook No.5.

Still scribblings, but something had evolved for there is a list of parts for plating. Also a date appears, 12-3-45.

Notebook No.6.

This begins with crude sketches of the breathing circuit and refers to tests on sodalime. Surprisingly comes the reference "Control test (Logsheet 8) disappointing", that is, a surprise reference to a logsheet, though only for an air trial. Then "See Logsheet 9 for first water trials". I should not have been surprised for I have preserved almost all my personal logsheets plus a number of operation sheets, and indeed 8 and 9 are among them. So are 1 to 7. No.1 is dated 18-3-45 and is of air trials at Bramhope (Leeds): those air trials included hurtling through the local hilly country perched on the rear seat of the bicycle-made-for-two with Nunwick in charge, chiding me to work a bit harder. No.9 is the formal record of the first dip, which was in a fire tank. Better still, the notebook rejoices in the first narrative.

"THE EARLY DIPS

"On the 25th of March the equipment was due for test in water. The air trials had been disappointing but the performance would be adequate for a quiet trial of weights and to get some measure of familiarity with the new type of apparatus. Nunwick had a date at Kettlewell or some place and it left us high and dry on the Sunday before Easter but Cooky" (F.J.Cook, office colleague) "was delighted to step into the breach as diver's attendant and right well he did his job, even though in unkindly manner soaked by a thoughtless diver who turned his spewing spillways on him as he fixed the various weights. In fact he got far wetter than the diver did.

"The weather had been fine and warm for at least two weeks, to cheer us on maybe. Maybe! Sunday was warm but dull, it rained now and again but in the afternoon it cleared and the sun shone. I had at a rather late hour written to Avro" (they had a factory a field or two from our bungalow, with the heartening almost day-long roar from the engine test- beds, welcome indeed in those dark days,) "asking permission to use one of their fire-tanks. We had checked them both the previous Sunday and found the Yeadon-end tank nearly full of muck, but that at our end was almost clear.

"A Mr.Bristow of Avro phoned to say only too pleased to help, and when we arrived (late of course, if only half an hour or so) he was there with a Major Grey of the works home guard and offered the services of his chief fireman should we need them. We erected Nunwick's tent alongside the tank and dressed for the occasion. But I have not mentioned how we got there. Shame there was no camera to record our departure for behind the patient tandem was a 12' ladder, at the end of the ladder the Nunwick Trailer, festooned along the rungs were the diving clogs and other such things while on top lay the tent. Pete" (the domestic dog) "was highly pleased and only with difficulty restrained from giving chase.

"Now back to the tank. The ladder was in and weighted down with fifty pounds of lead, though experience showed it could have been rigged without the weight and done the job as well. The diver climbed aboard the tank parapet and had his weights tied on. I was the diver and, feeling rather depressed and the more anxious the deeper I got in, I eventually submerged. The cold water made my unprotected hands and head ache and soon I had had enough and, not having stirred out of reach of the ladder, called it off, re-dressed and made for home." (Aching hands was an understatement, the log records too numbed to manipulate the gear.) "Unfortunately Cook could not stay long: after eating daintily and very politely a portion of the repast put before him, he departed. We are not accustomed to diver's attendants or diver's mechanics or what-have-you either eating daintily, or being polite, or ever leaving anything at all." (Would it be too unkind to mention that some attendants would eat all there was as slowly as possible "to make it seem more"? After all they were growing lads and rationing at that time was quite severe.)

"A big day had come and gone and left behind it apprehension and doubt. On Tuesday 27th, after phoning for more sodalime, a parcel arrived with four pounds of the precious stuff so Ray Nunwick and I went down to Otley to the open-air baths. With a fresh charge of sodalime all went well in sunshine, pleasant surroundings, and the company of friendly engineers who were busy getting ready for the summer season, painting and repairing. I spent half an hour doodling - literally - on the bottom, moving round in slow and fast circuits of the deep end, not truly deep for the water was a foot or so below normal, it was merely there to keep the tiles in good condition, but it was just right for me.

"Clearly, things were better and my spirits soared. I printed in large letters 'WOOKEY HOLE DIVERS' in the mud on the floor to acknowledge the memories that being underwater brought back then 'KELD HEAD CAVERN', upside down, in anticipation of things to come. Meantime the two engineers looked on rather perplexed, quite evidently they had not expected the outfit to work, while Pete, who had come in spite of Mavis's" (my wife, earlier referred to as May) "strict instructions, became agitated, rushed up and down the side of the bath and peered down into the water wondering, no doubt, whether he ought to jump in to save his Pop. A few people sunning themselves on the river bank stirred at these strange goings on, stared awhile then relaxed again. Evidently the sun was rarer and more precious than any such curiosities.

"Raymond was delighted: so carried away in fact that as the heavily-loaded diver staggered out up the vertical ladder, desperately holding on to the handrail in a do-or-die effort to gain the concrete, Ray held out his hand not to help but for a handshake of congratulation: diver nearly fell off with the shock and the reaction of his expletives as he realised what was going on. It was the Tuesday before Easter; we had got the outfit going just in time.

"Now Raymond had slipped his collar for the afternoon and it was well into evening when we arrived back so he had perforce to hang around until the night-school he should have attended was let out, else an angry father would discover his movements. So he stopped for tea. There was nothing prepared for him, while for us there was a fish dinner. So Mavis set to to knock out something and soon there appeared a huge plate of bacon, two eggs, luscious fried potatoes and various other tit-bits, my rations for the next week, and they smelt so delicious beside our miserable tasteless haddock and insipid mashed potatoes that I think he will never be forgiven. Just think of it, two fried eggs and luscious fried potatoes, luscious fried potatoes.

"Easter, 1945 KELD HEAD One 29-3-45 to 3-4-45

"Thursday was a day for making ready. First off was a load of heavy stuff to Horsforth to be picked up by Brown's milk lorry" (Brown was Nunwick's friend, hijacked for transport service for part of the way) "that took all morning. Next the Nunwickian trailer had to be strutted and stayed to face its task and sundry bits added or knocked off, then the bike needed attention. The weather, too, was busy getting ready; for weeks it had been mild and sunny, taunting us in our offices, beckoning us mockingly to come out and enjoy life. Now that the cage was open the weather became chill and it rained heavily. The river Wharfe was rising steadily and the wind sprang up.

"Friday dawned cold and wild; by eleven we had packed and left. 'We' were self at the helm, Mavis on the Daisy-seat, Pete in a box on the carrier and the trailer hung on behind." (An indifferent photograph exists of this caravan, as of many other scenes of the period, I have asked that the 'Balcombe Collection' - pace Farr - will be preserved awhile after I croak.) "The sun shone without heat, the wind blew keenly in our faces, so hard that we had to pedal down The Bank from Bramhope to Otley. It rained, it hailed, it took an hour to get to Burley, another hour to Addingham where on the hillside we struggled with wet wood to make a cup of tea.

"At the other side of Skipton our luck was in for Brown and his lorry, with Maggie Matterhorn and another already aboard," (Maggie Matterhorn, one of the NCFC lads, neé Harold Proctor but rechristened from the shape of his customary pot-holing headgear,) "hove alongside. Tandem and trailer were soon flung onto the milk churns and lashed down and we were whirled through the biting air to Settle, overtaking Ken and Ralph of our party" (Nunwick's friends) "struggling manfully against the blustering wind. At Settle we disembarked, loaded up with all our mighty weight of gear and slowly inched our way in rain and still more rain to Ingleton Station for two more bottles of precious gas then on to Westhouse. (Our load on this occasion had been such that on leaving Giggleswick we all but failed to push over the brow, Buck Haw Brow pronounced in the Yorkshire manner. Saturday was even worse but a scouting party, Ray and I, went up to Keld Head to inspect. Ray and his party had spent many weekends in a stout endeavour to lower the level of the stream, but so far had had little success. Kingsdale Beck, normally quite dry above the resurgence, was a fast-running stream with white horses and spume flying in the wind. The river rising from the corner of the Head gushed up with great force making waves which broke under the wind; from the auxiliary exits, too, it came rippling out; the pond was about a foot deeper than normal and looked like a huge brew of tea. We thought the least we could do would be to paddle round the pond and test the power of the current, but by afternoon when we returned the water had dropped six inches, the waves had gone but the current was still swift and eddies chased across the pool.

"At last I was dressed (it is a lengthy business), launched and set about the job . After some time wallowing about and checking previous observations I called for the light but it was then time to return. So the kit was stowed for the night and we went down for tea. I can tell you now first hand that the black abysses gaping under the rock walls looked very fearsome and suggestive of the lair of savage monsters. Visibility was two to three feet and likely to be much less with artificial light so it was not entirely with regret that I left the place to exchange for a mighty feed and the fun of the local dance hall.

"Sunday was a little better but it had been a wild and wet night. I essayed a descent, edging my way along the southern wall; the way down loomed dimly from the intense further blackness. Clutching my drum of rope I slowly groped my way downwards. Visibility quickly dropped from two feet to one foot then to about six inches from the light. Each stone on the slope seemed to be the last before the drop but after each there appeared another. The slope was very steep and the stones, about six inches in diameter, were perched precariously. When disturbed they rolled down out of sight with a queer high-pitched clink! clink! Soon the daylight disappeared, last seen as a dim orange foggy patch almost overhead; the sound of breathing and of the inrushing gas disappeared, a deadly silence ensued. It was disquieting and after another few feet I left my drum and climbed back with the aid of the rope anchored on the bank; the dim patch grew lighter and was daylight at last. The noise of breathing came back, and when I opened the gas valve, yes there was the rush of gas, all was well after all." (With a bit more experience I would have realised it was my ears that had not cleared: I was temporarily deaf.)

"After a brief exchange with the party on the bank I went back, reached the dark and quiet by the drum, and peered down. The slope still went on. A few inches at a time I climbed down following the little patch of light then suddenly a level patch appeared, sand and gravel. Halfway down I had manoeuvred to avoid a spur of roof which jutted down but here none was in view and I lay crouched on the river bed. So far there had been a measure of achievement and little would be gained by pushing on in such conditions. I had been asked by Simpson (British Speleological Association) to get a sample of water from well inside the rising for the Rural District Council which was thinking of installing a ram to supply drinking water to Westhouse. The sampling bottles had not yet arrived so I would have to make a further descent anyhow, so I went up.

"On gaining the bank I was already chilly and glad of a break for lunch but did not warm up, thanks to the inclement weather. Soon the sample carriers arrived. It was some time after the lunch interval had expired but Diver's Attendant was not to be seen. The bottle-carriers struggled with the weights and fittings and soon, disgruntled, I wanted to know where the so-and-so, my attendant, had got to when an offended voice came from the back of the tent 'I'm having my grub!' After levering him from his sandwich and getting trimmed again I went down. By now I had lost the touch of enthusiasm gained by reaching the bottom and did not feel happy about the descent. The neckband leaked and had to be adjusted. Going down, I thought that all was not well with the respirator, it was by no means free from trouble, but I knew there was not far to go and I would soon be back. I came to the drum but did not realise until later that it was no longer at the bottom but had been washed some way up the slope. By now I was sure the respirator was going badly so quickly opened the sampling bottle; I heard it gurgle as I sat there half dozing, sealed it off mechanically and slowly started to climb. It seemed ages before that patch of light above appeared and the difficulty of the last few feet came irritatingly through to my dulled consciousness; at last I broke surface but there was still the stretch to the bank to be covered; I started to walk it and came to the shallow; in a temper I threw myself down into deeper water on the other side and crawled to the bank.

"Once again in fresh air I quickly recovered and the sample of water was whisked off to Settle while we packed up and trekked back home to Westhouse. I had been using sodalime as an absorber, it evidently needs careful watching and a lot more experience in safe water before venturing any distance in a cave." I come back to this below.

"That night we had an enormous tea and settled down to argue on the manner in which stones fall and on the orbits of celestial bodies.

"Monday we spent on the flanks of Kingsdale in a tour of inspection of the pots and entrances; we cycled to Braida Garth, climbed up to Lord's Top and then across to Yordas with its waterfall in flood, got smoked out by our fire and passed on to the other holes on lower Gragareth, then to a late dinner and another hop - this time "a ball" with evening dress optional, but no-one opted - where after narrowly escaping being ejected, we shufffled and slid around until our soles smoked and eventually we retired to bed. Tuesday morning was spent in packing: we left at twelve, broke down at quarter past, retired in hail and rain to Reg Hainsworth's garage where I endeavoured to mend the broken gears, but without luck, then spent a happy half-hour at tea with the Hainsworths, returned by train to Apperley Bridge and pushed the long push home.

"Perhaps the weather will now 'tek oop aggen.'"

THE BREATHING DRILL

After typing out these notes I awoke during the night with one of those inspirations which is a blinding flash of the obvious. The respirator trouble had been attributed, at least by implication, to sodalime, that is carbon-dioxide excess, but the symptoms described here and elsewhere are of anoxic anoxia, lack of oxygen in the breathing mixture. This could only have occurred through defective breathing drill (or none). The logsheet makes no reference to breathing drill nor does any explicit reference appear until April, 1936, when Siebe Gorman, in demonstrating their Amphibian respirator, recommended three deep breaths to waste and about the same time in a letter to Haldane I described our drill as:

"Oxygen is breathed without dilution at the start of the dive, the lung air and bag air is expelled to waste ...."

(That would fail to meet the objective, anyway, for nitrogen in the dead-spaces of the respirator and in the much greater dead-space in the lungs would remain to dilute the oxygen.)

Thus even at that late date we were still very uncertain. My only previous information at the time on oxygen sets was from 'Deep Diving' R.H.Davis, and advice from the makers of medical breathing equipment; the former does not go into that aspect of use, the latter I cannot now recollect but had breathing drill been mentioned I surely would have been alerted to the dangers. The first reference to anything like a breathing drill on a logsheet was on Logsheet No.31, undated but after 17-11-45, "Gas on, lungs blown". The typical initial entry was "Respirator on, diver submerged". Now in later years the drill was the most important feature of the preparation routine, it dominated the whole process; had we in 1945 paid any such careful attention to it, I could not posssibly have failed to remember it even after 35 years yet I have no such recollection.

This is the problem: at the start of a dive the gas in the breathing bag will be a mixture of oxygen and nitrogen for the carbon dioxide will be removed by the sodalime. Breathing uses up oxygen and the total volume in the bag decreases and consequently its oxygen-nitrogen ratio falls. Suppose the diver starts with a full bag of normal air, four-fifths nitrogen; by the time the bag is empty, that is the diver is no longer able to take a full breath, ("bottoming"),the oxygen ratio will likely be dangerously low and, in most practical designs of bag, bottoming will never happen. Whodba at that time used the distinctly dangerous "on demand" system in which bottoming is the signal to admit more oxygen, a signal that might well never occur, so the diver would continue to breathe an oxygen-deficient mixture. The answer is to use a breathing drill by which the diver first replaces as much as possible of the original gas by oxygen and so ensures that, as oxygen is consumed, the fall in its proportion to nitrogen is minimised and, as there is only negligible nitrogen then present, bottoming always safely occurs. This is a simplified but adequate statement.

If, as it now seems likely, those early dives were done without any exacting preliminary drill then, apart from any other hazards of the game, I was indeed lucky to survive. Probably saved by being more than a bit chicken.

Notebook No.7.

The respirator was checked at Siebe Gorman's and found to have a breathing resistance at a flow, corresponding to hard work, of 5.4" w.g. The acceptable figure is 0.75" so the design was changed to to-and-fro to eliminate those exquisitely beautiful but inefficient valves and a larger sodalime canister was substituted. Even so, the resistance remained significantly higher than the 0.75" if my crude measurements were to trusted. On that same occasion we were introduced to Siebe Gorman's "Amphibian" which we were to borrow.

"AT SIEBE GORMAN'S

"Thursday, 19.4.45. The fourth day of the London heat wave. Slightly cooler but hot enough. John Beale" (office colleague) "and I met Cook at Waterloo and after some exciting phoning and dashing round to find train times, which should have been found before phoning, when I remembered to press Button A all was fixed. We arrived at Surbiton and it was quite quarter of an hour before we realised that the car which had driven up also quarter of an hour ago was the one we wanted. The works" (Siebe Gorman's) "are some 3 miles out but we were soon decanted at the end of Davis Road. The newness of the road and that its sole occupant was S.G.& Co. explained the mystery of its name; it was no coincidence.

"Sir Robert received me and, after preliminaries, handed me over to Mr.Gorman Davis. We all went to the Lecture Room, strangely small for such a big outfit. The Admiralty were in charge of the tanks; we trespassed once while waiting and got bitten for it. The one and only Burwood soon arrived, not a day older to look at though he must be well over sixty. It seems Sir Robert and he vied with each other in their claims to youthfulness. Sir Robert boasts he can touch his toes while Burwood cannot. Sir R. is 75, and he did it for us. Of course Burwood couldn't get a look in on that; I prodded his well cared for tummy and was sure of it.

"Mr.G. inspected my outfit and was impressed; he even said their dressmaking craftsmen would have to look to their laurels, and he was very intrigued by the porthole cover. We then adjourned to the nobs' dining room for lunch: very fine too, it vied with the Officers' Mess at Feltham in food and was superior in appointments. There were Gorman and Eric there and we think Jerry(?) but missed the introduction. There were also the Admiralty men - sorry, swobs, Admiralty Officers - one very interesting and interested who suggested adding bacterial research to our jobs and stocking caves with fish. He would contact a colleague back at Cambridge to see if they would be interested in our samples.

"After lunch I was manhandled into a hush-hush swimsuit (although Burwood assured us they have had an identical equipment since God knows how long,) and then an Amphibian was clamped on it. The goggles were a trial but might have been worse and, after some fun and games with the weighting, which included attempts to get to the bottom by hooking my toes under the rungs and suchlike, these things were settled to reasonable satisfaction; diving became much easier and I could just about move around. I found a seven-pound weight lying about, which helped matters, then The Bicycle. Now The Bicycle is a gadget with a saddle and two tiers of handlebars and huge pedals with vanes attached. I climbed aboard and pedalled but the pedals jammed so off again to inspect: it was just that divers have such thundering great boots that the pedals have to be even bigger and they fouled the deck when not properly pedalled. Soon tiring of this sport I found a slab of lead and was happy for a while chasing round the tank then tried hanging upside-down on the ladder and sprawling in strange attitudes, imagining some pipe, bedding plane or chimney to be the cause of all this.

"The goggles were still a trial and filled up rather quickly, when they were full up to the eyes I went up, after the jealous spectators had banged their fists sore on the tank glasses in endeavour to gain the attention of the purblind diver. Next they put me into a Mark II outfit which has a tailored bag to fit the shoulders, giving (presumably) lower breathing resistance, and with automatic outlet-valve facility for volume control by shoulder-wiggling. The Mark I has a downward-pointing flutter exhaust which can be raised by hand when required. The performance was not detectably different from Mark I so I chose Mark I on grounds of vulnerability of the Mark II bag under our working conditions....

"After that Sir Robert called for us and discussed our needs: we made a list and gave it to Burwood for despatch by rail. In the course of conversation Cook, after introducing his query with 'You do know something about high altitude work', to which Sir Robert replied, 'Yes, we have done some', is now satisfied (we hope) that elation from breathing oxygen is a hallucination of old-time schoolmasters.

"After farewells we were driven back to the station but got off with Burwood for a parting celebration at the nearest before continuing to our temporary homes. Another milestone."

That milestone, apart from improvements to Whodba, would be the availability of a second diver.

"GOLDEN ACRE

Undated.

"For the trial of the modified outfit we made a date - the first fine evening.... Thursday 24-5-45 started exceptionally cold but changed at mid-afternoon. Cook and I rushed off to Skyrac," (the domestic bungalow in Bramhope) "fed, packed and were off down the road by 7:30 with the trailer used as a handcart; Nunwick and Mavis would follow shortly. The tandem had no backwheel at that time." (We were heading for a local lake.) "We trudged to Golden Acre Park, saw the notice "W.D. PRIVATE" and went in. I had previously rung barmaid, manager, and cook, in that sequence, to find if it would be O.K., assuming it belonged actually to the hotel, and they had okayed it. Sorry if that spoils the effect. Down by the dam I changed and was nearly ready when Mavis and Nunwick appeared on the far bank; we hollered and whistled to no avail but eventually we contacted them as they appeared from the shadow of the Blue Lagoon.

"Learning from Siebe Gorman we cut down the weights but, alas!, left off the the wrong ones so with weighted feet I was left anchored by them like one of those lead-based toys you can't knock over. I tried to come back and after a fruitless struggle tried to come in on the rope but Cook, thinking I wanted more slack, gave it to me. I did get back at last. Eventually the weights were one at each shoulder and two low on the back. Statically this was fine but, after a leap to the surface in the deep part, the next thing I knew I was on my back and slowly sinking into the mud head first.... The lake was good but not ideal, it sloped gently down with a firm bottom, gradually becoming softer as the centre of the dam is reached. There are reeds but they are not a serious obstruction, the midges and gnats are a more difficult problem. The depth is about 15' at its deepest. It was a successful dip, over an hour until darkness and the gnats stopped play. We trekked home, testing the trailer to breakdown in the process, and were abed by 12:30.

"KELD HEAD Two"

Sundry improvements to the kit were continually being made, then off again on the long grind to Keld Head.

"Week-end 2 & 3-6-45. The previous weather had been thundery with heavy rain so the prospects were not good. Nunwick assured us that it had not been raining much over the other side of the Pennines. A party was arranged on the speculation of a chance to dive. Brown was to take us to Settle,

Reg Hainsworth from Settle to Keld Head and back to Windy Hill Farm," (Westhouse) "and possibly out again next day.

"Brown announced his inability to take us but Reg seemed quite excited to help." (He had a special interest in K.H., having attempted to enter in the past by skin-diving.) "After some prolonged - well, what is it best called? My office boss would have called it 'argy-bargy' - Mavis agreed to go with Pete by bus while Cook and I followed with the gear. On Saturday after lunch it streaked down again but after momentary waverings and a call to Reg to check on the weather and, as the report was not too damning, I decided it was on. Mavis left at three, Cook in his enthusiasm hurtled up from Leeds on a borrowed bike. Of course the departure was not without the preceeding days of hasty preparation, making gadgets and so on to the final assembly of all the kit. The Siebe Gorman outfit had arrived but there had been no time to unpack it. On Friday night the compass was needed, so one by one the lovely things were brought out and laid on the floor until last of all the compass itself was uncovered. Cook and I left about 3:30; there were showers to Addingham where the blue Dodge overtook us and went on its way with a bike or two reclining on the churns. I have often wondered why we had been so abruptly dropped; I had left arrangements in Nunwick's hands, maybe a beer or two should have come into the transaction. From Addingham Moss to the reservoir things went well, aided by the odd thirst-quencher and an interesting commentary from a miner-policeman. At Skipton we found Mavis waiting for her bus, at Settle we called on Cymmie, nursing his ills. (Eli Simpson, The British Speleological Association.) "Near Moorgarth Hall we met Reg Hainsworth and fixed for the morrow. Once clear of Wharfedale the afternoon and evening had been fine.

"Next morning the skies were grey at six, it was raining steadily at eight and continued so until teatime. We had left, a split party, by green van and tandem.

Ray Nunwick & Graham Balcombe, Keld Head, 1945.

Notebook No.8.

"The tandem found the joint exuberence of both Cook and myself too much for its gears and it was now a single-gear job.... At last, after midday, I got into the water... The water was pleasantly clear and it was with a measure of glee that from below the surface I spied my probe, dropped in near the edge of the pond and some yards away. At last I went down, the slope did not seem so intimidating or steep this time - what a difference when you can see the next step clearly!

"At the bottom, the point last reached, it was clearly the river bed. Eyes were not yet dark-adapted so despite the filtered daylight and the Ceag miner's lamp the extent of the patch could not be seen.

"The probe is the nerve-centre of navigation: a stick to poke around with, carrying a white streamer to test for current direction, a compass, a light and its battery, and, for lack of better position for it, the rope reel." (This would be the First Aflo - Aflolaun, Apparatus For Laying Out Line And Underwater Navigation.) "With its aid I went upstream, due west, along a sandy level bed sprinkled with small blocks. Soon I came to the end of the first part of the line, the remains of an Alpine line bought in Arolla, and I tried to pass the knot. (I was linked to the line by a lanyard and clip, there should not have been any knots.) "My fingers were so numb that after five minutes struggle I was no nearer to success so decided to pack it in. Taking a last look round I could see the Gothic arch of the fault rift ahead, scalloped from top to bottom, I was still at about 20' depth and the height was about 8' to the apex. Perhaps it was a lower system for the 'cymbals' previously heard indicated a shallow sump.... The sight of a delineated passage, however limited its extent might prove, was encouraging for to be in an unknown expanse of water with just an occasional flake or jutting piece of rock to mark a boundary is rather intimidating. I turned off the rope under a handy block and went out. It was very cold outside as well. After a spell of walking about with the cuffs off I warmed up a bit, but cursed the inclement un-Junelike weather for its lack of cooperation. Reg decided to go down to Westhouse for the Primus and Ray's Oxo cubes, but while turning his waggon round noticed the surface beck was flooding and came racing back to tell us. (The course of Kingsdale Beck along the valley-bottom is normally quite dry, the beck having gone underground, but occasionally ,as now, it floods.) By that time it was only 200 yards from us and we rushed up to see it. Down the river bed came swirling and frothing a stream of dirty brown water licking its way down the beck bottom, engulfing the deeper hollows in a rush, swilling out bits of the bank in its passage. One moment dry streambed, the next a four to six inches-deep stream. The wave swept on, progressing at a good walking speed, and split at Keld Head to empty its scum, froth and muck into our pool which despite a nine-inch rise on its own account had remained clear.

"After waiting half an hour to see what effect it would have on the rising, and it had none, I went down again, after more trouble with neckband, and quickly had the old rope out and the new one in the guide. Then on: either my eyes were not yet used to the poor light or the water was already thicker for the arch was no longer visible. The compass and detector still worked so I went through. What happened after this I am not too sure but after scrambling through a pile of large blocks and then on for some time I realised I was going up. The gas-bag swelled, I blew off some gas, heard it break at a surface and the full significance broke suddenly upon me - was this the end of the sump? Excited I looked round, or groped round, for a way up;I do not remember how I did so but I reached the surface and saw a stream passage chamber, no bigger than a bus, arched as the cave-passage below, with four-foot long white stalactites and a boss on the (true) left wall. I fancy I climbed a sandbank on my left to see out. The walls were everywhere overhanging.

"Dropping back to the streamway and picking up the course again, still west, I went on and on over patches of sand and more fallen blocks. The drum tended to catch but this was no longer acceptable as an excuse to turn back and I soon got used to freeing it. Travelling light is delightful. When you find a gaping hole, find the bottom then lightly step in; ever so gently you sink to the bottom like an air-borne feather. However, it is not all fun and games for twice in making my way against the current, presumably in a narrower part of the cave, the current won and swung me round so I had to drop flat, pick up the route again and have another go. It is comforting when climbing over piles of loose blocks to remember that one hardly weighs anything at all.

"To get back to the main job: somewhere on the way I found more surface, by blowing bubbles, and sought means to reach it. I had attached the weights by clips for experimenting in going up but trials in open water showed it is a difficult feat to remove them safely and in fact I now dropped one but recovered it then preferred to climb out. I think it was here I found a steep sandbank, tried to climb it but got switched off it by the current. Picking myself up I found the rope had gone slack and after pulling in a bit for one awful moment thought it had parted. It had not for the compass told me to about face and not go sneaking home like that so the rope tautened again and I went on to find a pile of blocks and making my way up through them saw surface just above. After many efforts I reached it and rose to look out but merely crowned myself on the roof above. Manoeuvring for a better position I found I was at the end of a chamber where roof came down to water. What was behind I cannot now remember but the cave continued underwater so I followed.

"By now the water was very murky and I could hardly see anything; the way went fairly steeply downwards and the rope was nearly out. I decided to throw in the sponge so detached the drum, not expecting to return for it and hardly expecting to draw it out.

"The return journey was specially enjoyable; after the line had corrected a few mistakes for me I began to have faith in it and soon there was a faint light patch ahead, growing bigger and brighter, eventually the entrance slope became defined and climbing it was delightful, fine yellow stones piled up in pleasant daylight. It seemed unduly bright but once out it soon became obvious that was only the after-flicks effect and in reality it was a drab and dull world to which I had returned and the rain was still pouring down; the landing stone from which I had first embarked, then some 3" above water, was now nearly a foot under.

"The impressions left by the underwater journey seem to have an elusive character. It is difficult to remember the sequence of events and there are gaps in the record, quite big gaps, and events of the imagination co-rank with real observations.... many details, events themselves not of great importance, ranked, by inability to relate them to real things, as unreal things and like dreams they quickly faded. There were other confusions of thinking too; on return I was sure they knew about the stalactite chamber whereas I had simply thought on seeing the place: 'don't I wish I could tell them about this; they'd be delighted', this passed for the telling and I was sure I must have made a double-trip in consequence. This is a curious study and gives warning that, in the initial stages at least, the diver's observations on many points, even seeming certitudes, must be very unreliable.

"Well, we were all wet, attendants probably more so than diver, the main diffference being that they were wet from the bottom up, he from the top down. We therefore skipped the undressing, packed up our dripping things as quickly as possible and made for the farm. But there was one thing that had first to be done; the blister neck-seal had to be deflated and, while some people found the idea of pumping up the diver with a bicycle pump a subject for laughter, when water was used instead of air and emptied from the nozzle at the front with the comment 'Excuse me, ladies!' it was a rare study. There was consternation and shock on the part of one of the lady members and general momentary embarrassment at the surprising reality of it all, except for the blasé culprit and Cooky, who pulled himself up quite six inches taller and rocked from heels to toes as he tried vainly to cover his merriment. It was Cookie, too, who while taking off the belay nearly fell in. The belay slipped and he swung, poised for seconds on his heels, before slowly rocking back alas! to safety, and it was he who again soon afterwards was nearly a diver, the victim of some horse-play while traversing the line round the top of the pond.

"Now Cooky and one Jack Parish were allocated the tandem and they arrived after a minor misadventure; Jack mumbled something about brakes but Cooky evidently knew better and described with great sangfroid how the road took a bend but the bike didn't and deposited them on the grass.

"During the evening it cleared up and the sun shone a while. Keld Head had won the second round for although as a dive it was successful as a cavern-hunting venture we had drawn a blank; however what we need is not necessarily grand open caverns but factual information on how the water gets from A to B. We now more information on the first 70 yards, or thereabouts.

"We left part of the kit with Reg, the bike and trailer at the farm, and like a gang of hoboes numbered off in degrees of disreputableness, we tramped to catch the bus, carrying our queer bundles of luggage. No wonder the people stood aside to let us pass.

"One day it will be fine and warm at Keld (cold) Head and the water will be clear as crystal but we are unlikely to be there on that day."
Such was our second encounter with Keld Head Beck. The third was soon to follow.

KELD HEAD Three Week-end 16 & 17-6-45

"After a spell of weather no worse at our side of the area than a fortnight ago and, with the promise by the forecasters of showers and sun, we set off again for Keld Head. Cook was in London, Reg was in Skye, Ray" (Nunwick) " would be there despite having had it in the neck from his girl-friend for it, and Ritherdon" (the engineer who plated Whodba's parts for me) "was keen to come.

"Mavis and I" (plus dog, I presume) "went by bus, or started to but bus was full, and at Otley we missed the connexion by five minutes. However, on Saturdays there is an extra which got us just beyond Addingham Reservoir before breaking down with the forward passengers in a semi-panic as clouds of steam belched out of bonnet and cab. Mindful of our own experiences there, we could but sympathise with the bus. The next service bus, half an hour later, took us on to Skipton where the next bus was not too overcrowded. At Ingleton I collected the gear from Reg's place and so to the farm.

"The evening was glorious; we went up to Keld Head, alas! but to find that the water was like sepia. It was heartbreaking. Still, we would have a go. Cows came to see what we were up to and we had second thoughts about leaving a tent up unattended until morning. So we went to see Jim Batty, the Keld Head farmer, to OK shifting them. Jim Batty was sympathetic but they were not his cows. Anyway we had a pleasant chat then snooped around the sink up the valley. The sink, like that of Goyden, is not very obvious, the water sinks in the boulders in the streambed. At last, with the ropes run out in the stream (no repeat of the Wookey tangle, please!), we left and got to bed on the stroke of midnight.

"Early next morning, breakfast at 7:45, we left for Keld Head and while I was dressing, Ritherdon and family arrived, which was just as well for we had lost the valve parts and his spare wheel provided substitutes. After more trouble with the neckband, eventually solved by keeping the band low and the dress high, I went down very slowly and in practically pitch blackness. It was as black as at Easter and from the bottom the daylight was not visible. It was a deal more pleasant a descent than at Easter, however, for there was now no doubt about the breathing kit. It was rather good fun to go down knowing that each step from one loose rock would be on to another loose rock and eventually onto gravel and to find that it was just so.

"What did appear from the trip was that a good light would penetrate the brown muck and not be reflected from it like from the white muck at Wookey. Methinks the car headlight stowed away at home would serve well here. Another thing was that the roof was found to go down in two bedding-plane steps, I hit them both on coming out! It was a pity but it would be daft to push on in water like that so I spent about half an hour frolicking in the pond, but the log-keeper quite forgot to log it.. Lying face down, sideways, upside down, watching the clouds and sunshine, and learning quite a lot, especially from one moment of panic when, falling down into deeper water from the centre bank, I momentarily forgot - or wanted to check - whether I had the mouthpiece and noseclip on O.K. and not until I took control of myself severely and put complete reliance on the kit did I come out of that panic and find myself lying flat on the bottom and all well.

"After that fun and games we went up the fellside following the fault while Ritherdon and family went to Yordas. Now Keld Head fault is very worthy, very wide and winsome, and in its lower reaches there are piles of stones, presumably fills, and higher up there are swallets and sinks just asking to be dug a bit. We must find out if the area has been prospected, and if not why not.

"We were back for dinner at two and left about three. Ray left an hour later by bus and won easily. We took 2 hours to Settle and 7 hours 40 for the whole journey finding a nice tea place, Coniston Cold Post Office, and discovering that the long hill on the side of the Chevin had been jacked up a bit. It nearly broke us. Thus it was a very successful and entertaining weekend, if you overlook the original object of the trip. The weather was quite the best yet and only a few chilly moments except the Saturday evening and night which were perishingly cold."

Keld Head had received us most unkindly and the jouneyings were indeed severe; we would give it a miss for a while.

Chapter 6

Alum Pot, Keld Head and Goyden Pot

Mary O'Neill, Ray O'Neill, Dickie Moxon, Graham Balcombe, Mavis Balcombe & Ray Nunwick, Alum Pot, 23/24 June 1945.

Rather depressed and rebuffed, we hankered for a change of scene and possibly a change of water but could we have a change of luck as well? We certainly have no claim to it but can always hope.

ALUM POT

Still with Notebook No.8.

"Week-end 23 & 24-6-45.

"Sunday the 24th June was an open day for The British Speleological Association, the Slaughter of the Innocents. Now Alum Pot has a sump, a black and sinister sump. Many years ago Reg Hainsworth had a go during a Conference Meeting and I took a look also. My own attempt was without any drive of conviction and failed to get more than a few feet in. Little did I realise I had been in water at least 30' deep (and with no idea of possible currents). How Reg fared I forget, but neither of us found new cave. This was to have been a weekend off, but a ready-laddered pot was too much of a temptation. Knowing Alum Pot to be a grand hole to look at and pretty easy to climb down - "a pansy pothole" says Cymmie - I thought it a good idea to let Cooky see the inside of the pot, and Dickie Moxon too," (another colleague) "to say nothing of Mavis. Then Paddy O'Neill" (another colleague) "and his pretty wife Mary wanted to come so it was fixed. We phoned around and got accommodation at the Golden Lion. Cooky and Mox arrived for dinner; they having travelled by train, and they whiled away the time propping up the bar and looking around Horton until the next-comers arrived. We were the next; having slogged with the tandem and trailer over hill and dale, we got in just after ten. Cooky and Moxon had been seen staggering down from the hotel carrying a small bundle between them - the weights - and the locals found it queer they should make so much fuss over so small a parcel, assumed them a bit loose in the head and cooed patronising 'good evenings' to them. Little did they know just how mad they were. Paddy and Mary arrived just as Mavis and I were debating how many sandwiches we could scoff and yet present the remainder as a plausible half. After much merrrymaking and some attention to the apparatus, we retired. It had been a fine-weather day and promised well for the morrow.

"On Sunday we were up bright and early or at least early; it was a morning of great promise; cloud mist hung over Pen-y-Ghent but elsewhere the sky was set fine for Yorkshire's second and probably last day of summer. Breakfast over, we trailed through Selside to be informed they had shifted pot a couple of miles up valley, becos it wer' a noosance. Being just a little bit sceptical, we went up the trod to have a look and found that if anything they had left an even bigger hole behind. It was a work of skill getting the trailer to the Plantation but we had a keen team and Ray still has vivid memories of working himself to a standstill on this trip - rigging ladders, hauling gear and especially heaving the trailer to The Plantation. Soon we were dressed and the tackle dropped down to the ledge where the tackle party was already waiting. This was still with the dew on the grass, too. So we went down Long Churn; now Long Churn and Alum have not really changed a lot lately so look up, for instance, Mitchell's pleasant description and it will suffice to add that for most of the diving party it was their initiation ceremony; we did not break any records though nearly broke some nerves and we did arrive at the bottom before the main party who were rubber-neckers for the moment but the rightful occupants of the cave.

"Dressing the diver was fairly simple for we had the parachute suit and as the Amphibian is carried down in one piece there was no delay with that either and soon the diver, with knees sagging slightly for which the weight of his kit could not entirely be blamed this time, took to the water.

"The tackle party had thrown a 25' ladder into the sump and the rungs floated on the brown froth on the surface. I started down the stone chute into the sump and fiddled about with the ladder and things sending some stones rumbling down whereupon the ladder sank out of sight. As I pulled the end it came up slowly and with considerable resistance then on letting go it was sucked back and came to rest with a perceptible shiver. Did that mean a small bedding crack with a terrific current? Was this one of those malevolent currents which by 'intentional suction', such as we poked fun at on the Wookey Hole work, are bent on sucking the helpless diver down some 'orrible orifice? Somewhat apprehensive I handed back my drum reel and put on an orthodox lifeline, told the attendants just what I thought of the place, and refreshed their memories on signals. Then there was a bit of trouble with the goggles, but not for long, and I started down the slope, hanging on to the ladder with one hand. I got under the overhang where the slope eased momentarily then suddenly found my feet overhanging plain water. Gingerly I went down until my chest was level with the ledge when a couple of boulders came rolling down past me, clink, clink, clunk, clunk, down out of hearing. Maybe the miner's hat should be brought into use again. When things had settled down again I went"

Notebook No.9.

"down slowly groping round with the probe. The water was murky, thick with floating bits from above, and yellow, making the light more a comfort than of use. Imagine my surprise when I came to the bottom of the ladder just a few feet below the ledge and found a great stone tied to it. I had never thought of that but was relieved to have the solution to the ladder-sucking effect.

"I do not remember much of my thoughts while hanging on to the bottom of the ladder with one hand and probing about except that it seemed to be a second Dolly Tubs. Naturally, I was disappointed; I had hoped for, but hardly expected, a quick dip and rise to air. More hope than realism for, with only a few feet fall between Alum Pot Sump and the rising, to expect a shallow vadose stream is hardly reasonable,... the character of the fault in which the cave runs as far as the sump does hold hopes that a section of deep water with great air spaces, like Wookey Seven, might well be met but with present techniques the diver would likely be the last to know of it. Firstly, the water was dirty but there could be some improvement by party control then a much better light would be imperative.... Next, the diver (at present) inevitably treads the bottom of all ways into the unknown; what is important is to explore the roof not the floor. These point to the need for evolution of new techniques and demand more experience than we have at the moment.... It is about time we left the bottom of the ladder. I went up but had rather a lot of gas in the bag; I had had no chance since the new kit arrived of getting used to its tricks hence I had on plenty of lead (21 lb) which allowed the gas bag to get quite full without consequence until the diver goes up. The bag ballooned and only by hanging on to the ladder did I manage to restore equilibrium, but in the first few unpleasant moments even the ladder thought it would come up with me. In those few moments I withdrew unequivocally all those unkind imprecations on the man who had tied on that stone! The surface was marked by the sudden intrusion of the roar of Diccan Pot waterfall.... At the surface I had another ladder tied on and lowered until the stone weight bottomed. This gave some 25' from the edge of the sump. The goggles then gave trouble; they were Flanagan swim goggles and where they crossed the dress they leaked and leaked badly" (naturally); "it was exasperating." (I cannot understand why professional people put up with such a crude amateurish arrangement; they did not for long for Dunlops were bringing fresh ideas to the diving world.) "Eventually I achieved a fairly good seating and went down but just over the edge one eye packed in; the other held on long enough to get to the bottom which proved just to be a ledge and the pitch went on at an easier angle. I was not tempted to leave the ladder without a distance line so after probing round I went up. The second eye failed after a few feet but it was not long before the roar of the fall told me I had got back to the right spot whereupon we soon packed up and slowly made our exit.... So much for that grand hole. We shall go again, I expect, when we are more experienced and 40 of the available 46 minutes are not wasted in adjusting goggles."

"We had arranged to have some lunch left out for us at the Golden Lion and so it was; it decorated the table all afternoon and had to be cleared away for the evening meal at 6:30. The gong was just being sounded as we sneaked in through the rear door, fearing the worst. It seemed, however, that our good hosts were more alarmed for our fate than concerned about the inconvenience so we ate well and departed, regretfully, for we had been made very welcome. Mox and Cookie stayed on for they had no bikes and there was no train until the following day. We had left Pete in kennels and now left the gear at the Settle headquarters" (Cymmie's place) "so travelled light and fairly fast in a glorious sunlit-moonlit evening to arrive home at one o'clock: a pleasant run as far as

Otley but oh, that Chevin!"

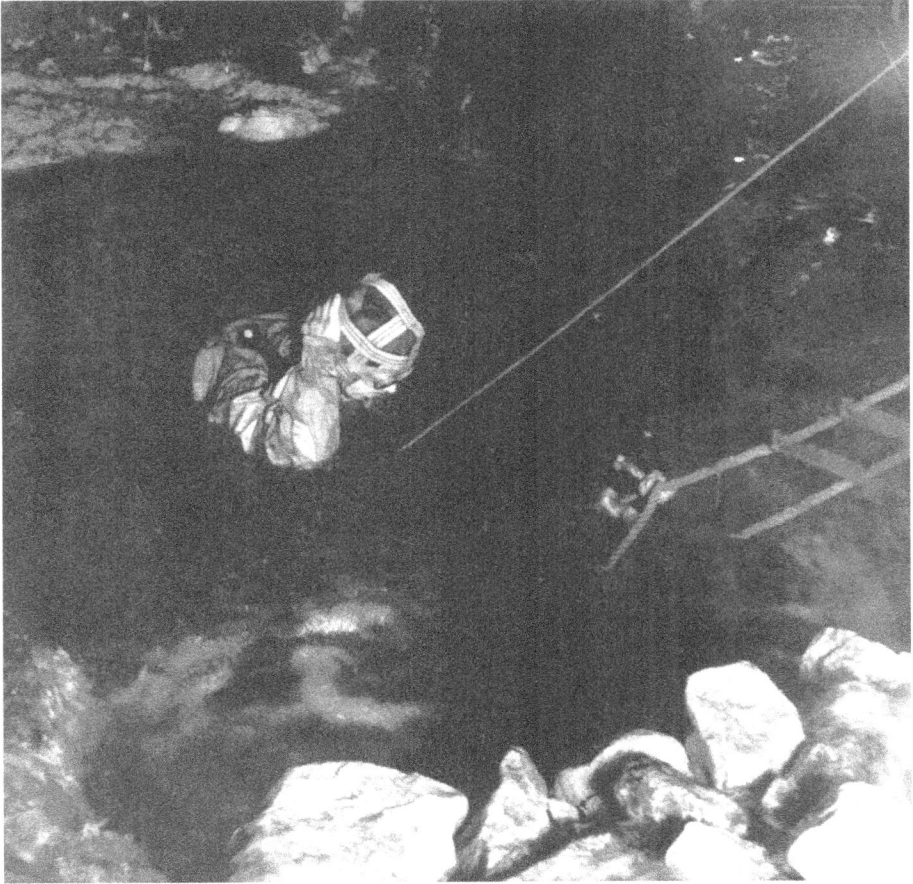

Graham Balcombe, Alum Pot, 24 June 1945.

MODIFICATIONS AND MISCELLANY

Modifications were being made continually to Whodd and Whodba but one to Whodd stands out above most. A Linatex sheet with a 4½" hole was let into its chest, two burly dressers pull the hole out until the diver can enter that way, then the hole would be sealed by a snazzy plug. Linatex was that extraordinary stretch material used, inter alia, to line our aircrafts' fuel tanks; the bullet holes would seal again. The modification eliminated the troublesome and time-wasting waist joint, was highly successful and as a bonus never failed to raise the spirits of the diving party. Over the naughty business of the modification itself, working with an open fire in the room and the naphtha bottle turned towards the window so the fire could not seeit, the veil should be drawn save to quote that: "The critical concentration for explosion was not reached but the c.c. for driving Mavis out was. How she suffers for speleology!"

Much of the time was now being spent in modifications or just plain looking after my job which took me away from home quite a lot but in the next notebook there is a pleasant little addendum to the notes on Keld Head:

Notebook No.10.

"the diver poked head and feet inside [an alternative entrance] but did not go inside. He found a 5" fish reclining there; a delightful moment. It lay still until he was within a few inches of it when, whizz! there was nothing but a cloud of mud."

Apart from further practice in the local lake, the next diving was the memorable trip to Keld Head.

"KELD HEAD INCIDENT Weekend 4 & 5-8-45.

"The days rolled into weeks and still no batteries had arrived or even been notified. On enquiry I was told they would be sent off the same weekend and, after a spot of bother, Britannia managed to arrange passenger train transit. Another week went by but nothing arrived. Renewed investigation and a new promise. Another week but nothing arrived. We had planned this op. for the Bank Holiday weekend: Saturday at Stainforth Foss, Sunday at Keld Head and thereafter as circumstances dictated. It had been really lovely weather for the last fortnight and hopes were running high. By Friday it was something of a crisis; phone and telegraph failed to locate the missing package and the trip was called off. Ray and his pal would be going in any case and Cookie would be joining them.

Mavis had been suffering from a bad tooth and swollen neck and was unlikely to be travelling. Later in the afternoon Cooky begged to be excused. Anyhow, he said his father wished him to go to Manchester but he would turn up at Westhouse if possible." (I think father had rumbled what he was up to.)

"Presumably he thought he could contact Ray by telepathy but must have had the wrong frequency for Ray bought in all the food, still expecting him. As time was fast running out, I started the manufacture of a battery-box and other fittings, hoping the drawing supplied was the right issue; the amount of work proved quite considerable. In fact I was soon flat out on a major project and realised the batteries might still be the easy winners. They were. They were delivered Saturday morning with the wiring only just started.

"At ten we went into Leeds, Mavis to her appointment with the dentist who found too much inflammation to operate but reassured her on the unlikelihood of worsening, so that let her in on the trip again. Meantime I went to the city centre for spokes and bulbs which later we found was just as well.

"By midday the wiring was in full swing, but with little hope of starting that day. It was fascinating work but nevertheless galling to be penned up in the rafters while outside the sun was blazing down in one of the warmest days of the year and, according to the weather forecast, right this time, to be the last of the present warm spell. At last the main task was over and collection for packing begun, with its inevitable trail of odd jobs, but it was not completed until middle Sunday morning despite being up again with the lark (the 7 a.m. buzzer on the alarm clock is our tame skylark; much more reliable than the little blighters in the field next door). I tried to weigh the trailer but a 60-lb maximum reading was too little to register the wheel loads; the whole thing was about 150 lb. The weather was still good, cooler and better suited to our load, and we had a measure of relief in that the gears were working again; back in the condition of first, second and a limping top. We reached Moorgarth Hall by eight but Reg was up to his eyes in work and could not help us up the last long slope. At Westhouse we met Ray and a Peter McKenzie; we were not sure which meal they were just finishing but they loaded us up with tent, primus and further odds and ends and pushed us off well and truly to the Dent Road.

"We pitched on the Scar side of the road, after a visit to Braida Garth, and just got things in before the rain hit us; for quarter of an hour it came down really hard and heavy then eased off, but it did not rain at Westhouse. That night we did about everything possible that a tenderfoot could do and, as for breakfast with a primus stove, I think we should call in JKJ for an adequate description.

"At last we assembled at the pool and I climbed into the diving kit. There were changes. A new neckband arrangement was successful. Next the entry port was plugged with the new Ritherdon Dishes and they worked, too. The goggles were tried with a smear of vaseline and they seemed to work. Further, the gas joints were O.K. immediately, and the lamps switched on to plan. In fact everything is getting arranged at last; the only fault was with the diver who, having been so long out of his element, was windy and wished himself anywhere other than at Keld Head. Once underwater, everything was so lovely that all nasty thoughts were soon forgotten and, peering down the entrance slope, I switched the light on and - behold! the way down lay bathed in the bright light" (48-watt bulbs) "showing up the gap in the bedding, the steep boulder slope, and the golden gravel at the bottom which now seemed only a step or two down. I went down gaily; I did not count the steps, but there were far more than two; there was the familiar hug of the water as it drove the dress close on me and pressed on my ears. At the bottom I hung around to get my eyes accustomed and played with the lights. They were good although two were by no means twice as good as one. The place is dominantly a bedding-plane cave and, strangely enough, I was quite unable to find the archway and soon lost myself in a northerly direction among the fallen blocks. Realising this I turned west and picked up the trail of gravel patches which marks the main current course. The new Aflo has a fitting for a current indicator, as yet missing, likewise the depth meter has not yet been produced; a pressure gauge had been calibrated but the attempts to seal it failed.

"Back to the cavern: the general structure is still predominantly bedding plane and only at one point is the way near to surface which seemed only a few inches away but beware of illusions! The light beam gave its presence away by doubling back in reflection; apart from this it was so clean that it was undetectable. I did not go up for undoubtedly it was the rift chamber with the stalactites I had already seen; maybe it is some 20 yards in.

"At about 40 yards the route turns north and soon I found the old drum at the foot of a boulder and a few yards of line still on it. The line had broken only a few feet short of the loop marking the furthest point reached" (we had attempted recovery from shore but failed) "so the previous estimate can be revised; the distance reached was about 60 yards only. I coiled up the old line, hooked the drum to my belt, anchored the working line to a stone and cut it for the point where I found the drum coincided almost exactly with my current full run-out, then I made for home and a new line. On the way in I had seen three fish, trout I think, about 5" to 7" long, the first quite near the entrance, the second some way in, and the third which I nearly touched was a long way in and in total darkness. Its appearance was quite normal; probably just a visitor. On the way out there was no sign of life and the whole route seemed strange, boulders to be surmounted which I never remembered from the way in and, what I had not noticed before, at one point the cave was quite small, in fact, everywhere the new lights made the cave look much smaller than before but at this point there was only just room to go through crouched down.

"Out on the bank they looked at me as if I was daft when I reported having brought the old drum back. With reason as there was no drum; it had become unhooked and dropped by the way. I did not see it again. It was lunch-time and we had quite a long break. Ritherdon and his party were with us; while they lunched from their car, we lit a fire and the gang fed by that then split up, Ray to fix a date with a girl-friend and we to collect the milk from the farm. Not only did we collect the milk but finished the churning, borrowed a thermometer, and hied us off to the sink to test the water which was not there; the dry spell had dried up the beck completely. Back at the Head the water was 49° but here and there in the exit it was only 48°. I was dressed quickly and went down again, full of confidence and with a new line. The gas was getting low in the working cylinder but there was plenty and here was a good chance to get used to the transfer technique.

"I followed the line without delay and located the end. The apparatus did not seem to be going so well but I attributed that to the absorber being on its second run, to the breathing pipe being rather long, and to the rate of working while coming in. Thus I was breathing quite heavily while groping round for the new rope end, to be tied on to the old, when suddenly the respirator choked; the resistance shot up to an impossible figure and I knew from experience that the pipe must have kinked; rapidly I passed my hand over it, but no, there was no trace of kinking. Alarmed and not knowing what the trouble could be, but knowing I could not last long in that condition, I tried more gas just in case. The working cylinder must have been very low for equalizing much increased the flow; I could hear it rushing into the bag but did not realise just how much had gone in. Still the breathing bag was distended hard as ever;" (no relief valve at that time) "I looked up for possible escape to a surface but could see none. In desperation I tried the tube again and again but found it O.K. then suddenly the resistance dropped to normal. At the same time the bag discharged so violently it blew the gag out of my mouth and away went a bagful of gas, some five to ten litres of it, before I succeeded in cramming the mouthpiece back again. It was fortunate it was pure water not pure sewage or something like that for I shipped quite a lot both into me and into the absorber. It was no end of a relief to get back to normal breathing but I still did not know what to expect. Would the wetting stop the absorber action? I had vivid memory of the earlier breathing tests when my breathing became so violent that I could not retain the mouthpiece. I stood a moment, checked the line, debated whether Aflo would be help or hindrance, then taking firm command of myself went very slowly with it to the bank. It seems that wet sodalime still absorbs quite well... I opened the equalizer once, perhaps twice, on the way and when I reached the bank the attendants checked and found zero-zero, both cylinders empty, which despite the accidental loss takes some explaining and gives an urgent warning." (I think the rule nowadays is to abandon dive when one-third supply used, leaving a third for the return and one third spare. I have no real idea how much was lost accidentally on this occasion.)

"There was no more diving and it was not until during the following night that, awaking from a nightmare in my sleeping bag, I found the cause of the trouble. It was simple, absurdly simple. Since last using - and getting used to - my outfit I had fitted a mouthpiece tap and must have nearly closed it accidentally and later, equally accident-ally, knocked it open again. The existence of the tap and its potentialities never struck me while searching the breathing pipe for kinks. Such is the effect, until accustomed, of the strange underwater existence. It will never be overlooked again, indeed, I shall probably have a tap-fixation for many a day. All this, however, is just personal tittle-tattle. What progress have we made since the drum was first left behind? Quite a measure but mostly in the matters of equipment and experience. The dress is vastly superior, though the goggles are a weak feature, and we have lights. In experience I have gained a lot, and I know I have a tap! We know fairly accurately how far we have penetrated Keld Head and have some slight knowledge of the form of the cave. We have also discovered fish living in the dark zone of the entrance.

"That evening, being Bank Holiday, we had a grand fire and stuffed our kites. Alas! either the stuffing or the diving had upset my stomach a bit and I had a rough night and morning so, much to Mavis's disappointment, we did not start home until one o'clock, just as the weather began to take up for it had rained all that time. The journey was not without incident for, after a long delay unshipping kit at Reg's, the back wheel of the tandem decided to come apart and by the time nine spokes had gone we pulled in for repairs. How provident we had those spares! The rain began again just as we finished the job and continued, off and on, until we got home. After beautiful rainbows at Skipton we had some excellent fish and chips at Ilkley, made a mad rush home without a tail-light, and arrived at half past ten.

"The journey is far too taxing and will have to be eliminated in some way."

We had one final look at Keld Head but paused on the way to give O'Neill his first dip.

"STAINFORTH FOSS & KELD HEAD Four

"... The weather for the week preceding the 15th" (September, 1945) "was a pretty poor selection and the water would be pretty thick; still, if we were to find out how useful Aflo's lights would be, we had better try them. Ray O'Neill" (yes, Paddy is another Ray) "was keen to come so we were glad to have him and to put him under at Stainforth Foss, a deep in the Ribble. Some luggage had gone in advance as far as Skipton which eased the burden somewhat. Eventually, managing to escape the rain which threatened ominously, we reached Settle, picked up the Amphibian and pedalled off to the Foss.

"It is a lovely spot to look at, to dive in, to sit by for a picnic, or to shelter from the rain under the thick leafy sycamores. We know, for we did all these things, and the smoke from our fire helped to mitigate the only drawback, the nibbling midges. Yes, nibbling midges, not the all-devouring kind to be found at Golden Acre. O'Neill, as the performer, had a brief instruction on how the Amphibian worked" (were he alive today he might say whether at that time he was told the need of a breathing drill) "then put it on and went for a walk along the bank to acclimatise. Then with Paradive, the parachute dress, and Sgamo, the Amphibian, and a good stout rope round his middle, he waded down the shelf into the deeper water.(The kit is illustrated as Plate XXVIII in British Caving.) It was an exciting moment for the onlookers too; I well remember my own first dip in the Mineries Pond on Mendip at tadpole time and this must have been a strange experience for him. He walked boldly and steadily down the incline, his dress ballooning with the trapped air, when suddenly he toppled over backwards and started to float away for all the world like a celluloid duck in a bath. He soon discovered that letting the air out of the dress still left his legs afloat and, after lying there a moment, presumably calculating the next move, rolled over and stood up. Descending again with more care he soon submerged and began to manoeuvre about the edge of the shelf. He had about half an hour with the usual troubles; could not keep down, goggles leaked, gave wrong signals and all that, and eventually came out well satisfied. Justifiably, for a first dip he made a very good showing.

"It was strange to be an attendant watching another go down in the water and disappear from sight; it gave me a special thrill to see his strange headpiece moving along some four feet under the surface and knowing it was the preliminary to great adventure.

"We reached Westhouse just before ten and Mrs. Whitfield was already abed, having given us up for lost. Actually it was only O'Neill who was expected but we reckoned on getting fixed in somewhere for it was too late to camp in comfort. We were invited to sleep in the hut, - a disused henhouse - if we wished, and did we wish! It seems some person had pitched a tale about having Ray Nunwick's permission to borrow his tent and had taken it leaving us the heavily-laden clouds to cover us up. We had hardly entered the hut when the rain, which had threatened all day, came down. It rained really hard from then until well into Sunday morning. It lashed the roof, found all the leaks and cracks, and did not ease up once unless while we were asleep. By ten next day there was a lull. The stream outside was spouting high into the air making washing up an easy if exciting process; we made off for Keld Head to see what it was like. The rain beat us to it and lashed us in fury as we rode down the final slope to the stream. Kingsdale Beck was a roaring brown torrent sweeping the flood fences out horizontally and overflowing its banks below them. The island in the Head was awash and the rising was a brown flood spewing from the hole and rushing out in all directions from it. The water at the rising was six inches above the general surface of the pond.... I attempted to take a few photos for the record but shipped a lot of water and had little hope of success. Diving was utterly out of the question.

"We returned to the hut, soaked, to attempt a dry-out while lunching and praying it would ease up a bit before we set out. Finally we could wait no longer (or at last we had finished our grub and were ready to go) and at three we moved off. The Ribble at Settle was characteristic of the day: a yellow-brown flood poured over the weir then swooped through the pool at its foot, rose and fell in a series of giant standing waves six feet from trough to crest, then flattened out to rush through the bridge and away, flooding the fields on either bank.

"Lo! the rain eased off to a mere shower and once or twice we even un-caped for a moment or two. At last, parting from O'Neill at Skipton, we reached Burley then through the floods at Otley to home again. It had been a disastrous day for would-be divers. 'Operation Fisca' had better have been named 'Operation Fiasco'."

We had said farewell, unknowingly, to Keld Head. Had we known, it perhaps would have been an occasion for rejoicing, for the effort and discomforture had been out of all proportion to the results. Well, maybe. But it had not been our final fling in Yorkshire. Let the record speak of the quite creditable but scarcely brilliant episode in Nidderdale.

Notebook No.11.

"GOYDEN POT, 14-10-45

"My own diving gear, all of it, was now at home at Bramhope and the season was drawing to a close. Now the GPO are members of the Post Office Engineering Department temporarily domiciled in Harrogate and calling themselves The Goyden Pot 'Olers, by virtue of their weekend labours in pushing forward the survey and exploration of that pot. They were mostly newcomers to caving; they carried a refreshing enthusiasm into their activities and had a markedly technical approach to the problems they met. Such people get good results.

"The GPO were to have their final trip of the year to Nidderdale at the weekend of l3 & 14-10-45 and to graft diving onto their project was more than just a possibility. They had been looking forward to such an event: Nunwick and I had at first intended my own first dip should be at Goyden Pot, not Keld Head, so my curiosity had already been aroused. It now became a race to get the equipment in working order. There was the neckband to make good, the waist leak to repair, the batteries to make fit for further service and the tandem to fix. The neckband was straightforward, soon patched up and the outer band solutioned to it. It turned out to be an improvement for the sorbo band is no longer needed.

"The waist leak was different; to find it meant flooding the suit" (doubtless there was a better way had I stopped to think) "which entailed a long delay for drying out. The leak proved to be due to a defective area of rubber in the twill sandwich, probably caused by wear as it was adjacent the stiff seam under the arm. That job was finished by midnight on Saturday. Meantime Mox examined the batteries as I had had to go down to London awhile. It seemed three of the six cells were flat; the whole battery consisted of three two-cell units and the cases were not insulated. I had housed them in a partitioned wooden box but this proved inadequate insulation for more than short exposures to wet conditions. With careful charging and discharging all cells (alkali-type) were brought back to serviceable condition. The tandem's back wheel had a chunk or two chewed off the Sturmey-Archer planet pinions which had not improved the rest of the works. We were lucky to have got home on it. Spares were available for the planet pinions and the cracked bits were knocked off the spindle pinion and, so long as one retained an excesssive optimism, the bike would be fit for the road. In spite of one or two alarms, it held out.

"Thus all was set. The baggage went by car, O'Neill and I by tandem, leaving Mavis and Mary to spend the day as they might choose. We were up at six, away by 7:20 and at the pot by 10:10. It was one of those rare still mornings promising a scorching day and so it proved. There was frost where the cold air had slid down into hollows by the Nidd but the sun was hot and as the day wore on it turned out to be one of the hottest days of the year, certainly one of the most magnificent days I had ever experienced, and this in October. As we passed Gouthwaite Reservoir the lake was still except for the almost undiscernable ripples, started by jumping fish and rolling on indefinitely, intermingling to give the reflections of the sky and land slightly softer outlines than their originals. It was by this we were able to say whether we or the mirrored landscape were upside down.

"The car party, Francis and Gort, arrived a few minutes later and the lazy blighters who had stopped the night at Thorope Farm (it was also an excellent way of eking out one's rations!) straggled along some time later. The organiser of GPO had organised in fine style; each member had written instructions for his day's jobs except the diving team which was an unknown and quite undisciplined factor in the arrangements. It took quite a while to get the kit ready for the descent and, admittedly, to recover from the ride, to loll in the sunshine, to stoke the inner man and to survive a mild attack of cramp. Meantime the main party went below to get on with the survey. The gear was not ideally packed, for we had not yet reached the pothole-diving stage, but the cave is a very easy one and the distance to the first sump only about 1,000 feet. Thus in three or four trips we were able to get the stuff as far as the bedding plane near the sump.

"The intention was to examine the sump at the end of Main River Passage as the only reasonable way to get to the sump in Lower River Passage for the route round Gaskell's Passage is a formidable proposition for divers. After lunch and another attack of cramp, this time not so mild and in the other leg, O'Neill and I - after soliciting the help of some cyclist rubber-neckers who decided not to get their feet wet after all - toddled back to the bedding plane and laid out the gear. I was nearly dressed by the time that the main party arrived from lunch out in the open air and we were informed that the Gaskell's Passage party were on their way to welcome the diver at the far end of the sump if he ever got there. First I made an overwater examination of the sump and noted a small rift running roughly SE along the back of the pool. Here a tree-trunk jammed under the rock formed the first obstacle. I was able to climb over it while unencumbered and the way on seemed to be SW from the far side of the trunk. This part of the pool is out of sight and not shown on the map but it is a minor feature. The water was flowing SW. Then, with the apparatus on, I succeeded in getting down on the near side of the tree down an easy slope with very little room to spare; the floor to roof distance was about two feet. I managed to worm down to six feet depth by Aflo, sending up clouds of mud - and leaving a trail on the bottom the shore party reported. The bedding plane went on and just groping for the best route I found myself turning NW; occasionally I would meet washed-in debris and always wished the rope would run out so that I could turn back for home. The way seemed endless; time and time I faltered, felt how much rope was left but it was always still a few turns so I felt obliged to run out just that bit more. Progress was achieved by lying on my right shoulder, lifting Aflo along a bit then crawling after it. At last the water became shallower and with mixed feelings I emerged to find myself in a sealed rift, hardly big enough to call it an aven, but bigger than the Little Bell in Swildon's Hole which it otherwise resembled. Disappointed, I ducked under again, leaving the scum and floating debris, and dropped into clear water. It had been quite a relief to move sideways now and again and get a glimpse of clean water though I cannot remember having seen any boundaries to this God-forsaken hole. It was consoling to think that if and when I turned back I would probably be able to see. I was using one of Aflo's lights and even if it could not show me where to go, it gave me comfort to be in a lighted place; without it I am sure I would have shirked the task. Well, I had run into clean water in a rather deeper channel, perhaps three feet high and at 10 feet depth by Aflo. Soon it took a steep upward tilt and I could get to my feet; the trapped air rushed out of my dress and soon I was out in a tunnel with a rush and splash of water at the far end. Was this indeed the far end or was it some intermediate point? If the lower end then where were the lower-end men? I shouted and listened, put out my lights and looked; I heard nothing but water and saw nothing at all. My line ran out at 10 feet down the tunnel where a tree-branch lay across the stream. I pulled at the branch and it dropped below the surface and jammed again, just too far away to use for making off the line.

"Reluctantly I turned back. The line now seemed to come from a different quarter; it had pulled over to the right, I tried to follow it but found the way too narrow and Aflolaun got jammed. It was a steep downward slope and some stones had shifted and trapped it. It took me some anxious minutes, or so it seemed, to free it. I went back to the full extent of the rope to reconsider. The line had passed behind a tree-trunk jammed in the passage so I went down left of the obstruction and the line obediently came clear. Once at the bottom, I found things easier; the line disappeared ahead into the blackness; I crawled along in clear water but cannot recollect how far ahead I could see, only that the line went always straight ahead until it disappeared. The passage seemed roomier than on the downward journey and I saw another fish - two small trout or some such had flitted across my path when I first took the plunge - and round me was dark brown rock, brown firm bottom,and clear water. It was encouraging no end and soon I forgot the misgivings I felt when standing alone and very, very lonely in the tunnel I had just left.

"The line was troublesome. I have never before been able to recover a line. I attempted to coil it into loops in my left hand while simultaneously hanging on to Aflo but my hand was now so numbed I had lost control to a large extent and soon found myself getting tangled in dropped loops. I lay a while to work out what next and decided to drum up. Lying down with the drum on its side the operation was successful, in fact easy, just a question of keeping cool (cool?) and not giving in to the urge to bolt for the shore. Moving forward half a dozen yards, I stopped and drummed up again, and so on till the bedding plane tilted up gradually and as I was about to drum up again I heard a shout, quite a loud noise but not intelligible. I dropped the drum immediately, went forward and in a few feet broke surface. The job was over.

"I had come out at a point roughly W of the shore party, that is, some yards to their right; they feared the line had slipped down some slim crack and I would not be able to exit there; they hollered a warning and O'Neill was dashing in to guide the line back to the old spot. The headroom was in fact about the same and if there is another crossing the diver should go in by the right-hand route (diver's right). The line was 100 feet long, which gives about 75 feet net length for the sump and compares well with the 65 feet on the plan though we had not proved the point I reached to be the known end of the water-trap.

"To settle this point, a few of us went round Gaskell's to have a look. Gaskell's is a filthy but intriguing passage. Two tributary streams in the past had united and parted again, one on its way to the main stream above the sump, the other below it, thus creating a by-pass. The going is very interesting, quite sporting, and finishes with a pitch. Here we found the tackle-party had made a most impressive job of the laddering; an enormous rope was securely belayed to an enormous rock and for safety given no less than three turns round another belay and from this dangled, just out of the sight of the emboldened pot-holer, two bits of string with rungs on them. It was GPO's first effort at a ladder. Anyway, it proved to have a safety factor of one-plus-delta so all was well. It was easy to climb, but made one a little circumspect and avoid bouncing down one edge hand-over-hand! We met the bottom party there and learned that they had doddered off downstream to the lower sump. Maybe they had seen the diver inspecting the debouchure at Lofthouse and thought he was to come upstream. Or perhaps they could not tell upstream from downstream. A kinder explanation would be that they took the Lower River for a tributary and expected the Main River to flow in lower down. Anyway that was their story so we might as well accept it. We took a look at the rising; it seemed smaller, no doubt because viewed from our higher vantage point, a ledge on the right wall. It was undoubtedly the same place and there was the branch jammed across the stream, two feet underwater and ten feet from the end.

"There was nothing now left to do but to make for the fresh air as any attempt at the lower sump had long been written off. So back we went, this time lightly loaded for there were many of us; and soon we were changed and on our way to a feed of feeds at Thorope Farm where Gaunt completely lost his reputation for having a large appetite. We had already been down to Lofthouse to phone our wives the O.K. so, after dinner, we waddled to the bike, laboriously climbed into the saddles and set off. It was a glorious night with the half-moon hanging low over Greenhow, following us as we rode down the valley. We rode quite fast, called in at Pateley Bridge to celebrate the crossing of the sump and arrived back home at midnight to close an exceptional day. We had ridden 30 miles to get there, done a pot, the diver had suffered ordeal by diving while the attendants suffered ordeal by waiting, then 30 miles back; in all eighteen hours of hard going.

"The sump in Goyden Main River Passage is no light task; its crossing was achieved only by virtue of the experience of Keld Head and Alum Pot, embodied both in the diver and his outfit. It is just as well we assayed it at the end of the season and did not try our hand there early on as we once intended. Even now an attack on the lower sump via the upper sump - the practical way - is an ambitious program but our adventure there this weekend has proved it possible."

That was our farewell to Yorkshire as divers, apart from one practice dip in a reservoir. The war was over, the fireworks spent and the rejoicing had largely died down. During our stay in Yorkshire the weather had been very unkind to us but it is a beautiful endearing county. As a Lancashire man perhaps I should not love it so. But it was back to London town, leaving the crags and heather-clad purple moors, the disappearing becks and the wild cries of the upland birds, for the jungle of bricks, mortar and concrete once again.

Chapter 6

Ffynnon Ddu and the CDG

Jack Sheppard & Graham Balcombe, Ffynnon Ddu, Easter 1946.

Early in 1946 I again contacted Jack Sheppard, Major Sheppard, now demobbed and free to roam. We both signified interest in further diving so plans were laid, or at least we would give them thought. I had my sights on Wookey, of course, but much had first to be done. We then had but Whodd-Whodba and Paradive-Sgamo with nowhere to practice. Willesden Baths most hospitably solved this last problen and we shall be for ever grateful.

Notebook No.12.

"AT THE BATHS

"... Sheppard was given ten minutes air trial with Sgamo which did not improve his appreciation of the outfit but did step up his appreciation of the cup of tea which appeared about this time. We then dressed him in Paradive and sent him below.... At first the goggle bogey was much in evidence and so was the buoyancy bogey... two more seven-pound weights... plus two more seven-pound weights gave him excellent control and he charged round the deep end, a full, clear and beautiful ten feet,... and so on until finally out of gas at the shallow end... as Sheppard remarked the outfit gives a false sense of security as all seems well until, quite without warning, you are suddenly and seriously out of gas.

"So much for the trial. Yeomans, the Superintendant, then told us he had a spare room upstairs where we could quite safely store our gear and, if we wanted obstacles, he could bring them up from 'below'; did we want to make trials in the dark, then he could fix that .... Well, could hospitality be more cordial?"

Next a meeting with Hodgkinson; the Captain, now a Wing-Commander, gave us the O.K. and a store of useful information on facilities about the cave. Then an oxygen supply was negotiated, and then more practice when this time the refreshment was Bovril and baked potatoes!

"... It was agreed to try at the weekend before Easter at Wookey but later it had to be postponed until the weekend before Whitsun to suit the BBC who wanted to do a program and, naturally enough, the Wingco would not let a chance like that slip; that would be silly."

THE CDG

The time had now arrived to do some organisation of diving effort. It would inevitably be that recruits to a cave-diving club would be members of caving clubs already, probably leading and very active members: indeed, such was desirable for we believed firmly that cave-diving should rest on caving familiarity and caving ability rather than on just diving ability. Surely this would lead to fears of poaching and to explain our position a circular went out to cave secretaries.

Then came a trip to Wales. I had had some tiny experience of limestone sea-caves as a small boy living at The Mumbles and was doubly cheered at the prospect of re-visiting the Principality.

Graham Balcombe, Ffynnon Ddu, Easter 1946.

"FFYNNON DDU, EASTER 1946

"During the months which passed between the departure from Yorkshire and repossessing our London home the restrictions on practical activity naturally fostered thoughts of a cave diving group. The response to various tentative enquiries was very pleasing. Ideas about a CDG took more definite shape and soon a proposal was launched for an informal group of cave-diving enthusiasts. Naturally, it would be a small beginning and, with some half dozen on the list, the first diving meeting was fixed for South Wales.

"We had been again to the baths and Jack Sheppard had met trouble with his ears, finding it impossible to get down to the 10' level, but fortunately that was cured by a short course of ephidrene and all was well. South Wales was chosen as there was to be a meeting at The Gwyn Arms, partly for a bit of caving and partly to form a caving club for South Wales, and Ffynnon Ddu, hard by, had been crying for a long time for attention. Ffynnon Ddu might well be the key to the problem of Pant Canol where the local lads, and some not so local, have been scratching for some time now. The whole area is very interesting and the people of the valley have for a long time cherished the hope that a great cave system might be found, a fair companion to Dan-yr-Ogof on the other side of the valley. It is a long time since I visited DyO and in any case I must have gone through it with my eyes closed, for I cannot remember much about it, but it is probably a fairly recent cave, carved out by the stream it now carries. Be that as it may, the Pant Canol is a very old system in which the present trickle has had little to say; it is a fossil, a relic of an age before the present valleys had been formed, when the area was a low-lying plain, or at least when the rocks forming the present hills were below the water-table.

"The chances of finding a sizable cavern depend on the possibility of getting through to the ancient system rather than to the cave of Ffynnon Ddu itself. Not that the Ffynnon Ddu stream is small, as cave streams go in this country it is quite as big as, say, White Scar where there is a large cavern on view to the public. However, these hopes, but only our own hopes, were destined to disappointment, as we shall see.

"Ffynnon Ddu is a beautiful spring whence the water bubbles over a stony streamed on its short course to the Tawe. The banks were sprinkled with violets peeping with big-eyed curiosity to see the strange doings of the latest callers. There was a nice flat-topped mound for those who like to loll in the sun, and the sun shone as I have only once known it at Easter. It shone all day and every day, almost. There was the shade of the trees for those who chose it. No such person being present, the shade came in useful for hanging out diving dresses to dry for there were handy low branches. Rubber, as everyone knows, is very liable to sun-stroke.

"After our first joyful visit to the spring we wandered over to see Farmer Powell who owns the land. He and his lad, Cyril, were busy ploughing over a potato field so we waited until the last few rows were covered. The Powells have a live and practical interest in caving and are stout fellows withal, for it was they who went into Pant Canol Cave while it was too dangerous for prudent cavemen way back in 1942. Powell said he would go first thing in the morning and bring the gear down to the spring. Mr.James, who runs the little station with one train a day each way (except Good Friday and Sundays, we are in Wales now, boyo!), would be only too pleased to turn out on his holiday to get the stuff out of the station. We patrolled the Powell holding, noted the depressions and places where Powell told us the water rises in times of flood, inspected the entrance to Pant Canol cave and looked into Penwyllt Cave.

"Penwyllt Cave is a joy to those students of cavern origin involved in the controversy of vadose vs. phreatic origins. Its ideal tubular shape with well-formed facetting tells of a main trunk full to the roof with fast-moving water. The upper portion of Pant Canol seems to be a continuation of this dead giant though much modified and weathered. Maybe it continued in its day down a route which in process of later erosion became Pant Canol itself, a small open valley. There are sinks probably into the same system up at Craig-y-Nos" (not Craig-y-Nos, surely?) "but we did not visit those.

"The organiser of the meet, Arthur Hill of Swansea, had fixed our party, and Frost as a fourth, at Nant Rhiw, the waterworks cottage, where Charlie Price lives and attends, among other things, to the chlorination of the Cray Reservoir water. He picked us up in his car at The Gwyn Arms and took us home where we were most warmly welcomed. The day had been rather poor and I had feared - and the forecast had pronounced - a break in the glorious spell of weather which had held now for several weeks but next morning the sun was shining and, with the sun in our hearts too, we wandered down to The Gwyn and from there we had a lift to Ffynnon Ddu. The gear arrived about the same time as we and soon it was strewn about in disorderly fashion - how much more careful one must be down a cave or when it is raining! -and eventually the divers went below. The water was crystal-clear; the descent was delayed by neck trouble, expected, from my new neckband but soon I was able to peer inside the cavern. The structure seen from the outside is fairly simple; the beds dip down more or less in the direction of the surface stream and there was reasonable hope that the passage would rise upstream with them and soon come up to a surface. Viewed from inside, no doubt due to the viewer as well as the view, things did not seem so simple. It was difficult to assess the shape of the passage; the place was littered with fallen blocks and the roof seemed more or less horizontal. Watching carefully for loose stuff in the roof, I crept slowly forward. The floor sloped downwards upstream and soon dropped away a few feet into a well with sand and gravel on the floor; it was roomier here; one could just about stand upright and a rising tapered tunnel went off to the right but I did not see surface. It must have been there for I got up to it on the next visit but it was so free from floating bits that it was invisible. Straight ahead the passage climbed steeply into a region of broken rock and a pinnacle stood in the way barring progress. Beyond it was a surface but again clean and motionless. My burgee had told me nothing except that I was making currents myself. By passing the drumline beyond the pinnacle I was just able to claim that at least a small part of the drum had 'done a sump' for it had broken surface.

"I left the drum and went back to report the failure. Jack next went down to have a 'look-see'. The sight of a diver underwater, and a cave diver at that, about to enter a real cave, was a superb thrill to me as a spectator though I felt uneasy while he was away and was relieved to see him back at the cave mouth. His main trouble was goggles which must have been exasperating. (Don't I know it; shades of Alum Pot!) His observations about a right hand passage differed from mine but this is by no means unexpected; when two divers make the same report we shall have made progress and they will probably be accused of collusion.

"We decided to remove the obstruction and collected all sorts of useless junk from round the valley, detonators that would not detonate, batteries that would not detonate them, and so on. However the problem was solved next day by some good dets. and a pukka exploder from the quarry, thank you Mr.Morris, very kind indeed.

"Saturday dawned fine again and we were back at the well just after ten: I went down to recover the line while Jack fixed the firing gear. I took a look at the side passage and found a surface. Here was something hopeful: I had shirked exploration yesterday for I was 'convinced' that it became too small to follow and so I relieved myself of the responsibility to follow it. After trying to wriggle up the slope and realising it would probably 'go', but that in such case it might keep me below for some time, I went out to tell of expected delay. I did get through; it was a tight hole and my gear clinked on the roof making me wonder what next if it should get caught. The new chamber proved to be very small, roughly cubical and horizontal. I cannot reconcile that with the dip but there is no possibility of checking that now.... I got out of the water and peered down a rift which came to a dead end. Did I prove it a dead end? No, I admit I did not; I could have taken off my breathing gear and squeezed down it to prove the point but I did not. I crawled almost out of the water, looked about, then slowly backed down to the roomier basement whence I came and felt much happier there. This scared feeling when esconced in an air chamber at the end of a sump will have to be controlled. It was the same at Goyden Pot when standing waist-deep in that lonely canal. 'What if Aflo fails?' is a foremost question. So far we have no independent lighting; this must be remedied. In the present instance it was mainly the Floyd Collins phobia; Floyd Collins was trapped in a bedding plane by an apple in his pocket; he was alone and he died there. So far I am not used to having a supporting diver; I must train myself to the realisation that if held up in a far chamber, with luck, there will be help at hand.

"I went to the bank and was presented with half a pound of gelignite neatly wrapped up, and as Sheppard grinned from ear to ear I went about, laid the shot behind that annoying pinnacle, fixing the cable down with a few odd stones. Ten minutes later, with the team posted at various vantage points, Jack twisted the exploder. The ground shook a bit and there was a dull boom but no tidal wave, dead fishes or anything spectacular. Soon the mud advanced on a broad front from the cave mouth and slowly crossed the well to the outflow.

"All afternoon the fine grey mud came down and, waiting, we first reclined in the sun then went up to Pant Canol cave with Mason" (archeological type from Bristol; we shall meet him again) "who detailed the story of its discovery and discoursed on many interesting features of local cave work and history. At tea time it was still a bit thick but I deemed it worth a trial so dressed and went below. It was hopelessly foggy so we wended to The Gwyn Arms where there was to be a meeting on the future of South Wales caving.....

"Sunday morning about the same time we were at the well to inspect the damage. Jack and I went down in turn; we found the obstruction well and truly laid in splinters but a mighty block had dropped athwart the passage cutting across the surface and blocking the way on. We had had our cavern."

Later:

"That afternoon we put down Bill Weaver" (a prominent South Wales enthusiast) "for his first dip. He was one of the keenest and we expect to hear a lot more of his doings. He had already tackled some preliminary experiments with mask-respirators though they were a bit off the track for serious work involving prolonged submersion. It was grand fun to watch someone"

Notebook No.13.

"else go through the ritual. Next we put down Mason, then Hill, this time in Sgamo. It is curious that all three should have the impression - quite vividly - that their apparatus ceased to work once the mouth and nose were awash; maybe a swimmer's acquired reflex.

"All three did the CDG credit but Hill was outstandingly good, once he was under we were doubtful whether we would ever persuade him out again. This concluded our mission; Ffynnon Ddu was finished, the new men had been given their baptisms, the rest was packing and going back to the daily tasks.

"It was during the packing that one of the cottagers of Gribath asked would we come in to supper? We explained how things were and that we couldn't manage it and she went away rather crestfallen, I thought. However, half an hour later, we were invited to come just for a cup of tea, it was already poured out, so in we went to find beside the tea a big rasher of ham. As soon as we were well into that rasher, two more were quietly slipped on each plate then pie and cakes appeared from nowhwere and so it went on. We then inspected the garden, the hens, the pig-sty (no pig, we had just helped to eat him up), and in all we had a very happy hour in their company. Let this be a warning that in no circumstances should the kindness and hospitality of these people of the valleys be thwarted, even if you are on your way to a meal; do not hesitate to dine with them when requested. This hospitality was characteristic of that we received on every hand, be it at The Gwyn, our temporary home at Nant Rhiw, at the well, at the farm or on the road; it was charming indeed.

"Little need be said of Tuesday, the day of the return to London; everything was timed very nicely (it just happened); the weather had broken at last but it only rained while we were indoors. We finished packing and weighed in at the station (thanks for taking the kit up, Bateson!), sent off that which was O.K. straight to Wookey Hole and to home that which was wet or needed repairs or modifications. We went by bus to Swansea and there we were separated; I was in the guard's van, labelling Aflolaun, Jack and Mavis were forward. At Swindon I found they had not been able to get aboard and had had to follow by the next train. It was only three-quarters of an hour wait at Paddington to link up again and make for home.

"As a speleological undertaking it was disappointing but definite; as a job of diving, satisfactory, limited only by the known and expected deficiencies of the gear; as a holiday it was unsurpassed!

CDG MOVES AHEAD

The CDG was now just beginning to move through the gears. By July, 1946, we were honoured to count Professor J.B.S.Haldane as our top member; a special class of membership was accorded to those who had crossed a sump (no fewer than 32) and the total membership was 36. (Not all those entitled as sumpers chose to take up membership.) The first "operation" at Wookey was set as "Operation Harridan" for 1-6-46.

"OPERATION HARRIDAN

"As the time for Operation Harridan drew near the weather, which broke after Easter and had been patchy and inclement from then on, decided to show its real intentions. During the weekend before the event it poured down as much water in a night as would normally fall in the whole month, so said the evening papers, while others said it was the wettest May for 75 years. At Wookey, Wingco Hodgkinson reported that the water was very high and pretty dirty; it was clearing quickly by midweek and he would ring us if anything untoward happened. It did. On Friday they had half an inch of rain during the morning which would arrive as quite thick mud by the following night, the night of the operation. We were still prepared to go and look but the BBC cable had not arrived so Operation Harridan was cancelled.

"It was customary in the days of the 1935 diving to blame old Pen Palach, the Witch of Wookey, for any such happenings; no doubt she can take the blame for this too. Perhaps we should pay more attention to Mossy's warning and not overlook to propitiate the old hag with a penny and some tobacco." (I half believe that Mossy took it seriously or almost did.)

Harridan postponed became Bung, nominally to seek the bung-stave of the barrel, lost by Balch long ago from the First Chamber, but really, among other things, to make acquaintance with the reach of the river from resurgence to the First Chamber and more. Sheer optimism, of course, but the reality was an undreamt-of surprise and caused Bung to be re-named Pre-History.

"OPERATION PRE-HISTORY 8-6-46 to 11-6-46 Whitsun, 1946

"As Harridan had been abandoned, a new op. was arranged for Whitsun weekend. The idea was to make it a practice weekend giving the diver some green-water acclimatisation, meeting new members of CDG and giving them experience with attendants' jobs, then more or less incidentally we would tackle the passages from the cliff-face (The Resurgence) to the Witch's Kitchen (First Chamber) and from The Witch upwards to the Witch's Parlour (Third Chamber), the wet passages of course, and to recover the bung from the barrel that Balch lost from Charon's sandbank many years ago.

"I travelled alone and rather lonely but the evening was pleasantly spent in Wells where, as a party of three, The Wingco, Olive his wife, and I, had dinner at The Star where Mossy's friend Buckle was unearthed from the kitchen; he was chef and a fine one too, judging by our meal. We discussed plans and prospects but might better have concentrated on the claret. During the next day a depression settled on me deeper and deeper and by afternoon when the gang had assembled I felt in no mood to do the job; that feeling of uneasiness which assails me when contemplating a dive, but so soon disappears when once below the surface, was at its worst. I thought of that vaguely barbaric picture taken at Ffynnon Ddu in which it seemed the diver was being led to be sacrificed to some primitive deity; I thought of The Witch of Wookey and of the victims that might have been led before that dripstone figure to their deaths but little did I dream that the following day I would stumble across what might be the very victims of that ceremonial.

"The core of the team was Stanbury, Coase and Bosworth, (the Bristol Exploration Club contingent), and Bill Weaver. We tackled the resurgence first, on Saturday evening. I found the water cold and unpleasant and would be glad when it was over for this time my bad mood was not dispelled as I cut beneath the surface. I admit no regret when the river channel narrowed down to a steeply descending hole which might be descended but was too deadly to warrant the attempt. The roof went down very steeply, about 30° from the vertical. The floor was the river's traction load; the lowest part visible was of large rounded blocks of conglomerate about one to two feet in diameter, grading upwards to smaller stuff, finally to a ridge of grit and sand, where, after its mad uprush, the spate had flattened out and behaved in more seemly manner. The whole area under the lip of the arch is covered with this grit and sand but in places weed has covered it to a depth of a few inches. The whole of this pile stands at the steepest possible angle and, as the slot is less then two feet floor to roof, to disturb anything would be just too bad.

"No doubt it is somewhat similar at the slope down to Six but that certainly seemed firmer in 1935 than this place is. To Keld Head also, but there there is enough headroom not to make a boulder slip so serious a matter. At the bottom of this hole, some ten feet deeper, that is about 20 feet in all, a roomier place is evident, though the roof itself looks deadly; hung with big loose-looking flakes. We packed up and went back in single file down the path to the mill.

"On Sunday we met at Priddy for some fun and games in Eastwater Swallet with the rest of the BEC and gradually I threw off my stupor and began to quicken with the old stirrings... After a hearty meal at the Witch's Kitchen Restaurant (as guests) we made for the other Witch's Kitchen and dressed for diving. The newcomers are all sound technically- and mechanically-minded men (to quote Simpson: 'just bloody engineers'; he said that of my Keld Head party when we failed to make the kind of progress he expected,) and dressing went well except for the neckband. And did that leak! At last I was below and very happy to be underwater, in Mossy's Green Jelly where she thought maybe a ghost lived. Five feet deep, then nine feet deep, under a low roof, down to the river bed strewn with lovely rippled sand.

"Crawling over the rocks down to this place I noticed the end of a bone sticking out of the sand in a break in the rocks and by it a black ring like the rim of a pot. Was it a find, or just a bit of rubbish? I was torn between going closer to examine them but, on reaching the river bed, I decided the find would keep and I went on, attracted by the green infinity. Everything was going well; the mud cleared almost immediately and the water was beautifully clear. It was a throw-back to 1935 but an even cleaner, nicer playground. Still onwards while the little drum of line spun happily as I progressed. This was a new flat-mounted drum which held about 100 feet of thin line and it was working well. I did not see the way up to the Hall of Wookey and found nothing to account for the cave noises of The Witch's Kitchen. The tunnel went straight on. getting gradually deeper, but the headroom improved until at last I could stand freely in a more broken chamber, 14 feet floor depth, and in front and round to the left - the passage runs nearly north-south - was an immense tip of boulders and mud, fine, loose and quaggy in appearance. The line was all out plus its stretch when I came to a halt, which proved the gang had efficiently tied the end to the drum. Ahead at the top of the pile of debris was a faint green glow, the lights of Three seemingly an enormous distance off; I thought I saw also something noteworthy to the left but could not be sure.

"After a long struggle to unhook the line, for my gloves, time and again, fouled the karabiner (a fault since remedied), I made off to a flake of rock in the floor and made merrily for home; at high speed with the tide. I must have shifted, for the land-party who having seen my lights pass Two, then from Three saw them turn for home, ran back to The Witch and arrived only just in time to see my lights appear under the arch. It was a memorable trip. A dead straight line, a good firm roof, a clean sandy bottom and visibility perfect. I reported most of this, while they drummed me up another line; I said there was a jerry down there in the sand which I would fish out later and was told that the shore party had seen me pass Two and seen me again from Three. Excitement ran high and even the sober Wingco was like a dog with two tails.

"I started on the second run and, passing closer to the bowl, could not resist the temptation to lift it out. Working carefully round it with my gloved fingers, sending up clouds of orange and sulphur smoke, it soon came clear away but, alas, the way back was difficult and I must have chipped a bit off the rim in struggling to gain open water; fortunately the damage was slight. The shore party had meantime rushed to Three expecting to see me make exit there: I hollered... they soon rushed back and there was double excitement. In a slot in the rocks I had seen something else. Down again I dived and brought back a skull, then two femurs, then another skull, miscellaneous lesser bones then yet another skull. All thoughts of a mere walk through to Three had long since vanished; the way was clear, anyhow; the only difficulty would be climbing the slope should it happen not to be firm. We packed up like greased lightning and disappeared out of the cave, bearing our treasure and the mundane means whereby we had found it. Everybody was on tip-toes; come and have a whisky, said Wingco, a double, a treble, and have a hot bath!

"After all this, and about one or two in the morning, I went to bed but could not sleep so wrote out a draft as a defence against, or for information of, the Pressmen. At last the excitement was replaced by drowsiness and I floated off; the end of the greatest day yet, both for myself and the CDG.

"On the Monday, Bank Holiday, there was a hurried consultation with Balch (Curator of Wells Museum and, as previously noted, the leading excavator of the cave,) Our find was Late Celtic and the circumstances probably unique.

Already there existed an opinion that The Witch of Wookey, that dripstone figure looking down the river in The First Chamber and around which the Christian legend has been woven of how a wicked witch was turned to stone by the Friar of Glastonbury, was in pre-Christian days the centre of some primitive ceremonial, maybe sacrificial. As evidence, apart from the eminent suitability of this grim figure to such a purpose, as god or goddess of the river, or of the underworld, both in its own fearsome appearance and its surroundings, there is a pocket cut away under the figure's side, grooves cut down obstructing ridges of stalagmite, and a hole in the floor where traces of wood were found indicating a stake to which the victims could have been tied. From behind the Witch is a flight of prehistoric steps cut down a dripstone cascade leading to the water's edge and worn smooth by the passage of feet. (Or so the story goes; my own observations of the place were not so clear cut.) Could it be that we had discovered remains of the victims themselves?

"How, then, did the relics come to be so far under the arch? The level of the river, some 9 feet deep in the First Chamber, is nowadays controlled by the mill dam at the resurgence... else the level would be some five to six feet lower.... This would leave a low arch exposed for some distance upstream with a platform of fallen blocks for its floor, awash or in shallow water. The relics were just beyond this platform and two feet deeper.... the whole region between First and Third Chambers must be searched as a check that the bodies were not accidentally collected in this spot.

"DISGRACE ABOUNDING 11-6-46

"The Wing Commander rang the pressmen who at once made haste to get the story and the photographs while we staged the next scene of operations. We assembled by The Witch and many were present; there were Gang and some friends, cave staff and some friends, the Wingco and some friends and the pressmen who had no friends. The work was only to be popping in and out of the water, raking out further bones and anything else which came handy (I cannot recollect whether I took any in first!), and duly posing for the cameramen when they called 'Halt'. This being so, and the scene of operations being relatively safe, I made the grave misjudgement of continuing to use the same sodalime.... I did not realise my breathing was unusually laboured... I just felt damned unhappy. I recognised things would be better if the sodalime were changed but we had left the funnel behind and the press were waiting for their flash shots so I carried on. My goggles simply refused to exclude water... at last I managed to get Aflo down to the 'grave' but could not work and came out. On the way out I bumped my head and lost my rubber cap, used as headgear and as a help to keep warm, but was beyond caring. At the bank, however, there were shouts of 'There it is, floating downstream!' and momentarily galvanised into action I grabbed the line my attendant hurriedly reached me....

"I was only half-present, merely grabbed the end and did not tie off to it; I plunged in, partially weighted, and was soon out of my depth. Then, and not before, I realised my position; unable or unwilling to behave as a diver I tried to keep on the surface and almost panicked on realising I was drifting down river to the submerged channel from which for me there was no exit; I was almost completely out of control and my attendant appeared to take no notice of my hasty signals to stop paying out line; it just came down yard after yard and for the moment I thought they had lost the end. The shock of it gave momentary stimulation; looking back I saw great loops and festoons in the water but beyond it appeared taut. With the feeling of a man narrowly saved from drowning, I hauled down the slack and came up slowly, hand over hand along the tightened line, to the shore. Of course, I had only drifted a few feet and the situation could not have been really serious but it felt otherwise. I was sheepish and ashamed of my exhibition but was assured I would not have got far; the gang was ready to a man to dive in and fish me out. I drank stimulating coffee while the gang reloaded the absorber canister, for Aflo had to be recovered. On breathing decent cave air the CO_2 headache hit me. I had

had worse in the early field-trials but this was quite enough to indicate how far I had gone.

"With new absorber breathing was easier but it nevertheless was quite an effort to go down to fetch Aflo and bring it safely back to land. With that, operations ceased. We packed up slowly. I was in bad humour; the gang, maybe by absence of any positive result from the evening's diving, set to skylarking and harnessed Whodba to the Witch for a photograph. Just as we had arranged everything on old Pen Palach, even to the noseclip, and one of the gang was down river in the Wingco's boat, another playing with the cave lights to upset the navigator, there was a crunch on the gravel path; the Wingco had returned. The lights-man had the wit to switch off the main light leaving The Witch in silhouette and happily the respirator could not be seen. Seconds seemed hours; the boatman made play of his attempt to recover the hat, the party suddenly became busy noisily collecting tackle and stowing it away. I took the first diplomatic opportunity to chat up the Wingco and, after what seemed an age, managed to draw him away long enough for the boys to cut down the ties and relieve Pen-Palach of her drapery then we trooped out like a lot of schoolboys caught at a prank, for the Wingco is no fool.....

"Anxious to recover my diving nerve, I spoke to Wingco and he agreed we could continue on Sunday night. Much phoning and wiring for Gang... a meal at The Witch's Kitchen Restaurant (I think we paid this time!) and off in haste, reporters and all, into the cave. My attendants are pretty good now and with further aid from Blaxall, the Cave Secretary, and Clare, a Guide, I was in the water in next to no time (you will be a fool to believe that; it is always a distressingly slow job, sometimes just not so slow as others). I had a smashing new bathing hat, a green one with the usual curly ornamentation, belonging to Mrs.H. The neckband only sprang the slightest leak and the goggles behaved themselves quite well. Soon I began my newt-like journeys to and from the sandbank-grave and for the next hour I scratched out piece after piece of skeletons from the fine brown mud.

"The work of disinterment is a delightful process. You work your gloved fingers behind or alongside the piece, partly scratch away the mud and partly fan it away, the water picks the mud up as an orange smoke which drifts away in the welcome current and some slides by gravity downhill against the current into the lightbeam. The fog grows paler and paler until finally the ragged edges drift away and disappear in the cracks among the rocks. Now and again there will be a little landslide for all the world like an avalanche in miniature; clouds of mud curl from its leading edge and spread out finally to attenuate and disappear leaving pale green water, brown rock and yellow-green sand....

"So ended the Whitsun Operation Pre-History, neé Bung. We have all learnt many lessons in the last few days. The attendants who eagerly bore the burdens of the weekend are much more skilled; it will be a great day when we can give them their send-off as diver-members."

CDG STILL GROWING

By September Sir Robert Davis was pleased to accept membership. At Ffynnon Ddu, whether or not spurred on by the excitements of the CDG effort there, an entrance to the cave beyond the rising had been found and Ogof Ffynnon Ddu is one of the big ones. A major improvement to Whodd was made by the addition of a helmet and facemask so eliminating those ghastly goggles and the neck leaks into the bargain; two new kits were mooted, thanks jointly to The Wingco and Siebe Gorman; the Group divided into four Sections to meet local interests, Derbyshire, London, Somerset and South Wales; last, but not in any way least, a dozen naval-surplus frogsuits and sundry other items of equipment were acquired.

In November Burwood and Wingco Hodgkinson made up our quad of Honorary Members and the total membership had risen to 48; first cave dips were becoming the order of the day. Morever, cave diving was being undertaken in South Wales by that Section. However, this record is mainly of the line that my own adventures took, so back now to Wookey Hole.

Notebook No.14.

There was a rather curious op. at Wookey in June that year called Scratch. I think it was to make a BBC recording for later transmission. "Scratch" was an oblique and uncomplimentary reference to the recording equipment. We carried a reel of cable through to Seven and, rather like the Grand old Duke of York, brought it back again. Neither diver can now recollect why and my notes of the time defeat me.

"OPERATION SCRATCH Weekend 21 & 22-6-46

"After ten days or so wandering easily about the Swansea Valley caving district Mavis and I made our way to Wookey Hole for Operation Scratch. We arrived rather late for our transport had broken down at the Swansea end and our delayed arrival at Bristol threw us into the busy hour with more delays. But we arrived and despite the hour there was a meal for us by kindness of the restaurant staff who had stayed on. Jack Sheppard, co-diver, had arrived earlier in the afternoon and was already made at home in the Wingco's house.

"We spent next day sorting out kit. The Gang arrived and speeded up the work and we found there would be time to put Jack down for a dip. He had made a mask for use with Paradive and had tested it to 2 feet depth in a water butt. He departed with Gang and a wheelbarrow to the cliff-face where he was given the gen on what precautions had to be observed in that place; The Mill was very sensitive lest damage be done to the puddling. Arriving there, we found a not-too-happy Engineer from the mill busy letting the water out. We soon became better acquainted; it seems that our final diving of Operation Pre-History had interfered quite seriously with the work of his mill; work had to be stopped and various pump leathers renewed before the plant was in working order again. It was clear that diving would have to be restricted to Saturdays only and on the weekends when the canal was due to be cleaned, and that is once a month.

"Sheppard was preparing for his dip as I walked down the valley with the Engineer and talked to his boss, Guy Hodgkinson (Wingco's cousin).... as we entered the mill grounds we met the barrow and its load coming out. It seems the water had just poured into the mask and put an end to the trial.

"Dinner was at The Star and afterwards we rejoined the gang and got the stuff into the cave. The BBC had got their stuff more or less in order, except that the recording engineer was still sitting beside his dead recorders, quite happy in the belief that a power supply would drop from Heaven or somewhere. His faith was rewarded for Stanbury took pity on him and hitched him up to the nearest lampholder. Inside the cave there were lots of comings and goings but nobody seemed to know quite what they were going to do and nobody seemed interested in what we hoped to do.

"Sheppard had put his outfit back 'as you were' and we tried to make some plan for the descent. This, characteristically, was at zero plus three-quarters of an hour. We decided I should go down tied by an 8-foot line to the B.B.C. cable drum, an unwieldy beast, and Sheppard should carry the drum and link on to the cable. After the usual bother we started down. I was in good fettle and the descent was exciting. I would slither down head-first until the line pulled me up then I rested until Jack came along and I moved on again. I had Aflo and kicked up enough mud for him to appreciate the scene á la Mossy. The Squeeze just is not. Aflo debunked this place and showed a gaping hole leading to Six; we must have been well off the best route when we first went through. This place seems to have become the collecting ground for the odds and ends of the previous diving; at least three concrete weights and one of the drums lie there. Ahead was the big block, heavily silted up but easily by-passed on the right. The whole of that chamber was more heavily silted than in 1935, unless it was Aflo showing us things we had never seen before. Above the block the tie-line did not seem to follow me; I waited but still no sign, so I went back a bit and found Shep pointing to his goggles which were half-full of water. We had agreed that if this happened that he would hand over the drum and return, which he did while I moved forward. Ahead of me there was the old lighting cable, the light itself still floating, and the old shot-rope with its clove hitch still intact round Belay 1 but rotten and parting at the lightest touch. It signalled the end of the known parts and, since Sheppard's trouble, quite a lot of enthusiasm for the job had evaporated leaving me feeling vulnerable.

"As I pressed along Six a considerable surface was showing but the gateway to Seven was still submerged. Passing into the gateway, I looked out at Charybdis, smothered in sand and with a steep ridge linking it to Scylla by my side. I looked down into a jagged pit, deep green to black in the gaping holes between the boulders. I looked into Seven to a great tumble of blocks lying in a disorderly heap along its length. The water was dark, annoyed-looking, and the whole chamber underwater took on a defiant attitude then the mud swirled up and blotted everything out. In a few moments it cleared, for the current was running fast, so I surveyed the crossing to Charybdis. It was steep and loose; I was burdened with both cable and Aflo which, once off the level, is a mixed blessing. I started to cross over and the deep green pit disappeared in the mud clouds. I rammed Aflo's battery box into the mud wall and waited until I could see again then pulled myself up to it. Gradually by this process, gaining more at each pull than I lost as the bank slid downwards, I landed unstably behind the rock. I could stand up and get my head and shoulders out of the water. Aflo came up too, and as it broke surface Seven was lit up as never before. Steep, clean prison walls, almost rectangular and holdless. I could not see the roof; I did not look back at the Guillotine, but I did see the far end, perhaps 100 feet away, clean, sheer and vertical like the rest, shooting straight up from the water.

"So much for the hope of a walk-through to the unknown. Wookey was fighting every inch of the way. I submerged and squatted there wondering what next: there came back to me fleeting memories of crag-climbing days when the going had been hard and the way on a couple of notches harder. I remembered the almost inevitable tangle of diving lines when turning for home in the past and this was no place for a tangle. I finally decided to wedge the cable drum in the sand then, with all the slack taken up, to go back to The Gateway. I started back into the clouds of mud I had kicked up, using Aflo as an ice-axe to steady me, expecting to shoot off down the slope at any moment and hoping that if I did I would not lose Aflo, or get tangled with the cable, or knock the mouthpiece out. The fall itself would be of little consequence but I could not be sure there would be no complications, even if only like being tapped on the head by the cable-drum! I moved down foot by foot and did not slide off; soon there was level sand under my belly and I turned round, changed over the cable and made for home in a yellow haze of clay.

"I had shortened the link-line before going on alone but even when only a foot long it caught up in everything possible so soon I decided to abandon it and link up directly with the cable; if the link is close to the knee there is no trouble, except in turning round; it seems to be good policy to keep the link as short as possible and re-hitch on going about, making completely sure not to lose the line while doing so. I swam fairly quickly down to Six, holding Aflo ahead to take the bumps, and the cable led true and sure back to Four for we hardly touch Five,it is rather off the direct route. It is hardly correct to say I swam; the technique was to lie down and kick one's way along by the toes, assisting with anything handy, including Aflo. Nor is it quite right to say the line ran true and sure to Four; it got hooked up a bit on an ugly-looking pendant and led me to head into the rock wall instead of the passage which, where we traverse, is rather tight. We could go into Five and turn but that would involve a belay and the diversion is not really necessary. Also, I managed to get Aflo hooked up on the 1935 lighting cable which has pulled across the bottom of Six like a clothes line. However, I am getting quite practised at unravelling simple hook-ups by feel and was quite happy about that one. I was escorted from the Three-Four arch and duly reported the salient features of the place as best I could remember them but for the life of me could not be sure of any dimension of Seven.

"Sheppard then had another go using my goggles but the gas cylinder leaked; he fitted another and that leaked, and yet a third. This hardly inspired much confidence so he wisely threw in the sponge. It took some time to recover from the shock of the realities of Seven and I was told the BBC were not a bit happy about losing their drum of cable. Soon, however, after pulling in the cable until it held fast, I went down to have a look. Visibility was patchy and I soon found the drum hooked up on the clothes line; it had followed obediently across the sandbank from Charybdis and down along Six. I freed it and went back for another pull. Again it jammed, this time among the fallen blocks of the deep. Next time in the blocks halfway up to Five then it came right out and the evening's work was over except for the clearing up.

"It is a pity there was no reconnaissance before the BBC brought its tackle along. Our experience on that evening should teach us a lesson we should already have known - that familiarity with a place makes a world of difference to performance. After the op., Sheppard, Hodgkinson and I had a discussion on the conclusions to be drawn and I took the line that the gear should be well-nigh perfect before attempting to get through that place again. That probably meant frogsuits and we must do our best to get them. H. and his co-Director had a meeting on the spot and voted up to £100 for equipment for the job so it is now a question of time only before we see Seven again, and perhaps Eight, for now we know that to make progress we will have to dive again from Seven.

"Tired and disappointed, we crawled to bed at two o'clock and slept. Next day we had a meeting and cleared up lots of questions with the gang, cleaned the kit and departed in glorious sunshine by the afternoon train which, in our own tradition, was an hour late."

There is no clue in the notebook to show what this op. was supposed to achieve. The logsheets are singularly unhelpful and we had not yet reached the era of the Operation Notices which set out, if cryptically, the full objectives of each occasion. The report made subsequently states it was an attempt to press on upstream and is quiet about the BBC's participation (we were very sensitive about The Media's interest in us; as cavers we found it unwelcome). Likewise the Letters to Members afford no answer. The divers and diving gained something from it; for the B.B.C. it must have been a dead loss, but that is just too bad. This was the ragged interim period before our objectives were clearly defined and when we were easily swept off course by events.

Notebook No.15.

OPERATION VERNON 20 & 21-7-46

The preoccupation for some time to come was with equipment, its acquisition, distribution to Sections, adaptations and the like. I notice we let slip a rather fine opportunity. In the notes of negotiations for surplus frogsuits there is this line: "Cameras available, £140, new." Presumably we, as usual, were too impoverished to take advantage. The "new" equipment ushered in the period of training, Operation Vernon, named after H.M.S.Vernon, the Admiralty training centre for self-contained equipment usage, and clearly the CDG men would soon be "pushing the sumps". The Bristol Exploration Club contingent were in the fore with Donald Coase as their star performer.

It was not until October that we returned to take up the challenge of The Witch.

Notebook No.16.

"OPERATION MAGNUM Weekend 12 & 13-10-46

"Time had slipped by very quickly since the last dip at Wookey Hole just after Whitsun; pre-occupation with the organisation of the CDG, which itself is a work of major magnitude, and the rehabilitation of our home are the causes. We had almost forgotten what it is like to be underwater; even had lost the fear of the great tumbled Seventh though we had not replaced it by any particular urge to push ahead..... On the

Monday before the op. I had a phone call from the Wingco and learned that Butlin's diver-demonstrator was interested to have a go with us. It was not until some time later that we discovered it was Butlin's rather than their diver who had shown the initiative and in this competitive commercial world there could have been problems so at least for the time being the idea was not taken up. We divers could be just lambs for the slaughter....

"The evening was left to CDG and a grand event it was. A terse program of operations was circulated to all concerned and we almost kept to it. London was represented by all three diving members and Mavis and Mary came along. Somerset had Don Coase and Harry Stanbury there and also provided most of the Gang. South Wales had Bill Weaver and his men. The long-distance people fed well at The Wookey Hole Inn while the gear went into the cave; everything was going like clockwork until there was a hitch in the Water Control Department. The sluicegate mechanism was broken. Consternation and who dunnit? We thanked our lucky stars that at the last moment Wingco had taken charge of the W.C.D. Even so, while the accusation was not made at point blank, the divers were sure they were believed to be the culprits. (I think a rock had fallen from the cliff face and unluckily pranged it.) The divers were all reasonably happy to go down without lowering the water so we decided to carry on; meanwhile the mill would see what could be done. They eventually succeeded in getting the level down nearly to the usual diving level and everbody was happy. Except the Wingco. The gang ploughed in and out of the mud with every sign of enjoying itself and having little or no care how much mud it sent downstream to foul the canal. So doubtless the Wingco's thoughts turned ever more to the possibilities of The Frogman....

"The Third Chamber at six o'clock was strangely ordered; everything was happening to plan, everybody knew what to do and almost completely how to do it. Figures came and vanished, spanners clinked and visors were polished. At seven the divers stalked into The Witch's Kitchen. I was first in the water, no trouble or fuss, the diving gear worked first time except poor Aflo; his line had been coiled wrongly and the drum would not run. That remedied, I soon wriggled down past the Witch's Burial to the sandy strips below. The place seemed darker and less welcoming than before; perhaps the water was off-clean, for the level was dropping; it was a cave tunnel rather than just a diver's paradise. I soon had the line tied off at the 100 feet point, probably on the same block but the tip of the block had pulled off last time. On the way in I passed a human femur lying on the floor and further in something that looked like a small but extraordinarily well-formed quern. This was too good to be true so on the way back I picked it up. It was too smooth for a quern, it was smooth as glass. There was a stem on it, too, like a large pestle with a hollow base. I did not recognise it for the bottle that it was and took it to the land-party, with land-eyes, to turn it over and recognise it. I did not get the chance of another look, so tight was the program.

"The shore of the First was lined with eager divers and their attendants sitting around on the gunwales of the boat and on the steps by the water's edge. So far, the water had not dropped much. I signalled to the nearest diver, Stanbury, and he waded in. I clipped his karabiner on the line and sent him down, following literally on his heels for he was soon head downwards on the boulder slope that leads to the river bed. ...Stanbury was soon tightly jammed, head downwards still, over the edge of the rock-shelf, Aflo weighting him down, the kara holding him back. I tried to slip the karabiner but could not shift it until I had hauled him back a couple of feet. I reckoned that, with two of us together, the hazard of losing the line was less than that of the karabiner. Harry, however, signalled that his visor was flooding so I sent him back and called on the next victim, Don Coase, who patrolled the length of the line at a steady pace and had a no-trouble run. We paused where we reached the lowest point and I directed Aflo for him to see the wide expanse of dark water and the accumulation of debris including the old bridge in the inner recess. He spotted a bone on the way in and handed it to me to carry. We went right to the end of the line, halted, then returned through the mud-smoke to the base. (He later wrote in my notebook a delightful appreciation of his first dive. It is on page 152.)

"Next was Stanbury again; we went down and Harry tore ahead but I managed to catch and halt him. We stood waiting on the bottom for the mud to clear and show us the dark green expanse of water on the far left that runs right under the dry way to Two then we turned for home. I was not happy; I thought the diver would give me the slip if he got the chance! Next was Ray O'Neill; like a flash of underwater lightning, or like that trout at Keld Head, he was away up the tunnel; he got some way ahead as I was negotiating the narrow corner and, alarmed, I raced after him, or after the light patch of mud ahead that marked his presence. We were a long way in before at last I was able to grab his heel and lay him. We stopped, rested and returned with repeated restraint from the rear, but I lost him again in the boulders and damn me if he did not overshoot the corner and go sailing down towards the lower tunnel! Exasperated, I gave chase again, eventually caught the delinquent and brought him to land. He dipped in more senses than one but should learn a lot from the experience and make a more sober and realistic approach next time.

"Last man down was Bill Weaver. His dive was sober and in good style so he went the full distance... I wish I had blacked out my lights to show him, and see for myself, the lights of Two and Three. I shall remember that next time. We had by now used up the allotted time for 'Vernon' and the explorers would have a go. In accordance with program I went into the Fourth to lay the first shot-line. We were in the Fourth where the Express photographer (allegedly invited or tipped off by the BBC) had set up his camera: 'I would like to take a photograph!'. No response. 'Do you think I could take a photograph?' No response. 'Look, boys! Can't we take a photograph?'. Voice from the darkness: 'Yes! Of a press photographer being thrown in the river!'. After the din had subsided and he had loosed off a couple of flashes, I squatted just underwater at the entrance to Five and looked at the way down. What from above water seems to be the left wall of the chamber shoots down below the surface then stops short... leaving a narrow slot between it and the block which lies on the slope below... I selected a route and slipped through this slot to the flatter bottom... a few feet down channel brought me through to Six and a few feet up the yonder slope the line ran out. I parked Aflo, dragged over a huge concrete block, anchored the line to it and returned to base. With the drum refilled I went down again; once more the sombre dull above-water would change as if by magic as the waterline cut my visor. Below was green still water with the light mud slowly drifting up from the First Deep. Down I went, no trouble, no fuss, no pain in the ears, just a hug from the water as I dropped again through the slot. A few whiffs of gas into the dress eased that and soon I was tying on the new line at the block, then to Belay 1 at Scylla, where I tied on again.

"I stood a while on the brink watching the mud float by. The passage here is quite large; the current bends down again from its upward sweep and drops fine silt over the portals of the Seventh. Charybdis towered over me on the right, cutting off my view, and to my left, steeply down, was deep green water. I took off the line-drum and tossed it down; it sank slowly to a ledge below and the mud rose up and around me. My job done, I went back to report all ready for the next diver.

"Jack Sheppard was soon off and disappeared in the brown haze I had left behind me. He was a long time down and we began to get uneasy. I went down to see and found him by Scylla surrounded by thick brown mud through which the lights of Aflo appeared as lighter patches. I do not know what he was doing, but he was O.K., so I went back. Five minutes or so later the murk brightened , 'He's coming!' someone shouted. As we watched intently, the faint lights waxed and waned for some time then Jack appeared, using his hand torch. Aflo, it seems, got hooked up in the line so he left it behind. He reported having followed the line about 10 feet down, was unable to retrieve the drum but he had pulled the line up.

"I went down for a final look round and to retrieve the gear. Aflo was just inside the dark hole and had unhooked itself. I took it to Scylla and left it pointing upstream while I sidled along the rock on the Charybdis-side of the drop. I pushed off and floated gently downwards landing like a feather on the big block. A delightful sensation. I saw that the drum could easily be reached so left it and pulled down a length of line from the festoons Jack had laid at the foot of Scylla. With this as guide for the return, I went down the second drop and further on to the end of the loop of rope; the way was not far but I cannot recall what it was like only that, ahead, I could see the floor flatten out then, beyond the farthermost slab of fallen rock and the low flat roof it had fallen from, I could see it rise again as if a sandbank stood across the path and turned it to the right for round the corner to the right the channel seemed to continue. There was the way on!" (Had I but looked up I should have seen the surface in the Eighth Chamber.)

"With mixed feelings, joy at what I had seen, joy at having descended at least most of the way to the Second Deep, satisfaction that I was at the end of the line and need not go farther (I did not pull it too hard lest it should give a bit!), I pranced - almost the right word - up the giant staircase back to the drum. I picked the drum up but cannot remember what I did with it; think I carried it in my hand and it was certainly without any difficulty that I regained the ledge by Aflo. I untied from Scylla, gathered up the festoons of line, and, grasping them tightly lest they should play tricks, moved down to the block, untied there and moved up to base, returning immediately to recover the first line from the block to Four." (I now completely fail to understand the purpose of this line recovery.)

"This over, we undressed, told our story then wended our way to bed, while the press reporter nosed around and asked questions but took no notice of the answers.

"Next morning we dragged the gear out of the cave, washed at least some of it, and hung it out to dry at Crooks' Rest." (A hut in the car park that Wingco had put at our disposal for gear and in which we kipped.) At one o'clock the party disbanded, leaving the London contingent to continue after lunch to pack those things they needed to take with them or would collect when opportunity offered. The journey back was slow and tedious; we were over an hour late at Paddington. Ray and Mary stayed on a day so escaped the tedium of the Sunday train. We were not sorry to be home and get to bed.

"On Monday morning the Express carried a report characteristic of the yellow press. It devoted ten inches to telling thirty-odd lies and completely misrepresented the whole affair."

(I suppose our unwillingness to cooperate was partly to blame but I am not disposed to excuse them.)

"It was a report that could do the CDG a lot of harm. During the afternoon The BBC contacted us through our office P.R.; would we call round to talk to them?... We did, and just scraped through a spot of rehearsal before the green light flashed - maybe you heard the rest."

Impressions on a first cave dive by D.A.Coase

WOOKEY HOLE CAVE, 12-10-46

"Having been dressed and loaded down with the respirator and weights, I sat on the edge of the boat, just beneath The Witch, and wondered just what I had let myself in for. At last Graham beckoned me, and after going through the drill of emptying breathing bag and lungs extra carefully, I slid down the bank into the water. Having vented my dress, I found I was too buoyant, and being slowly swept down stream by the current. Pulling myself back with the aid of sundry rocks I found Aflo thrust at me, and Graham then pointed upstream along the line he had laid out.

"The most outstanding impression under water was the colour, I was prepared for something exceptional from Graham's accounts, but this was amazing! A light green, with a tint of blue in it, that coloured everything, and gradually got deeper and darker into the distance, and seemed to shimmer gently.

"The rock where Stanbury had got entangled was no distance in and I soon reached it. As I passed I felt myself caught and after deliberating a second or so, I felt around and found my torch, which was hanging from a lanyard tied to my waist, had wedged between two rocks. It was soon free, and I went forward again down the boulder slope. Here the roof was rather low, and I felt my breathing bag rub against it. There was a canvas cover supplied to protect the breathing bag, but it was so stiff and unwieldy that we had decided not to use it. There and then, however, I made up my own mind, that in future I would always use it, as a ripped breathing bag would not be very healthy.

"When nearly at the bottom of the boulder slope, I noticed a bone lying between two boulders, so picked it up, and turned round to show it to Graham, and was surprised to find he wasn't immediately visible, being hidden in the sediment I had stirred up. He soon appeared out of the mirk, looking as grotesque as usual, but it was very comforting to know he was there. Giving him the bone, which he carried round like a good dog, I soon came to the bottom of the boulders and found a level sandy floor stretching away into the distance, with the line running along it and the drum visible at the end. What amazed me especially was the size of the passage, if such you could call it. It was more like a submerged chamber.

"Here Graham did a war-dance by me, and gesticulated mightily, but not understanding, I pushed on and soon reached the drum. Here I stopped and had a good look round. Just beyond was another boulder slope leading up, presumably, into the Third Chamber. It was rather astounding to realise I was only the second person to have been to this spot. At last Graham gave me three taps on the head, and after thinking a bit, I realised he meant me to return.

"To do this I had to let go of the line to turn Aflo round, and by this time being in a cloud of sediment I had a nasty second or two before I had hold of the line again, although I knew it was only a foot to my right. I then retraced my steps and groped back along the line most of the way, owing to sediment. At last the lights of the First Chamber became visible and my head emerged into air again. I was very glad when Graham shook my hand and intimated I had passed my test as a Cave Diver successfully. I was also surprised to learn I had only been under eight minutes, it seemed more like thirty.

"Hurry along my next cave diving trip!

26-10-46."

(Extracted from Cave Diving Group Letter No.4.)

It is a little odd that Scylla and Charybdis were the names I gave to two rocks hard by Seven: I had always been bottom of the class in Classics and suchlike subjects; it is far too late to make amends.

Chapter 7

The Changing Scene

Alpha, Janus, Acheron, Stoke Lane, Muckment.

As the Group slowly established itself, so the notebooks become filled with scribbled drafts of "Letters to Members" and the like. The newsletters began in May, 1946, and continued until No.20 in December, 1950 when my effort disintegrated. Typically, they began with a summary for those not wishing to read on - well, I suppose so - introductory pep-chat, membership news, equipment notes, technical points, operation reports, diving news from non-CDG sources, regularly in that order, and odds and ends to wind up. Often there would be appendixes, technical or otherwise. They give a fair summary of what happened in those early days. They were cyclostyled on the then demy-quarto paper and often carried plans or sketches; later issues showed that 120 copies were made so, if reference to them is needed, a little effort should find a file. For example, copies were sent to some cave club secretaries and may well have been preserved and at least one complete file has found its way into a public library. They were supposed to be confidential at the time, but doubtless there will be a thirty-year rule or the like. Non-confidential information was given in the form of "Reports", sent for a few coppers to anyone signifying the wish to receive them, again usually cave-club secretaries. They were reports of operation results, starting in pre-CDG days as Member's Reports to The British Speleological Association; the first (from memory) was a bit special, being a description with photographs of WHODD and WHODBA but the file copy is lost without trace. The BSA copy might have been inherited by BCRA, The British Cave Research Association. The BSA Reports graded into CDG Reports in 1946 and continued as occasional publications, ending, it seems, with a Derbyshire Section Report on Black

Keld, dated 6-10-49. Again, copies might be held by interested clubs, or the carefully ordered File Copies may survive my demise. Finally, there is a stack of Operation Notices which contain bits of information which escaped the other records: that file includes a number of Section notices.

Derbyshire Section had a number of op. notices and reports of their own publication; the other Sections were pushing sumps but were not so energetic in recording their work.

A brief entry in Notebook No.16 shows that The Cave was waking to the commercial possibilities of the divers' finds:

"However, Seven is nearer to base and accessible to mining and Wingco is very interested in it"

Thus foreshadowing things to come. There is also a note on the collection of wondrous goodies from the Siebe Gorman surplus stores, ending with the comment "Now has the CDG got its feet well planted?"

Swim fins appeared to be getting more serious consideration: I acquired some to make a personal assessment but concluded that with our current equipage they were a disadvantage. A further note helps to explain the rarity of Wookey or other ops. organised by so-called "headquarters":-

Notebook No.17.

"The work associated with the CDG is enormous; almost all my spare time, and a lot that is not spare or mine. It pushes diving preparations into the background until they scream for attention and it jeopardises connubial bliss." (It was about this time the virtual "Anti-CDG" association of wives was formed.)
The next op. recorded in the notebooks shows the growing spread; it was an op. organised and led by a Section.

"OPERATION ALPHA

OGOF FFYNNON DDU 16-11-46

"At Easter the place was simply The Black Well, now it has become The Cave of The Black Well. Operation Alpha was Weaver's first operational dip. The start of the story as I saw it was of a long struggle against time, the time being swallowed by the ordinary affairs of the CDG organisation until, almost too late, I had to decide that the correspondence should pile up while preparations were made.

"Reports from The Downend Group, which had used a light powered from base, showed the limitations of that system but a similar system was proposed for OFD. This made me think a bit and soon plans for streamlining Aflo were sketched out and Aflo II put into production. The weekend was preceded by hectic last-minute packing from which, as discovered later, quite a few essentials were left behind.

"Slipping off from work at 2:00 I arrived at Golders Green at 2:25 to find a singular absence of taxis. Apprehensive, to say the least, I hailed a delivery van; would he take me and my goods to Paddington? Why, of course! How much? Well, no more than a taxi. Done! So the old Ford coughed its way to my place to collect the burden then on to Paddington, the driver explaining the while that he did not normally drive that vehicle and that morning he had just taken delivery of, etc., but he got me there in nice time. Diving luggage usually runs into excess but I was able to sneak in the very much condensed Aflo as hand-luggage. The pick-up point was Abergavenny; after a short wait the cars arrived then away to Brecon and The Ancient Briton, welcoming hostelry at Pen-y-Cae. We jabbered and chattered, wondering what we might be talking about that same time tomorrow. It was exciting but we soon dropped off to sleep.

"On Saturday the advance party was Weaver and self with P. and H. as Weaver's aides." (P. could have been either N.Paddock or J.G.Parkes, H. was P.I.W.Harvey.) "Coase and

Lucy, the BEC complement, had had chain trouble and arrived late, dirty and ravenous, no food to speak of since Friday lunch.

"We four collected our kit and went in. OFD is a magnificent place, the finest I have ever seen, as judged from my present approach to caves, that is, interest in their form and origin. It starts with a descending passage in which the facetting shows that the stream that made it flowed uphill. All up the streamway, where the river has also carved recent marks on the walls and in the bed of the cave, there are ever present the signs that tell the story of erosion - corrasion - right down underwater in days before the valley of the Tawe had been carved. It is a veritable museum and a text-book for those interested in the birth and growth of limestone caverns.

"However, we had come to dive not to study the cave and we could not tarry. We reached the handy platform by the start of the dive, where the stream emerged from a lower passage, dumped our loads and returned with empty rucksacks to the entrance. It was three o'clock, zero hour, when we got there and there was lunch and the repacking of bags to see to. It was zero plus one hour when we set off again and wound our way past the hazards to our destination.

"On the dressing shelf we had three divers trying to set out their kit and get into their dresses, lots of bods trying to help them but mostly getting in each other's way, and lots of other bods parked on the opposite shelf or busying themselves starting up the high-power mantle lamp or the Primus for the comforting hot drinks. We were slow enough in dressing but at last Bill Weaver, feeling (I fancied) not quite so keen about the business as when I last saw him six weeks before, moved forward to the rising. I know that horrible feeling all too well, it peaked at Swildon's II, it is less marked at each new attempt, but as yet is far from lost. How different when the visor cuts the surface and goes under! He went down and a few minutes later reported that the open passage changes abruptly to a narrow crack that would not go. This was a blow. Nevertheless, we would have a look-see ourselves. Don Coase went down and after a while reported that the crack went on for some distance before it became too narrow to follow.

"Next it was my turn. I was not feeling too happy for I imagined it was up to me to go some place the other divers thought too dangerous. Once underwater the scene changed, once more from a repulsive black hole - maybe this one is not so repulsive as most - to a beautiful green and brown fairyland and my spirits rose a few notches but I felt the discomfort of every breath and every irritant of the kit. Definitely, I was not at ease. I beat the oxygen supply, too;" (I now had a metered flow) "I kidded myself it was because I had started with a nearly empty bag and the way was downhill but there was more to it than that. I soon found the narrows and wriggled a way through; the cross-section of the tunnel was a rude figure of eight, the centre marked by projections quite rough and sharp. The way through was first at low level then high level and so on but with confidence I think we might have gone either way; it was just the fear of those sprags which might trap us fast. Aflo was good, far better than its predecessor and the piggy-back instrument light did just what was required.

"I went down this figure-of-eight tunnel with its fairly uniform six feet height and two feet breadth, its smooth roof and slotted floor, and its thick white calcite seam like a traffic line that occasionally went crazy and shot over the pavements and up the shopfronts. It brought me to a hole about six feet deeper then the tunnel continued in almost circular form at a lower level and almost along the strike. I had been travelling compass south down the first leg of the tunnel and now it went due west. In ten feet it changed shape and projections halted progress. I left Aflo and moved back a yard to reconsider. I tried again and began to wonder how I had got so far first time and would have been happier to go back and make sure the route was really possible and preferably easy - as it proved to be on the second dip, that is, when I was covering the ground for the second time and knew all was well!

"After wriggling about, head downwards, for a while, I decided to prove that to go back was possible so looped the line around a splendid point of rock, just etched out for the job, and managed to grasp Aflo, yanked it out and made for the shore.

"There was a short council and a welcome cup of Oxo with the divers on the ledge then Bill and Don went down together to have a look and took Aflo with them. Bill's lighting gear did not work so well for we had forgotten one of the links for the battery and were one cell short. Don was some time getting his face seal right; meantime Bill hung around the little chamber. It was uncanny to see his light shining through the murk; a pot-holer was down there alive and probably fairly happy, down below the surface inside a rising in a cave. How often have we looked at such places and been galled by the thought that the cave went on but we could not! How caving tactics are changing! Soon I had fixed Don's mask to his reasonable satisfaction and down he went; the light below flickered, then was eclipsed by Aflo's beam as it lit up the brown fog of sand they disturbed. Then they were gone and nothing was left but the twitching of the wire to say they were still moving.

"They returned to report that Bill was too big to get past Coase's Narrows but Coase himself had been down to the pit but mask leaks sent him back in a hurry, leaving Aflo sitting on the edge of the hole. There was no real need of the line as a tracer; the current was clean and strong and it quickly swept away any sand or mud that might be kicked up and, for the most part, the hole was swept clean but for the traces of stringy stuff (algae?) clinging to the roughnesses of the walls, which brushed off as we passed, and but for the sandbed in the little chamber. There was no chance of mistaking the way; there was only one and no doubt about it. However, we overlooked the line's most important property - as a signal line. On my trip George Lucy at the base gave me a clear and sharp signal which so surprised me that I did not recognise which it was so sent back two bells ('I am coming up'). The smooth, greasy, stiffish wire transmits the signals well.

"We drank more hot Oxo at the base then, remembering Aflo, its owner called on Leading Diver to salvage the poor thing, bringing forward all manner of sophisticated argument, or sophistry, to show why Leading Diver and not Owner should do the recovery, like, for example, it would be another dive towards his Trainer Diver qualification, very valuable experience and so on until it was plainly evident that Owner had no desire to go in again and was shirking the job. Bill, however, was willing to go and soon was a patch of brown light fading into murk. He soon returned for his bulk was too much for that narrow passage and he could not make it. So Owner then put much the same arguments to Don but less forcibly for I was beginning to feel the stirrings myself. He too soon disappeared leaving me hanging on to the sensitive lines which twitched and shifted uneasily as he trod his way down.

"The rest of the party was probably feeling cold and subdued by now for interest had waned. I was left in near darkness accompanied only by the suck and gurgle of the stream as it washed around my feet and licked at the battery box. The mud from the little chamber drifted quickly past and was gone but the wires still twitched occasionally. After a minute or two it seemed as if Don were holding the wires for they see-sawed to and fro; I gave him a signal and was surprised a moment later to receive a tug that nearly pulled me under. The diver was alright, thank you!. More twitching and pulling then suddenly they fell limp and slack; I pulled in a bit and they followed without resistance and lay as dead in the stream. I thought maybe Don had unhooked the other end so I did not pull any more, just waited with a sneaking anxiety which mounted with the passing minutes. At last out of the darkness a faint light appeared, then mud clouds, then Don's head came out of the rising but no Aflo. It seems that on the way out his bag-cover had fouled the relief valve and he had blown up to the roof at a moment when he had let go of Aflo. Unable to sink again, (there is a way, but he did not happen to think of it,) he had to leave Aflo while he made his way, bumping and scratching along the roof as the current wafted him home.

"By now I was almost eager to get underwater again so I popped down to retrieve the light. How different was the second dip, the strain of unknown terrain had gone, my breathing was quite unconscious and I floated happily down the pipe thinking how futile is the emergency torch compared with my bonny Aflo and wondering if it would delay the party unduly if I tried to go on a bit farther. Soon Aflo was in sight but rather dim. I thought at first that the water had not cleared but soon found the battery was on the way out. This decided me; I picked up the load and was in turn wafted up again by the current. Within a few minutes of reaching the surface Aflo had cut out. So that was that. We changed out of diving apparel and slowly the party got off the mark; as bundles were made ready, a section of the party took them out until finally the last four, with an inordinate pile of clobber, struggled downstream, expecting and hoping at every bend to find the advance parties on the way back to help them. We reached the exit before they had started back.

"We had been underground just on six hours; it was ten to ten and grub was timed for ten so we dumped our kit in the barn and beat it as fast as we could to supper at the Ancient Briton, just half an hour late.

"As mentioned earlier, Operation Alpha was Bill Weaver's first undertaking; the organisation and preparation was deficient in a number of ways as is to be expected; it resembled some of my own early ops., and I was contributor in no small measure; in my rush of preparation I had failed to make the usual check-list for the kit and overlooked a number of items including, believe it or not, the visor for the face-mask" ("helmet" in the original, probably an error) "and we spent most of Saturday morning trying to get a substitute eventually chipping a disc of window-glass in the Ystrad carpenter's shop. The carpenter himself was not to be found; it was the kindly Welshwoman, his daughter, who saved the situation by inviting us to help ourselves.

"The main lessons immediately learned were on lighting and heating, on organisation of transport parties, on packaging of kit, the essential need for checking down to the minutest detail and finally the need to restrict the number of divers to those needed for exploration alone. In the longer term, just as the diving at The Well might have spurred the search for an alternative entrance, so the diving at the rising within might have hastened the discovery of the by-pass route which led to the great cavern beyond. The venture was also a supreme experience for the divers and such beginnings were the foundation of the successful cave-diving of today.

"Ogof Ffynnon Ddu is a magnificent cavern, a text-book for the student of cavern origin, and a fine playground for those who just want to play. It played us a slightly shabby trick by closing in like that but we bear it no grudge. It was a grand trip, every minute enjoyable and informative. The Sherpas may well not entirely agree which makes us all the more indebted to them. The occasion has also started a new train of thought; the origin of the large pots that straddle the river for the unwary to plunge into is not known. (There are lots of unwary ones who suddenly disappear to come out spluttering and abashed; even Bill, Leader and Organiser, who was known to have kept his upper half dry as far as Fourth Pot, was discovered to be completely soaked on arrival at base but no-one actually saw him take a ducking!) We should send down divers one day to record the pots in detail... the splendid phreatic pipe prompts ideas on direct observation of the generation of facetting... the curious slot in its base needs detailed description. Cave-diving could have quite a different future from the mere conquest of water barriers, important as that will remain. At first we desired to overcome a rather repulsive obstruction, then we found a beautiful world below, now we find excuse to dally there in the cause, for once, of true speleology....

"The people of the valley one and all gave us of their best efforts and a splendid welcome; it was a sorry moment when we had to drive off up the hill and away. We made for Gloucester, missed the train but spent a jolly hour or so at The Huntsman before I was decanted at Temple Meads for a long, cold wait for the night train back to Paddington. It was a dreary journey but at last, at ten to six, I crept to bed and dropped off to sleep."

Three months later we were back at Wookey Hole. The interim was divided mainly between "office" work for CDG and equipment work. The op. did little to broaden our basis as a diving unit for the diving was shared by Sheppard and myself but it did generate excitement and interest.

Notebook No.18 has nothing significant for this record.

Notebook No.19

"OPERATION JANUS 22-2-47

"Janus happened not in the month of the God of Gateways, but that was secondary. We were at a gateway. We chose first to push the route through The Giant's Staircase but never returned fully to explore The Seventh. That February the country lay in the grip of frost and snow the like of which none of us could remember. The news that this much-postponed op. would be on came at very short notice and in the two days available there was the usual hectic rush to collect kit which had long since been dispersed into the general disorderliness of the workshop. Aflo, now Mark III, was given a little tittivation by the provision of a spare bulb carrier and changing the drum for one carrying thin field-telephone wire with distance markers. We had been lucky in obtaining some army-surplus wire. Unlucky, really, for the waxed sheathing proved vulnerable to attack by a hitherto unknown alga which then exposed the steel core to rusting but it reflected the general pinch-penny character of the work. To mark the wire, the supply drum was neatly racked in the domestic loft, the end passed down the hatch through a fairlead of sorts. I squatted at the head of the stairs and yanked down length by length and affixed the plastic markers as Mavis entered up a tally on the understairs cupboard door. We rolled off 400 feet which lay in the passage, apparently a hopeless tangle. Then, fitting a drum in the lathe in the upstairs workshop, the wire fairly whistled over the banister and the drum filled at an alarming rate, never a kink from start to finish. The drum would not take it all, 130 feet were left over.

"That stage over, I toddled off to Paddington with Aflo and the dress-drying rods and dumped them. It was snowing quite hard, cold dry snow like a postcard from St.Moritz but with trolley buses, instead of skiers, doing the graceful Christiana turns from Finchley Road into Cricklewood Lane. There was little time for the rest of the packing so the stuff was thrown hopefully into a trunk to be finished off next morning. Finished it was and, although rather less than usual, it was a colossal weight and I just managed to stagger with it to the bus stop. At Cricklewood, where I changed buses; the conductor started to hand it out but it had become accustomed to comfortable travel and refused to budge, 'Lumme, mate! What 'ave yer got in that?' he said, as we struggled to get it out between us. I then dumped it with a builders' merchant while I called in at the office for indeed it was just a call that morning. Staggering at last into Paddington, I found Jack had arrived on time and we reached Wells unnoticing, for we were engrossed in some problem of high finance or the like. Suddenly the door was flung open and a voice called 'Come on, there, out of it!'. It was the Wingco; we rushed madly round to the luggage van, not knowing where we were, but we had to get that kit; we threw it out of the van and all was well.

"At Wookey, Bill Weaver and the Diving Group were there in force. Bill had done most of the sorting and improved my breathing tube by shortening it... We finished off the kit in fading daylight and popped off to The Wookey Hole Inn, just half an hour behind schedule. Then to the cave where ops. began slowly. Jack and I had changed into diving underclothes at Crooks' Rest then had to hang about the cave waiting for the anti-dim and cutters we had left behind, then for the lowering of the water which had lagged even more behind schedule. At last we were ready and Jack, as Leading Diver on this occasion, checked leaks, did his breathing drill and went below. The water was still off-clear but we were treated to the grand spectacle, first a diver partly submerged and groping into Four then, as he fully submerged, becoming a flattened and distorted figure silhouetted in his own lights, his outline wobbling in the ripples he had left behind him. He looked like some elongated jelly-fish disappearing into the green. He appeared to go horizontally and grew smaller, and his lights fainter, until he at last disappeared from sight under the wall of the cave chamber leaving only the glow of his light showing pale green below the undercut wall. Then that, too, disappeared and we settled down to wait.

"His job was to run out a tracer line to The Gateway and to Seven, then to proceed beyond or return according to choice. We waited anxiously and after some minutes he returned using his hand torch. It transpired he had no choice for his helmet valve was leaking water (it proved to have a bit of grit under it) so he left Aflo on the sanded-up block in Six and came back. While his attendants were locating the trouble, I vented and went down, feeling in pretty fair fettle. I had had my moments of misgiving earlier in the day, but not anything like on that previous occasion, rather like clouds passing over the sun compared with thunder skies. The new line was fine and it was a thrill to see each white marker come into view and pass. In Six poor old Aflo was sitting on the sandbank with both lights blazing away; I picked it up and went on to The Gateway. Instead of tying to Belay 1 there was a handy block, the big one used for the drums in 1935, so I tied on to its iron ring without significant loss of line length. I looked at Charybdis; it seemed closer and more friendly. I smiled inwardly as I thought back of my fears of it on the night of Operation Scratch. How different it seemed now! I had been down that hole and knew it step by step to the bottom; it had lost its power to scare me.

"The surface we had wrangled over in bygone years seemed to be the near end of Seven. But I am still not certain, for when I reached Aflo in Six I did not recognise the place; visibility was poor but I could hardly find my way to The Gateway, it was only as I picked out the old lighting cable, then the floating light fitting itself, that I was sure of the direction... yet I was not sure of my destination. The questioned surface might yet be farther on. I stood at The Gateway for some time, debating which way to go, for it was Op. Janus and Janus looks both ways. I chose the hole, poised wondering if the weight of Aflo would make any difference to the thrill of it, and jumped then passed gently down the Giant's Staircase to where the way flattened and the roof was low. Along the dimpled conglomerate platform then down onto a slippery mud slope where Aflo showed 18 feet depth. I do not remember much beyond except a fish-shaped bed of river grit telling me I was in the main river channel then, later, deep water where the roof rose high and curious bosses of clay, 'weathered' like wind-riven rocks in gritstone exposures, stood about the floor. I could not be sure of the height for the water was murky; that which might be an underwater roof might easily be a higher roof above the surface, the expanse of water encouraged the idea. It might be The Eighth.

"The line drum kept on spinning and I realised I was far from home and the scale of the place began to awe me. Ahead was a bend in the way, I was travelling East, I would turn the bend then stop. The channel turned North. On the right I remember a steep mud slope, ahead a tumble of giant pinnacles and blocks,, like Charybdis's sisters nattering over some long past event. I turned off the wire, switched off and parked Aflo, noticed the depth was 18 feet again and beat it for home.... Back in Three they lifted my visor" (we must have been using the new Siebe Gorman equipment,) "and I told them where I had been, that I was disappointed; the cave seemed to go on for ever in deep water, in fact I agreed we had had our inner series. I was suffering from the strain of that journey, especially the return without lights and felt a little sick, just a nasty feeling in the pit of my stomach. I asked Jack if he was going down to have a look round, and to bring back Aflo," (I must have left it with a further push in view) "and learned that he had had ear trouble, and he too was feeling a bit sick. His respirator was giving trouble for he was panting continuously underwater.

"I lay down for a while, until I was sure my sickness was passing, then hopped down for Aflo. This second journey was not so leisurely and I saw nothing but the floor over which I crawled, walked or clambered. At the far end I tied off the line to a second and more secure belay, snipped the wire off short and went out, strangely enough, finding quite a measure of difficulty getting up the Staircase.

"Operation Janus had not been a great success; Janus had only looked one way, into the hill; and had not seen much of promise. We staggered out of the cave - this time I tried the experiment of undressing at Crooks' Rest. We parted after a not very enthusiastic discussion of the event. It was not until the early hours of next morning, lying awake thinking things over, that the significance of the clay men and the mud slope struck me. My attitude had been 'how disappointing, the cave is going on for ever deep under water' but now I was better able to reason. Such deposits would occur if a free surface stream plunged down into spacious submerged channels, and especially if that stream had stored up a mass of clay and rubbish durings times of flood and in normal times slowly eroded it away. Just such a system exists between the Third Chamber and The Witch's Scullery where the sandbanks of Three are an ample stockpile which the stream is slowly cutting away to deposit in the Scullery. A closer study of the Scullery deposits should give information to assess our chances and guide our progress in the higher reaches of the river. This will set the direction of our work.

"While waiting for the water level to fall at the start of the operation, when the water was still about a foot above its lowest level, the famous noises of the cave were heard coming from the direction of the Second Chamber, as if from the water-hole there. Whether there were any disturbances at that surface we do not know, we were busy dressing and could not go to see for ourselves. The plopping was quite loud and might well frighten anyone not prepared for such sounds. It sounded like 'the running of a hundred pigs', said Wingco, who had a close-up vantage point. At last we have some fairly definite information on this phenomenon; that can give us a starting point for investigation. We can watch for it from below, and having found it, can probably control it, measure it or even use it!

Notebook No.20 is concerned almost entirely again with equipment and deskwork but there is an entry on Wookey: it was in the period of great flooding after the freeze-up, an operation already twice postponed. When at last we arrived, I was in my usual rags and with the heaviest load of gear ever carried by the Great Western Railway, well probably, and had attracted interrogation by the police near Paddington; the river was recorded as "a milkman's dream", actually the visible range was six feet but useless to us, so we set about other things.

The developing trend in deepwater chambers raised again the problem of surfacing. I was still opposed to using fins, an opposition probably based on my own failure to achieve satisfactory buoyancy under cave conditions. Currently we would need more than just to reach surface, we wanted photographs as well, so turned to floatation devices of various kinds, finally inflatable rubber dinghies.

Notebook No.21 is pre-occupied with equipment problems, including testing methods for sodalime, but also holds the notes on Operation Acheron with its less amicable undertones among the teams. Acheron was in the Llygad Llwchwr, source of the Loughor, near Trapp. It was on forbidden territory; we had to get in unobserved.

"OPERATION ACHERON 5-4-47

"Easter, a CDG meet with South Wales Caving Club. It had been agreed that CDG should join the SWCC in their meet at Glyntawe. It fell naturally to our South Wales Section to organise the CDG op. and, in their words, to 'lay the law down'. This they proceeded to do but forgot to mention any of the arrangements to SWCC - Weaver was the man in charge - and soon had their worthy secretary in wrathful mood, as SWS cut across his accommodation arrangements without ever a 'by your leave'. However Weaver is well-known, and they knew it was not our Group attitude to cross them.

"After a long period of uncertainty, during which Bill seemed to go out of his way to misunderstand and cross swords with us in London, in response to a frantic wire to discover the arrangements, we heard that we would have to find our own way to Glyntawe and so on. On Thursday it was taxi to Paddington with 'one and a half' trunks and miscellaneous packages, a full train to Neath, where we joined Jack Sheppard to find that the evening train going our way had been cancelled, so taxi again. We eventually arrived at Smith's the Waterworks and settled in.

"Friday morning was spent preparing kit, the afternoon run to Llwchwr stopped by breakdown of the transport. During the evening there was a pre-Acheron meeting at The Ancient Briton; not sure how we discovered about that, for Hon. Organiser now requires us to be thought-readers!

"Saturday, day of the op., we were running a bit later than program but only by minutes at the meeting point. Then to Roderick the Draper's for the Aflo batteries which had suffered in transit, and then trouble started. For twenty minutes I knocked, and the dog inside barked, until my knuckles were sore and the dog got hoarse and stopped barking. The rest of the party was itself obviously delayed at The Ancient, for it had not yet come round the bend but it soon did, with a roar of motorcycles and a clattering and banging of cars. The convoy drew alongside and added its din to the banging of my helmet on the door. The dog gave a few last despairing whelps then retired, for there was sound of movement within. The door opened, Roderick the Draper emerged and we got our batteries. Then one of the cars broke down. Eventually we got to the cave and sneaked in. Aflo was rather a devil, but we got it there. Three divers dressed and in the Fourth Chamber played in the milky water which was almost too shallow for leak-testing or venting dresses. Further inside is another small chamber, a fresh clean-looking place with dripstone, and the river rises in the SW corner. Visibility was about a foot so we did not take things very seriously. We slithered in and out in turn or in pairs. On my own second dip I started down the mud-hole where the water rises, guided to the spot all the way from The Fourth by the white particles floating in the beam of the light. Where the floor dips I dangled a moment then slid a few inches until well and truly on the slope and added a new diving experience. I was on a live line, payed out from the base, and on the slope I only just remained put; any small movement and down I slid a few more inches. Naturally, base continued to pay out the line and I wondered what my attendant would do if I tried to signal 'Stop'; it was not comforting for I had no idea of what was below. A deep pitch, perhaps, and I was heavily weighted. Soon I discovered that Aflo, properly used, could serve as an ice-axe and make a good brake; by digging its sharp angles into the mud it holds quite well. So down I went to

-10 feet where I paused hoping to look about. I could see the right-hand wall, smooth and rounded with a knobbly spike lower down. All within reach but nothing beyond. Enough for the moment. It reminded me of another occasion, but in very different circumstances; Sheppard and I were descending a steep slope of grass in The Lake District, the grass slippery in the hot afternoon sun; we stopped for a rest; the day was very hot and we both fell asleep, but we did not slide and on awaking found it was just as well for just below was a very considerable sheer drop.

"I signalled to return, did not get the normal response but the line was eventually drawn in as I ascended and floundered into The Fourth. Then I followed Weaver down to more or less the same spot, he with Aflo, but this time, having more faith in the mud slope, I found little trouble, but my mask leaked unpleasantly... We went out and packed up, Weaver a convert to Aflo as a third hand.

"The op. was conspicuous for the improvement in packing and organisation; save for the sundry hitches mentioned, everything seemed to go well to plan - overlooking the unwisdom of allowing transport parties go in guideless! At last we were outside but in pouring rain. It was chucking it down, the lane was awash, the vehicles started only with difficulty; one bike had to be abandoned. The journey back was easily the worst feature; I was relegated to the back of Lucy's bike, and we ploughed through pools while the rain lashed by the wind beat first one side then the other. The cars had trouble at the water-splashes which had risen to torrents, one car was being hauled out by brute force when the rope broke and laid us all flat on our backs, at another crossing a car was nearly washed away. The streams and rivers everywhere were muddy and racing, reminiscent of that Easter in Yorkshire when The Ribble showed its strength, and I for one was mightily glad to get indoors as I had no protection beyond my pot-holing clothes.

"Sunday was Operation Vernon again; it rained and was miserably cold... The Craven Pothole Club were very interested in the dressing and many old friends called to see us at the spring...." (Monday was devoted to sight-seeing and a bit of "dry" exploration, i.e. not more than waist-deep, in Dan-yr-Ogof; on Tuesday we returned home.)

"A pretty miserable Easter, but no-one seemed unduly disappointed, they got wet and cold, and got warm again, and knocked back whatever was available. The food was first class. The organisation was thorough, it must have been an enormous load on the Hon. Officers and Helpers, they have our warmest thanks."

Notebook No.22 is entirely devoted to equipment matters but slips in a mention of a booster pump. That was a magnificent acquisition (actually we got two but do not enquire into the details of how, nor how we got away with the equally irregular filling of high-pressure cylinders) and it upstaged operations enormously.

Notebook No.23 finds diving almost squeezed out again but records a further spreading of our activities in the discovery by the Somerset Section of Lower Stoke Lane (Coase discovered that by the "duck and go through" process without any respirator) then another trip to Wookey, successsor to the aborted last visit.

"LOWER STOKE LANE SWALLET 2-6-47

"I called at Bristol on Friday on my way back from Land's End Radio and there met some of the members of the Bristol Exploration Club, a growing and energetic body of local caving enthusiasts. They had recently discovered a new passage in the swallet of Stoke Lane, near Shepton Mallet. They asked me if I would care to come along and look at it. Surely enough I was glad to since, apart from anything else, the passage ended in a deep pool of water which is a feature of special interest nowadays for we are developing the technique of underwater exploration. So on Sunday morning we set off, five in number. We changed into our caving attire, which would disgrace any self-respecting scare-crow, and disappeared down the hole.

"This swallow-hole engulfs a small stream from the valley above and the stream reappears at St. Dunstan's Well about half a mile away. The part of the cave already known is perhaps 800 to 1,000 feet long. Scarcely anywhere is there room to stand up and in some places the roof is so low it is a tough struggle to get through, maybe some 9 to 10 inches from the floor and the various jagged projections are decorated with torn shreds of clothing and are liberally plastered with the mud carried down from the slimy crawls just above. Most of the way is through passages which the stream has deserted but, here and there, the stream crosses the path and we slithered through it taking the opportunity to wash out some of the mud which had squelched between our fingers and oozed up our sleeves in the so-called dry passages. Not far from the end the stream disappears under the right-hand wall except for a mere trickle which continues with us. This curious feature, in its nature an overflow or distributary, was an encouraging sign for it suggests that sooner or later it would lead us to the main stream again which, indeed, it did. We followed the passage to its apparent end.

"Now it was here in the boulders on the floor that the BEC had discovered only a few weeks ago that a way could be made down through the floor and the passage then went on for about another 200 feet where it came to a dark pool with low down-hanging roof. By submerging to the shoulders I was told it was possible to get through round a double corner to a small pit where the roof came right down to the water. We clustered round this termination to decide on a plan while the two who still smoked lit up.

"Then Don Coase, leading adventurer, went forward, squawking vociferously as the cold water rose above his belly then his armpits, and he disappeared round the corner. We waited rather anxiously. After a few moments he called back for an underwater light and another 'bod'. I happened to be next in line and, regardless of my protests that I was only a guest, I was pushed in. I found him standing up to his neck in the pit and with a grin of glee from ear to ear. He had found a hole and thought he could feel surface at the other side. Yes, he was sure of it and struck the wall at the other side with the lamp. It rang low and clear. He tried to touch the roof with a stick, found floating in the water. No, it was beyond reach! It seemed reasonably sure that the barrier in front of us would not hold us back; we had come to reconnoitre for pukka diving with respirators, but it looked as if we could manage without them. Coase then announced his intent; one more torch and one more bod was wanted. Harry Stanbury followed with the torch and stood behind me. Coase said he would go through and did. He took a deep breath and sank slowly down. As he turned sideways I could see the blurred pale patch, that was his face, fade and disappear. He had gone. Then there was a muffled shout; a moment later he reappeared and beaming with delight he announced it was the main river passage as we had hoped. Coase went through again and a few moments later his light flashed back, the signal to follow. I took a deep breath and sank after him. As I went under I thought what a crazy idiot I was and wished I could turn back but not actually willing it for I could not really stop myself. I went on and as I passed under the archway I wondered if my clothes would snag and trap me but I rose safely to the surface at the other side.

"Soon Stanbury followed; I guided his head clear of the rock roof for he came up rather fast. So reinforced, we set off down the new cave. Our lights were poor and did not do justice to the passage which, after the first few yards, was of considerable size and we moved fast downstream. After a number of scrambles and turns we came to a chamber piled with boulders up the left-hand wall and, at about 25 feet up, there were some big stalactites hanging from the wall. We passed on, keeping to the streamway where the roof provided some protection should those boulders move. As a matter of fact that chamber would probably be the safest place in the cave in the event of flooding for it would easily be possible to climb the slope to comparative safety near the roof about 30 feet up.

"Below the boulder chamber, the passage closed in somewhat and at one spot we thought we were nearing the end, but it opened up again and just beyond was another chamber, this one about 20 feet high, and the stream ran to ground among the blocks of a rock-fall. There were a number of possible high-level passages and the choke itself might go but for the present trip we had done enough and sped back to the trap, ducked under and were back, shaking with the cold, to tell the other two our story then back out as quickly as we could, and that was slow enough to be sure, to the surface and sunlight where we changed leisurely and washed our clothes before making back for a meal at The Belfry, the most appropriately named headquarters of the BEC."

(This item appears to have been an article for publication, or maybe broadcasting, but its fate is unknown. Something very like it went out on BBC's "Eye Witness" series.)

There had been delays and op. postponements, mostly on account of bad weather, but at last our luck changed. We had to investigate the mud slopes and the like in the Witch's Scullery before returning to Eight, indeed Nine had we but known it. So the curiously named op., "Muckment", was put on.

"OPERATION MUCKMENT 5-7-47

"The water was beautifully clear when we arrived to resume work after the long interval since Janus. The water was low in the valley stream but, as we found later, the mud cleared quite rapidly. We were a team of three now; Coase was there for his final Trainer Diver dip, as well as to make sure, we hoped, that there would be at least two working divers all the time. The program was to lay a number of fixed lines along the most important features of the underwater chamber between One and Three which we have named the Witch's Scullery then to survey the place by measured offsets at fixed intervals along the line.

"We started later than usual as the visitors in the months of Double Summer Time continue to arrive until quite a late hour. Quarter to eight was zero for going in and the last party of visitors was still inside as we carried our gear into position. By 9:20 the first man was in the water, Coase, in a Coase-Balcombe combination, most accurately following carefully given but entirely incorrect instructions, proceeded straight across the river, under the wall then left. I followed hard on his heels but did not recognise the place and found it rather tight. Trying to wriggle over the lip I knocked my by-pass open, and how!, everything blew up hard and jammed me between roof and floor; only after a long delay (like a split-second or so) and much fiddling could I locate the valve and turn off the gas, an unpleasant reminder of my unfamiliarity with the kit layout. Down below, just past the old bones corner, Coase's mask showed half full of water, so we returned. The way back seemed even worse and rather alarming, obviously I had boobed but when the water cleared I found the right route....

"We had another go and methodically and easily laid the line to the point of Magnum. It was an error to leave Aflo at the far end of the line so I slid off and shifted it, finding to my delight a jaw and a skull partly buried in the sand... then we waited again for the mud to clear. This was not a good start and caused considerable delay. Next Balcombe-Sheppard laid a line; I stepped over the old bridge" (a wooden structure washed in from Two) "and got nicely wedged in an attempt to enter a gully along the far wall. Then I went North along a creep to tie off on a second old bridge. My luck was in again for I found there a splendid femur waiting on the floor. While reconnoitring from there, I thought I saw a long descending channel with a hollow in its flattish roof which might have been the Cymbals Centre, I left Aflo to explore it and looked North along the next stretch to be lined. This, too, seemed to be a long defile and gave me the impression that we were a long way from the Third Chamber.

"The Sheppard-Coase combination then laid another line but my long channel, '50 to 100 feet long', proved to be a short steep, glutinous slope to the ceiling! There was no anchorage so Sheppard reeled back the line and dumped it. Time was flying and we were already getting tired and cold. Balcombe-Coase would do one more line and, after some delay in transferring line at the far end, Coase gesticulated excitedly, pointed to a crescent of light high up ahead, so up towards it we went. The slope was easier than it looked and in a slot among the boulders I spotted a couple of skulls, showed them to Coase, but was feeling distressed and did not tarry; we went straight out to what proved to be the Second Chamber. We passed on the way sundry less ancient relics, such as toffee papers, a broken bottle and later Sheppard noticed a packet of sandwiches with the wrapper waving gently in the watery breeze!

"Coase had collected one skull, a broken one, to add to the collection. My sodalime was spent - the relief on going to air was immediate; it reminded me of Pre-History when I had just about had it below the Witch. Sheppard, in spite of ear-trouble, went in again but failed to find the remaining skull. We abandoned further work for the night, it was already one o'clock; the survey would be a long job, it would have to wait.

"The operation has simultaneously shown us that our technique is improving and the diving routine is sound but that all underwater work is very slow indeed. There were a couple of interesting but unsettling experiences. Sheppard's ear trouble is still with him and he suffered severe head-ache afterwards. On my trips there was a squelchy noise somewhere in the back of my nose while crossing the deepest place and, on taking the nose-clip off while resting, my nose ran for a while as in a severe cold. This happened twice and on the third trip at the same spot my ears were painful for a few moments. There was also the inevitable spot of bother; Sheppard fell over on landing, most of us usually did, but he was in the presence of The Wing Commander. The Wingco fumed as he saw mud clearly discernable in the wake of the accident, and wanted to know if all that was necessary. Well! But much worse was to come; our Controller of Operations pranged a light switch and was the Wing Commander wild when it was reported! It was the Fourth Chamber light and 1,400 people on the morrow would not be able to see whence came the river. Was he wild!... He calmed down a bit after I had read to him the proposed statement for the Press Association. In the synopsis, however, where I had made reference to 'Wookey Hole Cave, Somerset' he thought 'Somerset' unnecessary. It seems the great Wookey Hole did not need putting on the map. The BBC, when they got the story, thought otherwise and we now learn that Wookey Hole is 'near Cheddar Gorge'; that'll larn 'im!

"Our gear is now in the old office; we stowed it or set it out to dry then left after whiling away a pleasant couple of hours with the excavators, chatting with the publican and last but not least, the farmer, then home via Bristol to a bus strike in London. I swear my trunk was over the railway weight-limit."

ARCHEOLOGICAL ADVISOR

The discovery of bones with such a wide distribution made rather a nonsense of the idea of Victims of The Witch. The further archeological work of collection, preservation, identification and classification was taken over by E.J.Mason, well experienced in excavating, aided by members of the Somerset Section. They had much fun as well with a water pump used to "excavate" the First Chamber; a long preliminary schedule of the finds appeared in the Letters to Members and in Proc. Somersetshire Archeological and Natural History Society, Vol. XCVI (1951).

In the original record the various lines were lettered; as the sketch-plans are not reproduced here, the letters are omitted. Sketch-plans also appeared in the Letters to Members and in Operation Orders.

The work at Wookey was suffering somewhat from the geographical handicap of divers living in London while the helpers lived in the locality. There was, in consequence of the usual frantic rush, inadequate opportunity to develop those regular exchanges and fruitful crossing of ideas such as happen in course of happy times in a pub or the like; op. objectives and arrangements tended to be entirely the unconsulting product of the London end. As the novelty of the work wore off it was hardly surprising that occasionally in some dark corner might be heard whispered the comment "Führer". The gang were much imposed upon, staying on at such late hours, cold and often hungry, to ensure the job went through. It is to the great credit of the Controller of Operations, Dan Hasell, that the party was held together so well.

Chapter 8

Peak Cavern and back to Wookey Hole

Notebook No.24 is also pre-occupied with equipment but there is a mildly amusing record of a clandestine visit to the Womens' Swimming Pond on Hampstead Heath with our recently-acquired boats. Why the Women's? We had just been given the bird at the Men's so waited a while, as it was closing time, then we sneaked into the Women's just after the Amazon-in-charge departed, for that pond was well screened from prying eyes. Our efforts to control these lightweight craft contributed to the entertainment, our own and that of the poacher-fishermen who soon had gathered in the gloaming. We also sorted out the defects for the boats were far from new.

Notebook No.25. The scene now moved to Derbyshire, where that Section was pushing ahead fast, though as yet no-one there had yet achieved Trainer-diver standard. Coase of Somerset took the actual lead but I was happy to be included as a passenger.

"OPERATION BETA I 17-8-47

"In November, 1946, it was Operation Alpha, the first scuba-divers' operation run by a new man. Now in August, 1947, it is Beta and it was Coase, who had recently attained his Trainer-Diver ranking, who arranged it. At first the idea was to tackle Giant's Hole during the week when the BEC were having a look round Derbyshire but after consulting Grainger" (himself a giant among Derbyshire pot-holers) "interest was switched to Peak Cavern which would be better suited to our standard of achievement."

(Not sure what Grainger meant by that but surely enough we were greenhorns.)

179

"Once the idea had rooted, the usual rush began. Aflo III was not available so a new and more compact model was put on the stocks, Aflolaun Mark IV. The first gas pump to be got working was rushed into service and, from a big massive brute of a 110 cu.ft. cylinder, we filled up 14 of our 6 ft. cylinders before calling a halt with 30 atm left and when the pumping time was 12 minutes per pair of small cylinders; by then it was right hard work. Weights were needed so they were cast. Then cylinder plugs and carrying containers were made and the packing itself done; thus we finished at just short of midnight on D-Day Minus Two. Meantime something had gone wrong with the dispatching of the kit and Aflo III became essential after all; frantic calls to the Somerset Section" (Aflo was at Wookey) "and Aflo arrived. Coase lugged it from Paddington while I scrounged a charger to fill its batteries with amps.

"Coase had sent most of his stuff on by parcel post and told with great glee the story of how he wrapped up his lead weights into a neat little parcel and carefully planted it on the Post Office counter. The counter clerk smiled at Coase and went to pick it up. The smile vanished very suddenly when the little parcel failed to move and he saw Coase grinning at him. Rather taken aback and suspicious, he then slid it to the edge of the counter and finally into the parcel chute. There was a horrid clang as it went in, a succession of sinister bumps then an awful crash as it landed at the bottom, maybe in a parcel of eggs or china. Coase and the clerk stared at each other for a moment then Coase turned and beat it. The sequel came days later; the address, Pindale Farm, is a mile or more from the Post Office and there is no postman; the postmistress has to deliver; no bus, no bicycle. Stacks and stacks of parcels addressed to one D.A.Coase and, to cap it all, that innocent-looking one. The look in that postmistress's eye as she at last handed them over told what she thought of diving gear by post, and more, it gave a pretty clear idea of what would happen if she ever came across anyone with the name D.A.Coase!"

(Clearly bordering on the apochryphal but Coase swore it was true. Doubtless some part of it was.)

"Apart from our own kit it seemed a good idea to take a few things up for Grainger and his lads" (The CDG Derbyshire Section) "so out of the loft came a couple of kits to be added to the pile by the front door.

"On D-Day Minus One, by a bit of luck, a passing green van picked up the pile and dropped it at St.Pancras. Bill Mack" (an ex-patriated Derbyshire man living not far away) "was also going by train and between our two tickets we managed to smuggle and wangle over 3 cwt of kit on the 2:20 for Hope. At last we were off, sweat dripping in the heatwave weather in which the whole country was basking. On the journey up, a little girl of perhaps eight years snuggled up to me closely as I read to her of Snow White and the Little House in the Wood. We said goodbye to her at Millers Dale and rolled on to Chinley where either we had missed our connection or it did not run, for we were given both explanations. We had an hour to wait, until 8:14 and the pub did not open until 8:15.... We cooled off considerably while some kind railway porters fixed our kit aboard the train - a whole platform truckload of it. I had parked my personal kit on that truck for the time being and it all went aboard, rucksack gaping open with camera and what-not within. Careless work on my part but it all arrived safely.

"At Hope there was no reception party, not even a lone motorcyclist, to show us the way. We found the farm as it grew dusk but none of the party was about. Grainger had called and would come back later, so we ate and waited. The party arrived in odd bods then came Grainger and we plotted our plans for the morrow.

"Early (?) on Sunday, Mack and I toddled down to Castleton to collect a van or taxi to get the gear to Peak Cavern. We had just about exhausted possibilities when Lewis and Marjorie Railton hailed us. They were on their way to Pindale Farm to pick up a message I had completely forgotten to leave for them.... They took us to the railway station and we manoeuvred the kit aboard... and so to Peak Cavern. We arrived before Grainger but were more or less expected and were made welcome. We learned from the custodian's small son, who was already in his caving kit, that a British

Speleological Association party was coming and that he would be working with them. This was interesting news indeed. We stacked and sorted our kit by the entrance hut and there met Cymmie" (BSA) "who, I must admit, did not seem overjoyed at meeting us. He was looking pretty fit but he did not tell us of his intentions. Roughhead's son seemed to scent that there would be far more fun with our party and attached himself to us; all the way in he was prominently in the lead; he enjoyed the trip no end and was proud of his role as guide.

"The way in is easy; just follow the path to the dressing place. Plenty of room everywhere and no-one was worried about mud on paths or where we went, provided only that visitors did not see us go beyond their limited traverse. There was trouble with Coase's dress for a neat hole had been nipped in the helmet... A quick patch and we were off along the pile of debris the old miners had brought down from the roof.

"Coase was Leading Diver, he was using Aflo III, since his 4B's" (no explanation offered, it is too rude) "was a non-starter from battery trouble. He sank down the ridge to the left; a gurgling and a rushing of bubbles broke over him and died away; a few sporadic escapes floated up as he fiddled with switches then the dark pool was cut by the lights beam; it was green, deep and spacious. I followed him round his boulder traverse. To the left it seemed deep and (at least at the moment of submerging) rather awesome so we were careful not to disturb the rocks which formed our precarious path and, for myself, I hung rather tightly to the wire just in case! Round the nose, sand hove into view; a firm safe bottom and the way opened up ahead. Don led on at a good pace; at last it was my joy to follow on a new runout behind a good diver. We went about 100 feet and halted. We had agreed 'just to have a look round' but this place was so temptingly clean and safe, such a delightful place to dive in, that I, at least, was loathe to stop. We thumbed each other 'O.K.?' and as we could not discuss a program I grabbed Aflo, pointed its beam upstream, thumbed 'O.K.?' again, was okayed in return and off we went. The way went on, always enticing, always a secretive bend just ahead. The compass showed a fairly continuous S to SSW direction until we were brought to a halt in a bell chamber. There were rocks strewn on the floor and a thin layer of mud over them; they did not reach to the roof, in fact, the way on looked easy.

"As I rose on the platform of rocks some gas escaped and bubbled upwards; it must hit the wall about six feet above my head for, when we looked up to inspect, a film of mud had travelled across the bell at that level and shut off the view. Aflo said the floor was 6 feet deep; the muddy water was about 11 feet higher, or negative five. This was curious; we had expected to find something like this at Wookey when the water is down but not in a system in which the level has not altered perceptibly for months. 'Torricellian' might be a good name for such a place. Another thing which struck us both was that although the tumble of blocks had been derived from this chamber, its walls were smooth and tapering just like those we are accustomed to attribute to simple solution.

"We fiddled around for some time trying to find a way through but despite first appearances it was not there. Each and every spot looked easy from a few feet distance but each time the breathing bag snagged. At each point where I stuck, I was still convinced that a foot or two forward there was plenty of room until measurement showed it to be only 1½ torch-lengths. My thumbs were rapidly becoming numb - the water is 46° - so I signalled Don and, after a struggle for my cutters with a dead thumb, he cut the line for me and we tied off, taking Aflo back with us. The way back was long but cheerful; clouds of mud but clear patches at the sides. It was grand to know it did not matter much if you did hit the roof, except should you prang your skull on it, for it was sound and safe. Soon we gathered on the debris pile to tell our tale (after an uneasy moment when I could not tell whether it was I was going up or the debris going down) then on to the base for respirators off, cuffs off and hot coffee. Grainger had laid on the drinks unprompted, though what his wife said, when he cleaned out the glass and china cupboard to take the stuff pot-holing, we did not hear. Enough that it was mighty fine coffee and warmed us through.

"At this juncture Pengo (?) got busy with his camera and flash-powder; when he had finally satisfied himself, we collected our stuff and marched out. The cave route is much longer than Wookey but much easier; no steps, no stooping, in fact it is everything a diving party could desire...

"Back at the entrance, we took a look at the Swine Hole; a rising which would superficially appear to be an external tributary to the Great Chamber efflux but the facetting shows it is the reverse. It appears to be a backwater of The Styx which goes to ground farther back in the cave. The BSA were busy scratching at the streambed and their level mark at the Swine Hole showed they had succeeded in dropping the level there by six inches. We had a yarn with Cymmie who okayed the suggestion to look round the sump, and look round we did. We assembled then piled on our BA's. Coase led and soon we were under a surface, alas, only a few inches of headroom though it did rise to a couple of feet at one spot in a roof joint. At the edge of a slope leading down into a fair chamber, the line ran out. The drum had been wound in a hurry and had not been marked, also the winding tackle did not run very evenly, so the full 370 feet could not have been on the drum, however, between the two trips we had run out the full amount, whatever it was, maybe 350 feet.

"The drum from Aflo IV was pressed into service and it fitted nicely: I took over the lead, hitched on and made my way down the slope under what looked to be a rather dangerous roof. Still, by going left to a vee-groove and then down it, we by-passed the ugly block in the roof. On the way down the line knows a quicker way, of course, so we kept low down on the way back. The bottom is the lowest yet, unless Wookey has some places I did not measure; here it was 24 feet by the meter with the roof of the archway only some four feet higher. Coase had a mask leak and returned but I was anxious to see it through and, in any case, I had to find a belay. At the other side of the arch, which was quite short, there was another nasty-looking chamber, a twin to the first, with steeply sloping boulder-strewn floor. The stream may have gone down the dark hole on my right, low down, or that hole might have just been a dark hole anyway. I tied off to a miserable bit of rock and not very securely either, - cold, dark and a rising tide in the facepiece all had their effect - then went back to land to report. It seems that on our first report someone had dashed out in excitement, and maybe with a touch of malice, to tell Cymmie that the way on was 15, or more, feet down. Pity we did not invite Cymmie to the op. Circumstances did not seem exactly propitious but maybe the various parties might have buried the hatchet for an hour or so." (Alas, these petty jealousies!)... In the Swine Hole we both noticed sandbanks in the first chamber and a black but small hole from which The Styx might rise but that is doubtful. We saw no other likely spot and between our two visits the main-chamber water became clear, also the water in the second chamber was clear. The general distribution of sand and rock is strongly suggestive of an active streamway. The hollows are swept clean, the sand lies in ridges or banks and the mud we disturbed was heavy, there is no general obliteration as in other places; as the mud clears it leaves clear patches between definite mud clouds. We really must get some gen on the way mud disappears. Wookey would be a good spot; if we can have observers at the Resurgence we might learn a lot.

"So we packed up and went on our way by the Railton Service, back to the farm, most carefully leaving my helmet and lamp sitting on the wall. It had been a grand day, in some ways disappointing, in others very satisfying."

(The next day was spent in training with the Derbyshire men; eventually we set off home, got a lift in an empty truck that had lost its way, grabbed some fruit from a shop to allay the hunger, just caught the train and after a few vicissitudes were home before midnight.)"

Quite a slice of the same notebook is devoted to a struggle to adapt Double-Entry Bookkeeping to the needs of the CDG; I eventually worked it out and thought I understood it but I fear no-one else agreed.

Notebook No. 26 is filled more generously with diving. The Haldanes joined us on an op. and the Muckment program went on and on with, however, a moment of lighter relief from Dan-yr-Ogof.

"OPERATION MUCKMENT Two 4-10-47

"We thought M2, by virtue of its special interest, the ease with which spectators can watch progress from One Two and Three, and its suitability for visitor-divers, would be an excellent occasion to invite our VIP's to an op. We chose wrongly; Haldane was in Switzerland and Davis was unwell. The date also clashed with the Wessex Cave Club annual binge. The meet was moved to 4th October....

"Our trunk had gone on Friday to Paddington (no, not of its own volition or motive power) and on Saturday there was Aflo to load with its batteries and sundry other things to do. Even the bus trip had its problems; when a bus conductor says: 'take it inside, it might get damaged', front-and-back mounting of one's impedimenta can be a decided embarrassment. I had left with 1½ hours in hand but, with the odd call to make, arrived at Paddington quarter of an hour late; dumping my load at the barrier, I hared off to the left-luggage office to find a party casually having many articles removed, most of them cached in the wrong places and not to be found. At last our Mr.Casual, the attendant, took my ticket then came back and whanged my box on the counter with a resounding crash which raised my ire and he got a mouthful. I had meantime grabbed a porter and truck, so having quickly sailed in and out of the labelling booth, we ploughed up the platform and got the kit aboard at minus two minutes. Jack had given me up for lost and had handed over my seat.

"At Wells we were met rather coolly by Wingco and ferried to the cave. The party was late; what part had arrived went off in search of that which had not, what time the cunning divers beetled off for tea at The Cave's expense. This seemed to start the disintegration for we never pulled into step that evening. Diver Three (Stanbury) eventually arrived after a delayed trip down Swildon's with some small boys. We got into the cave, there laid out the kit and got down to discussion of the program. It was then that the Wingco expostulated 'What, make exit in Two and walk down the cave path? Most certainly not.'

They would have hundreds of visitors the next day; someone might slip and break a leg then claim compensation.' 'What, then, was a diver to do?' I asked, going all hot and cold and thinking that now the crash had come. 'Go back underwater!' was the reply. Whereupon I let him have it fair and square. He was visibly shaken. I told the boys to get packing for we had finished and we were quite ready to go without further ado. He knew we meant it and started to come to terms. We reached agreement on post-op. cleaning down and M2 was on again and dressing began at 20:00.

"Diver Two (Sheppard) had a handwheel-leak that could not be stopped; Diver One took over while washers were changed and when his next turn came Diver Two found his ear or sinus trouble back again and had had his diving. Coase took over in Sheppard's kit. Our rota was badly upset but we kept going. We tabbed our lines and ran out new ones, popped out in the Third, then popped out in the Second with hardly a drip or splash of mud to mark our exit. We had looked at the roof and deemed it sound enough. We collected or noted old bones. One diver (that was me!) dropped his line-tabs and had to grovel around until he found them. He also forgot his nose-clip and generally behaved to the delight of his log-writer who had some scores to settle. We linked up lines but had trouble with mud which was slow to clear, for the river was very low after a dry summer of glorious scorching sunshine. We found the way to Three leads deep under the river's left wall along a lovely sandbank. We retraced our steps and ran a line to this 'new' part of the chamber, but hardly had we got going when we found we were steaming straight back into the main chamber. Our line showed up under the rock wall and the spectators said it was a magnificent sight as the divers churned their way along the river bed. Another fine sight was when Coase and Stanbury hove into view in Three (I am seeing things like this for myself now); Aflo was dazzling white as it shone up at us through the water, the light becoming greener and deeper the further from the beam, and the two figures apparently without any thickness were crouched behind it; the light got brighter and the figures got bigger as the seconds passed until they came to the surface and the magic spell was broken. It was magnificent; a caver's dream come true.

"But listen. Not only did we lay and tab our lines, Stanbury had noticed a queer object like a coffee pot standing erect in the mud. He pointed it out to me where it lay beside the line. I felt carefully round it, rather sceptically, for it might have been any old tin can, but perhaps - well just in case not, I left it there, noting the position carefully, then followed on. We were on a new run-out and we had no idea what difficulties might lie ahead and which might endanger any treasure we carried. On tabbing the line later on, Coase and Stanbury brought it out. It was a most curious vessel, the like of which we had never seen before. It was double-conical, base to base, the lower cone truncated to form the bottom. The axial neck was broken but still plugged with what seemed to be yellow ochre. The handle was tall and slender, its upper part broken off. Through a hole in the side we decanted the water carefully, so as not to lose any contents. Inside we noticed a small triangular plate like a fragment of glass and were puzzled. We rushed the vessel down to the House, hoping to catch the old man before he went to bed, but failed by an unfortunate margin." (It proved to be our oldest artefact, Roman.)

"We then got down to our job again and finished work at 01:15 with not a single survey reading taken. Harry Stanbury was wet through from a leaking helmet valve and he was cold. I was beginning to get ear trouble and was not sure of my kit; the regulator was playing tricks... Don Coase was ready to continue but we agreed to chuck it in: the weather was against a survey but we had done a good evening's work so off to The Belfry, to tea without milk and a cold bed.

"I rose early (for us) and wandered over to the old camping site by Fair Lady Well to commune for a moment with the ghosts of the 1935 party, not forgetting Ting, the little watchdog, and Matthew Walker.

"Jack and I breakfasted after a fashion and left the others snoring still as we walked down Deer Leap to the cave, to clean and pack our kit or set it out to dry. We lunched 'on The Cave' and Balch arrived to see our latest find; it was very different from what he had expected. It was something new to him and he was very pleased; his pleasure and his hypotheses made the Wingo 'even pleaseder'. Wingco phoned a message for me to the Press Association" (I had set up a "special correspondent" relationship with them) "and when I had occasion to ring him from Westbury he almost gushed, offered me my expenses and welcomed us back for another do.

"We had sat in conclave with him that morning and told him things about his cave; let him know we had other irons in the fire and that the task was no light one. He seemed quite surprised to hear of proposals to photograph The Seventh, or even to lay lines to it, though I had told him before, written him, and put obtuse comment about it in the CDG Letters, likewise, he had no knowledge of the roof fall in The Scullery and quite clearly takes little notice of what we say or write. The upshot was an O.K. to regular ops. and we settled for that.

"Thus the air is clearer; some straight talking in the cave had done some good. ...."

The next entry in narrative form shows no addition to CDG's experiences but part of it might well be recalled.

"OPERATION NUTHOUSE

"News came from South Wales that Dan-yr-Ogof cave would like us to examine an obstruction in the outfall and, moreover, would pay the expenses of the essential team..... (When put to the members a division in the ranks appeared; one group was willing to dive for pleasure and suffer the martial planning and discipline at present deemed necessary, the other put the pleasure paramount and found the Wookey type of programming distasteful. To neither did the DyO proposition appeal, it pleased me to discover, and the proposition fell through. On subsequent enquiry, we found the cave had £5 in mind.)"

The discussions arising from the proposition were very helpful in guiding the tactics at Wookey, so the notes record, but in retrospect I can observe little change.

Instead of Nuthouse we had Muckment Three.

"OPERATION MUCKMENT Three 1 & 2-11-47

"Honorary Member, Professor Haldane, wished to come along. Yes, he would dive but Mrs.H. would not. Out went the program after invitations to Siebe Gorman had been declined. Everything was soon laid on and the kit dumped in a pile at Paddington, so much the easier for Coase's help, and on Saturday I wandered off to work with merely a haversack slung over my shoulder. Of course, I forgot bits of the Professor's kit and had to return for them, eventually reaching the office at 10:30 to sneak out again at 11:15 but had to reconcile them by conceding a day off my holiday allowance! I arrived at Paddington with 20 minutes to spare. At program time, 12:10, Sheppard and Mack were there but no sign of Coase or the Haldanes; actually, Coase was seeing to the luggage; I had wasted my anxiety over him but I was still concerned about the Haldanes. I took up my post by the barrier and the others boarded the train. I had never met our guests so would not recognise them; the minutes passed but no sign except for a couple of nice-looking persons attired in clothes which seemed appropriate for pot-holers but outside the lattitude I expected of a Professor and his wife. I tried to catch snatches of their conversation and should have recognised their connection with our party; obviously they were not genuine tramps. I was inwardly sure the answer to the question 'Are you Professor Haldane?' would be a roar of laughter and I failed to put it. They moved on. As the clock moved up to zero, I felt I had no alternative but to wait a decent time to make sure our guests would not be left stranded... The train departed and I hung on for another ten minutes, telephoned to check and found they had left in plenty of time so abandoned the waiting.

"I took the next westward train and dropped off at Bath catching up the party timewise but they were on a train; I was on my feet. I got buses to the edge of the city on the Wells road then thumbed ineffectually for five minutes until, at last, a coal truck took me to Radstock, six miles nearer. At Radstock a large car hove to to ask the way, I borrowed their small-scale map as security; now they could hardly refuse me a lift and I took over as pilot. If their journey to Weston-super-Mare went a mile or two nearer Wells than it should have done, the more fools they for not being able to read a map! Two people gave me another lift to the outskirts of Wells, stopping en route to collect some turnips from a field on Mendip top. They said Varmer had told them to help themselves, who would not? I soon filled their bag for them, that was my contribution to Lending a Hand on the Land. Then I had to walk quite quarter of a mile before the next lift to Wookey Hole. By that time I was almost affronted at being decanted at the Bakery and not driven into the car park! The Wing Commander (already equated by Mrs.Haldane to The Archangel Gabriel) was mightily relieved and, after apologies, I joined the gang for tea.

"Kit preparation was behind-hand, but we were only about quarter of an hour late getting into the cave and the program started a few minutes after the scheduled time of 19:30. The first run had two objectives: in clean water to make more careful note of the boundaries of The Scullery in ts upper parts then, to provide a fitting spectacle for the guests, including Hodgkinson's who were many. We succeeded in both.... (line-tabbing then continued until visibility failed)... When The Prof. had been pushed and mauled into his dress, for he is a big man, the water was milky but one could see about 10 feet... Now The Prof. is oxygen-sensitive even at atmosheric pressure, as the result of his work for the Admiralty two years before. He had not appreciated that we would be using oxygen but decided he would be O.K. if he did not clear all his nitrogen. He was without shadow of doubt the best qualified to decide this so the op. went on.... It seems he misjudged the effect of a cave-dive and travelled far too fast... " some way in "he gave me the pre-arranged 'thumbs down' signal of trouble so I grabbed him and made for the exit into Two. It was tough going, he got caught in a line and ripped it off its belay. I had to drop Aflo and the mud we kicked up blotted out everything. Weaver came astern and pushed as I pulled. The slope was steep and difficult, the line slippery and now it was loose, but we rose slowly, Haldane helping himself feebly. I was apprehensive, but soon the mud was illuminated by the lights of Two, then I saw my charge, his head hard against the roof and his face in the sandbank! It could have been screamingly funny. We were on the edge of safety now and I pulled him free but not before the press-man got his shot.

"We repaired to the First Chamber and divers went down to rescue Aflo and repair the damage. They found the water like pea-soup and lost one another. Coase came out of Three with the recovered Aflo, found no Weaver so went back to look for him. Weaver had come out in One, found no Coase so went back to look for him.... Knowing the mess of loose lines and mud, I was uneasy but soon Coase's light appeared as a dirty yellow patch under the arch of The Witch's Kitchen and he was doubtless relieved to find Weaver now safe on the bank. We suspended operations for an hour and after much nattering went out for a breather. Haldane was adamant that he would like to go down again and he was the best judge. We dallied on the moonlit road, as Wingco saw his guests off and Haldane treated us to a model of tact and diplomacy in his handling of the press-man, then we got back to the job. In the First Chamber the water was slightly milky as Coase and I went down; we made good progress for about 50 feet when, suddenly, we broke through into clean water. It was splendid; the water through which we had come looked like a great white cloud stretching from side to side of the chamber.... We stood in the edge of the cloud looking right and left and watching with happy imaginings the scene at our feet where trails of mist drifted slowly along the hollows in the floor. We were like a pair of giants standing astride some Swiss mountain range, watching the mists lying in the valley bottoms.... we collected another skull and a recent tin can then made exit in Three.

"In Three we picked up the Prof. and marched him along the sandy bottom to Four, carelessly letting him collide with the archway. In Four we picked up the inner line and went to the edge of Five, standing there as we flashed our lights around. It looked homely and was a beautiful sight, Mossy's Green Jelly world of 1935. On pre-arranged signal, Coase went down and thrilled us, me at least, with his descent over clean grit to First

Deep, over the ridge of rock which is like the bottom knife of some huge shear, then to lose shape in the clouds generated by his passing. His light shone through to Six then disappeared. We waited a minute or two and First Deep vignetted the returning light; I was keen with expectation then noticed my companion was unsteady. He swayed and fell over. I know how easy it is to get off balance and how well-nigh impossible it is to save oneself; the usual way is to go on falling then get up again but I had the last trip very fresh in memory so was uneasy. In spite of the Prof.'s head, shoulders, body and knee stand above all others as a physiologist, I had not taken him more than six paces away from safety on this trip! I yanked him into the air space in Four and asked if O.K. Eventually getting confirmation, we turned and made for home leaving Coase to make his own way out. The Prof. is a tank-diver, we think, and his passage of Three amused the boys no end. Bolt upright, with head and shoulders out of the water, he stalked slowly along with his submarine companions, like a couple of sharks, breaking water from time to time in his wake.

"With that the party ended. It was about three o'clock, the Prof. was ejected from his dress and went his way to hit the hay for a well-earned rest while we trundled out the gear and wound up with the usual Operation Seven Brooms which, below the thick layers of trampled mud, laid bare the pathway proper. So much for the story of the mud that divers bring out.

"Sunday morning... we had a meeting with the Wingco... and arranged for Archeologist Mason to be allowed to cut a trench through the sandbanks of Three to check the latest theory that this might have been a burial chamber, the source of all those bones...."

So the party dissolved once again, the London contingent to a farewell beer at Paddington, after a splendid week-end.

The next Wookey Op. was Muckment Four, for the survey was hardly started, and there were other interesting things to do down there.

"M4   15-11-47

"The M4 program was a little ambitious, a composite,
first to make best use of clean water conditions for picking up
relics in The Scullery... then B2, successor to Bung which
showed that to enter by The Resurgence would be rather
hazardous, B3, a recce downstream into the same region, M4
to get on with the survey and J2, Janus Two, a recce upstream.
"From previous experience I had found I quickly
saturated my desires to be underwater but Coase is made of
sterner, or more inquisitive stuff, and kept us to our tasks. It
proved to be an all-time long, logged from 16:00 to 03:45. The
shortest dive was 4 minutes, the longest was Bill Weaver's with
84 minutes. One wonders how long the gang will suffer these
impositions.... At The Resurgence we prepared for fun, for we
did not take the op. too seriously; it was an opportunity for new
divers and rubber-neckers to have their fill. The patch of ground
by the sluicegate was thick with bods, jostling, weaving and
milling round like ants and equally devoid of apparent purpose.
The place is always quaggy and soon was like a mud-bath...
The excavators from Badger Hole were there, and wives and
girl-friends too, all adding to the crowd until it became well-nigh
impossible for a diver to move or an attendant"

Notebook No.27.

"to force his way to or from him. Despite this, Coase and
Stanbury got ready and took the lead, keeping well to the left
wall (diver's left)... It was already dusk and the play of lights
was not lost on the spectators, at first clear beams, then brown
clouds from the sandbank at the throat obscured them. The
divers reported the hole had possibilities. At last Lucy and I
were ready... we went to the hole and looked, flashing our lights
about, for there was one Aflo per diver now. Yes, the hole did
look a little bit larger, especially on the diver's left; with a bit of
careful work it might go. We about turned and went back to the
bank.

"Then Coase and I had a go, scrubbing B3 to gain the time."

The record goes into a maze of detail on various, now unimportant, aspects of the evening's work. Coase did get down to the river bed; in my bigger outfit I failed to follow or to find a better alternative way down. Then we moved on to M4 to make a survey of the lines we had already laid, interleaving with items for the Archeological Section. Coase and Weaver brought out a Romano-British pot of considerable size, broken, but they were able to find practically all the shards. In the survey, distances were taken from the markers on the lines, directions by a 6-inch compass, heights by a captive ballcock with calibrated 'kite-string' and depths by meter.

"J2 was to be a recce in Five and Six. I wanted a clean-water check at the far side of The Slot, Coase wanted to check out Six and Seven and Weaver wanted to look around, too. In Four there was a diversion: there is a round hole just below high-water mark. I took a look but omitted to note its compass direction. It goes steeply down seemingly to the back of Five, a narrowing water-swept pipe, the clean sand lying in streamers behind the knobbly projections. I seem to remember seeing something like this before. I left it and went to The Slot. There was no surface to Five beyond that point. We found Five and Six were strangely off-clear; Resurgence, Scullery, Three and Four had been brilliantly clear yet in Five and Six was this opalescence which was difficult to account for." I took a few bearings and watched the other divers then "Weaver arrived... and we waited for Coase to return; he at last appeared at the Deep and quickly joined us. We sorted ourselves out and spontaneously raced for the base, laden with our Aflos, not too fussy about direction, our heads bobbing up and down to get a new bearing, and off again, finishing up somewhere on the rocks in Three. So to packing up and Seven Brooms again. It was well after 4 a.m. that we left for the hills, eventually to sleep."

Larking around in the higher chambers was indeed a delight and was valuable experience, especially to the more recent divers, but perhaps we should get back to the more serious business. The next op. was to be a continuation of the Scullery Survey plus another more serious look upstream. There is much in the original notes quite irrelevant to the growth of CDG and of little intrinsic interest, but a nostalgic interest to me and to those who took part. Most of it will be recorded, simply because, if not, when the notebooks are destroyed the story will have gone for ever.

"M5,J3 Muckment 5 and Janus 3

"December the Sixth seemed to come hot on the heels of the November meeting; perhaps the slightly easier tempo of events in between had caused time to slide away unnoticed. As usual, the packing was left to something like the last moment, held back this time largely in the hope that our non-magnetic cylinders would arrive to solve some of the survey problems. Thurday found us busy as usual, Bill Mack on his own kit, Don Coase with me blowing up cylinders and marking line. Alas! we most carefully marked a full reel in 2-fathom instead of 10-ft intervals; really inexcusable.... it meant that Friday was spent in putting it right again, plus pumping a few more cylinders, so that the kit was packed too late to get it to Paddington and this meant another day's leave lost for Saturday. We assembled in good time (12:05) and the journey to Wells seemed quick. The Archangel dropped us at The Star, for tea, amid a characteristic assembly of individuals forming residents' afternoon tea groups. We started by overloading the coat-rack which gently tipped over into the hall then we braved the down-the-nose looks and sat down, our 'Good afternoon!' being received in stony silence. (The old lady at our table to whom we addressed the greeting was stone deaf.)

"We rushed for the five o'clock bus, Don Coase with a sole flapping noisily as we strode along, but there was no bus so we set off on foot, glad that it was not raining. We saw a bus marked 'Wookey Hole' and hailed it. It was only going as far as St.Cuthbert's Mill but if we liked we could go to the top of the road for a penny. Thinking the top of the road was only a few paces away, we walked on to realise we could have saved 10 to 15 minutes and the ride would have been a bargain.

"At Wookey we learned that Sheppard had not been able to make it so, with Weaver out as well, it would be a 2-diver op. We got cracking after sorting out the kit and found Mason and The Archeological Section busy cutting trenches in the First and the Third Chambers but not with much success. The cave was dryer... but the mud was clearing quickly. The Archeos. were disturbed that their petrol application had been turned down and wished us to support their appeal.

"It fell to me to start the M5 run, re-marking one of the lines. Passing... through clear water to a little sand-patch among the rocks, I saw a flat broken bone with huge teeth set in it, just showing above the sand. This was something quite new; it was where we must have walked time and time again and obviously had smashed it. Working carefully, I got it free and Don took it out to the delight of the Archeos. In and out went Don, femurs and tibias, human now, and a splended female pelvis, all from the same spot. The human bones were blackened as usual but the horse's jaw was not (or deer, if not a horse) save for the crown of one of the laterals.

"It was now Don's turn to go fetch things; pots were our ambition, and I followed with a sieve to carry the bits. It was fine to watch him in action, creeping inch by inch over the area where he and Weaver had collected the last lot and where they thought they had seen another which was almost intact. He found shards, and some pieces of skull (palate) but not what he sought. He returned to One with his finds and I re-fixed a torn-out belay... it struck me later that the old waterlogged planks down there were not only unsightly, and might be covering something important, but could themselves have value in the story of the cave..... We reported to Three then made off for Six. It had been very cold hanging about in The Scullery and I was almost glad to get on the move. We nosed around Four, confirmed that Five is completely trapped... and slid down to Six; there was the surface, still and clean, and so close we could readily see through it to the walls of this high and narrow rift; it lay on our right, clear and unmistakable, the doubt of twelve years standing dispelled, and it its stead was a knowledge of a new place waiting exploration, and explored it soon would be for it is an inviting not a fear-inspiring place. To the left of First Deep was another small surface... It may have been that in the early days the difficulties we had at First Deep stirred up enough mud to obscure the main surface and the smaller could easily be in doubt even now .... A ladder would seem to be the best way up .... The mud we had disturbed shut off the way to the left so we went on to Seven, by Scylla, and looked again at Charybdis.... We had added a marked line from Four to the block in Six, 80 ft exactly. From there to Scylla is about 25 ft of fine mud ...

"Unable to see for the thick yellow blanket, we made our way back to base, a journey which had its moments as, for example, at 'the 360° bend', a spiral turn round a knob in Six about which I had moments of misgivings and Coase turned a complete circle, then again in Five where I kept too far to the right, rammed myself between roof and floor, while my sketch-pad chose the same moment to get entangled in the wires. Back in Three we discussed our findings and decided to pack up; it was half past eleven, my sodalime was at its end and neither of us felt keen to continue.

"The mood of the evening had been very happy; the party was small and the strain on us all was less than usual. Things we wanted were not buried under someone else's kit, or body; there was room to move about, and there were intervals for hot drinks .... The attendants, however, went on strike... and left the divers to pull themselves or each other to pieces which, after all, is not a very difficult job. Then the whole party dropped into a sort of knitting circle; the kit just lay strewn around for half an hour while we talked in groups. At last we got moving and cleared everything out in two jeep-loads. Like the beer and the rum, the jeep was Luke Devenish's and it made light work of an otherwise arduous task and left us with just sufficient energy to stagger up the hillside to Hundred Acres and so to The Belfry and bed.

"Next morning early, about nine, some of us got up, not bad after a three o'clock roosting, and we spent the rest of the morning getting breakfast and drafting a press report but at last we got down to Wookey Hole, cleaned up the kit and chased off into Wells in nice time for the train. Both divers thought the weekend had not yielded a full crop of fruit and that it was the divers' own lack of enthusiasm which was at fault. Maybe the more positive excitement of breaking surface in Six will keep us up to the mark next time. It certainly is an exciting prospect.

Notebook No.28 is almost fully occupied with the problem of surfacing, with inflatable boats as the current answer; it carries notes on S1, the first attempt to surface, then manages to squeeze in the start of that op. with the crazy title B3,M6,J4,S2, but which is left to the next chapter.

"OPERATION S1,SIDESPLASH 7-2-48

Probably named from the splash of the boats on breaking surface.

"They say it was the wettest January for five years. It was wet without doubt, and The Axe was reported to be in bad condition. On Thusday evening the Wingco phoned and we agreed to let the proposed arrangements stand, provided the water was not worse than the previous occasion, but we would abandon hope of the M and J work unless the water cleared in the meantime. On Friday the report came through of 10 ft visibility, improving rapidly. So all was well for at least S1. I had already got one trunk from the practice baths to Paddington... at last the kit was ready, too formidable a pile to take via the office and, still cogitating, I retired to bed at midnight.

"Late as usual next morning I decided it would have to be a taxi so left a note for Don who was calling later for the cylinders and went to get a cab and damn the expense. There were to be only two divers for S1, Weaver woulc not be travelling, leaving Coase, Mack and myself to meet at the station. We were met at Wells by a Guide in a neat hat; he was doing service as chauffeur, and slowly we got under way. The jeep was at our service again which makes things very much less tiring; after many and usual delays the divers were dressed and ready, by 20:00, taking an incredibly long time....

"There was a mildly reprehensible excursion when first Don Coase jumped in without his weights but was buoyant enough to swim ashore then next time jumped in with only half his weights, was about neutral buoyancy and could make very little progress. We watched him from the bank and burst with laughter at his desperate efforts to swim for the bank as the current swept him downstream. It was no mean current, either.... I was ready and tested for leaks, having already somersaulted in once and proved O.K., so he was in no real danger but, nevertheless, we have never seen him swim like that before! The water seemed so clear we thought we would try a Pre-History just to see if the floods had brought down anything fresh. But conditions were much the same. Visibility was about 7 to 10 ft, just enough; the current was strong, no real handicap to progress, but ensured visibility did not noticeably drop. We could stand and kick up a cloud of sand; the sand would settle immediately and its burden of mud vanish downstream. Higher up the current was another matter; we had the greatest difficulty in making our way against it.....

"I was wearing Sefus and consequently less than my usual clothing and found the water perishingly cold (it was 49°), it struck straight through and for some time I did not cease to fume inwardly at Don's slow and careful progress as he minutely scrutinised every inch of the way .... I found a tibia trapped under a rock and broke it trying to release it, it was deeply incised where it fractured, I thought from chafing, but on land they concluded it had been gnawed by rodents. After a wait to warm up and a curious period of hesitation whereon I passed the initiative to Coase; Coase deemed we would never stand against the current at First Deep and it seemed that S1 was marked for scrubbing but at First Deep we hardly noticed the current save that we could not make the water muddy... Coase unfastened V4" ("Vunghoochi IV", transliteration of fwnghwchi, "my boat") "which obediently stood on end, like a grotesque snake under his spell, then on opening the gas valve the boat shot up with increasing speed out of my sight. Up went Coase after it (up the tail-rope) and for some time I could see his feet thrashing and his light moving about. After a while he slid down again and I went up with little difficulty and thrilled by expectation. My head came out of the water and in the light of Aflo IV I found myself in what I can only describe as a homely, hospitable chamber. It was very narrow, so narrow I could only just turn the boat round; short, about 40 feet, and not awe-inspiringly high, about 30 feet. The rock of the walls was a rosy, warm hue. I felt quite happy there bobbing about hanging on to one end of the boat, for there was no purpose in boarding, even if I could. Then I sank back. Coase packed, I unhitched the distance line and we went back to Three where Wingco was waiting for us; his two Swiss maids had a basket of thermos flasks full of hot soup and Pep Powell" (no relation to Mossy) "was keeping her kitchen flag flying with lashings of hot Oxo.

"At last we were off again, my turn to carry Aflo and boat; it was Don's turn to chortle as I stumbled down to First Deep. I reckon I must have disappointed him for the boat (V3 this time) behaved itself well and I could hold it and Aflo in the same hand and avoid any spectacular bits of technique while threading my way through the boulders of The Slot, for instance.

"In Seven I looked round for the surface. The old lamp swung up somewhere but the place did not look like our chamber. I stepped along the block that forms the rim of the Giant's Staircase and onto which the sloping sandbank debouches. The bank was curiously marked with a series of slots, rectangular in section and about 1 inch square, running down to a focus behind the rim-block. It was the bank I had crossed for Scratch but looked quite friendly now and Charybdis stood beyond, rather sullenly I thought. Above was surface. Out came V3, and with its bag hitched to Aflo, it too stood on end; a twist of the cylinder valve and I was left grasping a sliding line. The line stopped and I tied it off and went up. It needed quite a good haul to get moving, a lift from the breathing bag would have helped, or maybe I should have slipped a couple of weights, leaving them in V3's bag. By the time I reached the surface my visor was badly misted and I was feeling the effects of the exertion. I found V3 had tied itself up in its seat-strap and it was a struggle, a blind struggle, to free it. Then my efforts to climb in and sit on the strap proved unavailing while handicapped by Aflo, which I could not park; a snaphook and line is needed. The seat-strap, which also serves as the ladder anchor, cut into the side of the boat and the fat bulges of its balloon-like walls grabbed me fast, while the whole contraption squeaked and squealed like a child's balloon when it is pinched, and we know what happens when a balloon is pinched. I managed to get a fair view in spite of the handicaps. I had enough water in the mask to wash the visor down but had to relinquish my hard-won position to do the washing and, when I did, the effort to get back steamed it up again. Seven is a rift chamber strikingly like Six but bigger; 60 feet long, 10 feet wide and 70 feet high by estimation. To have called it 'Great' was an exaggeration, perhaps forgivable in the circumstances. I dropped down and left Aflo, hoping to do better with only the emergency torch, but by this time I was clearly fatigued and unfit for the job. I had another quick look round then dropped down to let Coase have a go..... The light buoy never left the drogue pocket but it was a pleasant comfort to see V3 lit up, however dimly, and rocking at the surface.

"Coase seemed gone for ages, meantime I got steadily colder and miserable. I counted my gas pressure by the new technique... it was about 70 atm; I waited a while and began to feel vaguely uneasy so turned the gas on again, bypassed some to waste and felt better but even colder so signalled to Coase who was still flapping about up aloft ...." (There was a bit of bother getting the boat down but eventually it was stowed back in its bag) "... and we returned to Three. I was damned glad to get out of the respirator, breathe some decent air and sup some hot Oxo. It did not take me long to get out of the kit and be ready for the exit either. Thus we wound up S1 having made some small progress..... The Mendip-top party got its lift on the jeep; it was raining hard and at destination Lucy called for his log-writer to record his dive! Coase and I lorded it in the back of the Archeo's car.

"It was the usual four o'clock as we turned in and ten o'clock when we turned out. It was nearly one before we set out for Wookey Hole, via The Hunters' Lodge and Rookham. The rest is the usual routine but, unusually, we were ready two minutes before the hire-car called for us.

Chapter 10

Forward to Nine and Eleven

John Dwyer, George Lucy, Edmund Mason (with skull), Graham Balcombe, Bill Mack & Tony Setterington, Wookey Hole, 10 April 1948 (Luke Devenish).

Still with Notebook No.28: there is the more ambitious, curiously-named B3,M6,J4,S2 operation, each component full of potential in its own way. For reminders: B is in the lowest reach, Resurgence to One, M in the middle reach, One to Three, J the farthest penetration, while S is among the surfaces of Six and Seven.

"B3,M6,J4.S2   13-3-48

"The routine was much the same as previous recent ops. Part of the kit was at the baths and had to be cleared before seven o'clock. In fact, I had the load at the station and was home by eight. It was a little surprising how, even without cylinders and batteries, the load is still a mighty one. V3, some lead for Mack and suchlike oddments and it was back to the old staggering pile.

"On Saturday morning I dared to arrive at the office in ski-boots and polo-neck sweater to chair a meeting. H'm! But it was the juniors who were most startled.

"There had been a longish dry spell, indeed, for the last few days the sun had been most expansive and 'The Little Summer' in March was the talk of the country; it was like June and a good June at that. It was a shame to waste the afternoon in a dingy railway coach. However, there was a diner on the train for the first time, post-war, and it was not long before we found some compensation, nominally to celebrate the return of the diner. The team for the op. was not according to program, any more than was the date. The date had been twice postponed a week at a time... and now Harry Stanbury had contracted bronchitis. Bill Mack had been pushed into the gap as the only other available diver who had done his five hours in cave conditions. Pushed is hardly the word; the door was opened and in he jumped in one bound. He confided later that an hour or two before zero he began to wonder if he had done right. Probably his feelings were like mine as I sighted the line of hills at Whitsun, 1946; I hope for his sake they were not nearly as morbid: at least he would be in fairly reliable hands.

"The Wingco's waggon met us at the station and dumped us at the diving room, Crooks' Rest. By six we were at The Inn, the kit all ready for transport. At half past six we set off and jeeped in two loads to the entrance. In One we sorted the kit and Don set out his boat while I assembled my P-Party kit. When I went to set out my boat, I could not find the vital cylinder connectors and soon I was convinced, horribly, that they were lying back at home. Feeling as small as when I forgot my mask window, if not considerably smaller, I secretly found satisfaction in what had hitherto been an intense irritation. For at the gates we had been confronted with a fait accompli; the press photographers and an author seeking diving colour for his book on Wookey Hole were on the spot. I suddenly became thankful for their intrusion, reckoning they would probably slow down an optimistic program so that, in failing to do S2, attention would be diverted from the inexcusably incomplete boat.

"While waiting for the M6 diver, Coase took a look downstream and went in some 75 feet..... On starting M6 I found the compass quite unreadable. It was hand held and it was hard to believe the bubble... which was also unduly large... we topped up with methylated spirit; it turned milky, but the compass was readable. I took sights as best I could down the line but... a prismatic type is called for. Even so, the readings we took seemed consistent and probably good enough for our purposes."

Notebook No.29.

"The party had expected me to emerge from Two but the line was straight as a die so I just took one bearing and passed right on. Emerging in Three, I was informed I was for the high jump as the Press were waiting to photograph me coming out of Two... for the next half hour it was nothing but posing for them, 'Just one more, boys'... 'Now I want a colour photograph' and so on.

"At last the Hen and Chicken were allowed to get away (Coase was the Hen and Mack the self-styled Chicken). They had already patrolled The Scullery without finding any evident cause for The Cymbals of Two and now were away to check the south wall of Six. They returned, in due course, to report that they had found a new surface in Six, about the same size as the first, parallel to it and nearer to Seven. Don and I then went down, originally to look at the north wall. From First Deep visibility was finer than ever I had known it but the cold struck through and chilled me to immobility. I was cold enough after

M6 and had not warmed up since. Now it sapped all my interest in the job. We stood looking this way and that and Don wandered off, hard left, for a few feet and returned to report another surface. All the enthusiasm with which I had set out had vanished and I was in no mood to force myself to carry on. I signalled to Don to come out and we retired to Four for consultation. We decided to send up V4 in 'Six-Two' and Don dived off to get it, meantime, I crawled out onto the sandbank but was too depressed to take a look round while I had the chance.

"Don returned with V4 and we went down; after another chilly wait V4 went up and, when Don was aboard, I followed. Both the surface and the dome at Six-Two were very similar to Six-One. The little surface in the program was the north end of this stretch .... Don was comfortably esconced in the boat, which only holds one, and looked supremely happy there. My mood of dejection was by no means dispelled by this find, although at first it was a great relief to swing up to the surface and, holding on to the boat, to breathe ordinary air... I had seen enough for a first look round and was quite content to let Don note with better measured accuracy the points of interest in the place.... While preparing to send up V4 we had a good look round, I stood on Pulpit Rock, which is flat-topped and some feet in diameter, and I was convinced that just behind the rock there was a deep steep slope which went down fifteen feet or more, although Don had not seen it, and it called for a current to explain its existence. On the way in, when we first went down, I was also struck by the appearance of the sandbank in Five. It was a sharp ridge, not just a bank piled against the west wall, and it dropped away under that wall to a considerable depth, again some 15 feet at a guess, ending at what might be a low arch leading to another chamber. Such a place called for a current to explain it. Is it possible that the stream we see is only a part of the river and that the rest dives behind The Scullery and rejoins somewhere below One? It seems unlikely, yet how can such a hole exist without a good current to keep it clear? ....

"It was late when we came out, after one o'clock, so we packed up put the clocks on for Summer Time, made to The Belfry for some food, not exactly 'as mother makes it', then dawn was breaking..... I felt damned ashamed that in such splendid conditions I was such a brake on the party and must tackle the problem of keeping warm as a first priority ...

A practice session at the baths is recorded for (a) a clothing check, not very intelligently tackled (I merely tried to put on more "ordinary" apparel), (b) weighting trials (c) fin practice (d) surfacing trials with lifebelts and (e) surveying practice. There clearly was no brilliant discovery or achievement. The next narrative is of a successful push downstream but of another failure upstream.

"*J5,S3   10-4-48*

"Summer certainly seemed just round the corner as Coase, Mack and I made our way by the usual route at the usual time to the usual place. At the cave there was a change, however, for the restaurant was open and we had a civilised tea with the gang (at our own expenses). After kit preparation, and a quick one, we jeeped the stuff to the cave entrance and manhandled it to the First Chamber. Coase was itching to get to his B-op. and did his successful damnedest to be ready before me. Aflo III was in trouble; the batteries had been charged at the cave while tied together so that the cases shorted. Aflo IV had also suffered shorting, leaving Mack's awful Aful as the only reliable illuminant, reliable we hoped, between the two of us. Coase dashed off on his private op. while I tested my weighting, as I had put on an enormous pile of clothing, and while testing I made a minor contribution to the survey of The Scullery. Suddenly Coase's light was seen coming up river. He came ashore and reported finding a skull a few feet beyond the reach of his line, which had run out at 130 feet. In accordance with procedure, the main op. was waived and we set off to retrieve the skull; Coase led and I followed with the sieve. Mack should have been his bearer but something had gone wrong with his dressing so I collected the job. The water was not yet clear but most of the silt had subsided. The B-Reach (it never acquired a better name) seemed to be a low-roofed passage and must have been wide; I could not see the sides. We went over smooth and almost level sandy bottom to the end of the line. Don tied on a new wire, purloined from Aflo III, but we could see no sign of the skull. We waited for the mud to clear but, although it thinned, we still could not see. We moved towards the west side of the river; the roof arched down gently until it pressed down on us as we lay down flat and waited. Still no clearing but we moved some way downstream. Don was still ahead and now, as we were out of the main current, the silt was thick and impenetrable; I groped my way after him, occasionally seeing a brown glimmer from his Aflo. I was using a hand-torch and I occasionally touched his feet. As I gingerly felt my way where the bottom slopes steeply downwards I felt a change in the floor; there were slabs of rock in the sand and - no, that was not conglomerate, it was too smooth. I felt it carefully; it was like a skull. I called on Don, and his Aflo showed it was indeed another skull, the tenth so far. I carefully worked it out of the riverbed and transferred it intact to the seive from the place where it had lain almost completely buried. It was too dangerous to the relics to prang around like this in the murk so we made exit, to be met by a flash as a camera recorded the now familiar scene of diver with skull.

"So to J5 and S3. J5 was to examine Crowberry Ridge (the sandbank in Five) with The Slipway (the long deep groove west of the sandbank), to patrol north end of Six and Six-Three and to examine the contested deep hole by Parson's Rock (The Pulpit); S3 was to surface in the Sixes and in Seven. The Slipway was much as estimated, about 20 feet long descending to about 13 feet depth but there was no way on. Coase had discovered Six-Three, so it was his privilege to make the first ascent. I led to First Deep, tied on a branch line, trailed it to the sandbank hard left, then reeled out sufficient to reach the surface, we hoped. The bright copper ball (a surveying float) looked strangely out of place down there and it was only unwillingly enticed up the steps in the overhanging roof to the surface. Coase passed by in a cloud of mud, his legs tarried a while at my eye level then disappeared." (There is no actual record of his using his boat; I think he was trying one of his other surfacing devices.) "He was some minutes up aloft then another wave of mud, followed by the red-brown glow of his light. Talking facilities are still very limited so discussion was deferred and we resumed the J-op. I rounded Parson's Rock, trailing a line, and found the deep hole was illusory; it was a few feet at most and the place became known thereafter as Balcombe's Folly, or B.F.Corner. I re-met Coase at The Gateway and we returned to base, I by the route by which I came, crawling exceedingly slowly as I reeled back the line, eventually meeting Coase again at First Deep. It appears the diver with his Aflo, crawling flat on his stomach (to simplify reeling), presented a curious sight. He was almost completely immersed in the mud but the Aflo float bobbed up into the clearer water a few inches above his head and his backside would occasionally heave into view above the mud-level. Meantime Mack was in reverie in Four or Five, watching the mud-clouds float gently by.

"Back in Three we replenished our apparatus for the ascent in Seven. Aflo III was for emergency only and Aflo IV was finished. It was the crazy Aful which carried on. But, alas, at The Gateway the mud won; visibility was nearly nil; I could not locate the bridge with any assurance. We waited and waited, but the mud just circled round and would not disperse then Aful got tired and its glow gradually redder, which was no fault of the mud, so we returned defeated. Nor do I think we were sorry for the methedrine to keep us awake had long since worn off and I, for one, felt like lying down in The Gateway to sleep rather than going out on a boating trip. The experience showed us we had another problem and would have to find an answer. We would have to reach Seven without any halts or hesitations or the reverse undercurrent, which sweeps up the mud and obliterates everything, would defeat us again. It was three o'clock as we left the water and it was daylight before we were ready for bed. So much so that a party of us went for a stroll round Mineries instead but on our return sleepiness overcame me and I settled down to a welcome snooze in the Belfry bunk.

"We had been blessed with splendid weather and that Sunday was no exception; after our tramp down to Wookey Hole over the fields and the sorting of the kit we sat for half an hour by The Inn in brilliant sunshine then had a pint, or possibly a couple of pints, to aid the pleasant dozy feeling before we got back to the kit and off to Wells for the usual train.

Looking back over recent ops., I thought it was high time we ceased messing about and began achieving something. We knew of the big mudslope at the far end of Eight which should betoken a stream from higher level, possibly even a surface, but had made little real advance towards exploring that area. Now, at last, "Forward" is the cry.

"OPERATION AVANTI! 24-4-48

"On the Sunday of J5 we were told that would have to be the last of the inside ops. owing to the increasing number of visitors to the cave, and that would mean no more ops. until Autumn. However, a last one was squeezed in by cutting down the usual interval to two weeks. Program was: no Bung, Muckment or other delaying ops. but Avanti! There was just a little more in mind for we could hardly leave the inner chambers without going for a sail and the boats in Seven would be a safeguard also..... We travelled down in brilliant sunshine by the usual train and on the railway embankments the few early flowers were already giving way to the masses of their later brethren and the trees were clothed already in their new leaves..... At the cave we had no jeep and the restaurant was closed... Once inside the cave we started dressing and I soon found my frogman trousers were missing; Lucy dashed off to find them... and at last I was able to proceed...

"We had decided to do S4 first and leave the boats in Seven as an emergency depot and, with previous failures in mind, had brought snaphooks with us. As we shuffled through Six, snap! the line was fixed and onwards we went, cursing the 'laying-out-line' part of Aflolaun. The trouble with it was later found to be a flaked turn on the drum. Normally this risk is avoided by tying the outer turns with wire but someone (like the B4 diver?) had robbed the reel of a length and made off the lazy man's way. I reached the bridge block, snapped on the boat case, lost some seconds in finding the valvewheel, then away went V3 but alas! only to blow a connection. It drifted up only too slowly and not until I went up after it did I find the pipe waving free, the cylinder empty and only a whiff of gas in the dinghy - and that still escaping. I reconnected the tube, used the second cylinder, settled down to hand-pumping and at last had the boat fat and rigid. In climbing aboard I forgot first to park my weights in the drogue pocket. I had already signalled Coase to come up so to move out of his way was first priority; being weighted, I could not mount my boat in my usual way and my swimming efficiency was near zero; when I did manage to move a couple of feet I just as quickly drifted back. I gave up and just warded off V4 as it bobbed up alongside.

"In the struggle to get aboard I overstressed the starboard underrail, to which I had attached Coase's Aflo, and the anchorage parted. Down went Aflo IV over and over to the bottom and lay there beside Charybdis but still giving enough light to see things dimly.

"Coase took a poor view of this, but controlled himself well, even offering to go fetch. I think affection for his box of lights was the moving consideration on the spur of the moment and only afterwards did his wrath at my bungling rise to normal intensity. He slid down and, hanging on to the end of his ladder, was just able to save it from the edge of a gully where it hung precariously. We soon shed our weights and masks in preparation for a sail then paddled about noting how the place had dwindled since last we viewed it. We noted a possible anchorage for a permanent line on the west wall. Coase did some sketching then I replaced my mask and hung on to the last rung of the submerged ladder and was towed round the lake. Gone was the undercutting of the walls at the far end... the sandbank beyond Charybdis was there, steep and fine, I could touch it with my foot. It sloped down to a gully which runs close under the east wall, from Giant's Staircase to the south end where it shallowed out and vanished. There is no way out of Seven except by the routes we already know.

"The tendency to fantastic estimations is serious. At first we thought it only occurred underwater but now it is cropping up in kindred circumstances, for example, on breaking surface as we first see a new chamber with our heads only just above water and it is making for great uncertainty in our observations. We need a simple amphibious method of measuring distances.

"We left the boats and went back to base to refuel. Then 'Avanti!'; with that queer niggling feeling inside for the excitement of it all, we slithered and stumbled into the water, checked each other for leaks and were off. We sank down through First Deep where the water was clear. Across Seven the water was beautiful. Being in the lead, I at least had a fine view of The Staircase... without more ado we slithered down block after block towards Mudball Alley. The water behaves strangely here; the mud we kick up tends to go back upstream for a few feet then stays more or less put. I was able to get frequent glimpses ahead but immediately the mud closed in again. Coase following me saw nothing but felt every block in the roof, or nearly every one, with his head!

"We turned the corner into Mudball Alley and such was my own excitement at seeing it in clear water, and indubitably with a large clear-cut surface overhead, that I forgot to look left to see what lay there and just stood guffing bubbles, watching them as they slowly wriggled to the surface. I sent up three good guffs but did not see them really reach surface. It seemed ages while they were going up and each time I either lost my balance or for some other reason could not look upwards as they broke. The bottom is 26 feet deep, our record broken by 2 feet! Swine Hole was 24 feet. The walls of Eight rose sheer out of the deck; here is a first-class place to go boating. The roof above the surface seemed immensely high, but beware! What, I wondered, awaited us at that surface? Now was not the time to experiment, so on we went.

"Rising up at the end of the Eighth there was the mud bank to our front and right and it too led to a surface. The smooth, rounded and polished mud looked treacherous but excitement rather than caution ruled us. I signalled to Coase, 'Up!' and he promptly agreed. I fumbled with the line while tying on and at last had a belay serviceable, but doing no-one credit and off we went. Don first, as it was his Aflo paying out the line, (mine had by now jammed solid); he kept hard against the right-hand rock wall, partly for assistance from holds, partly because the mud elsewhere was so repulsive. I soon found the mud not too horrible to climb direct and made left towards the larger part of the surface and a good landing. Don was heading for some nasty rocks but as we rose so did our excitement. It was a matter of moments now. Recklessly I grabbed Don by his breathing bag and yanked him off the wall and we stood with our heads above water.

"In front was a rampart of muddy pinnacles rising ten to fifteen feet from the water's edge; what was beyond we could only guess but the roof soared up to a great height and away into the darkness. As we rose out of the water, so our feet sank deeper into the mud until it was almost imposssible to move. However we could just reach the bank where immediately the mud was hard and we unweighted each other; by now the excitement was displaced by all the intense irritations we experience on coming out into air. This is quite usual; it must be coupled with our inability to balance when freshly out of the all-supporting medium to which we have adapted and we become intensely annoyed at our failures.

"We parked Aflo IV at the foot of a ridge and started to climb with, of all things, that clumsy Aflo III. The ascent was not hard but it was exasperating and it was not until our respirators were off and lying on the summit, where the climb ended at a small platform, that I, at least, returned to normal. Before us at slightly lower level stretched a long expanse of sand, dipping slightly to the east. Its surface was pitted by many craters made by the drip from the roof, most about 4 inches deep. Beyond was the far boundary wall, rising slowly at first then steepening and shooting up to the roof, leaving one or two deeper ways on only to peter out at quite short distances. Left and right, the walls ran sheer up to the roof and up there were two huge wedged blocks, or part of the roof, waiting somewhat sinisterly I thought. The sandbank at the top of the sloping floor on the right finished at a narrow raised shelf against the wall. At its lower ended it finished at a beautiful green well under the east wall....

"Was this The Axe again or just a waterlogged hole? Surely all that sand must have come up through it? That can only mean that the main river flows along that way and is deflected round the northern boundaries to appear again at the hole we came through. One day we shall make sure of that! But time was flying and the base would be anxious, worse than that, Mack the only diver there would in duty bound to come to our rescue if we badly overshot our time. So we started back.

"Respirators on, line tied off and cut, we tobogganed down the mud, a black wave advancing before us. After a while I picked up the line at the belay but was not quite sure of it for an earlier line continued some way upstream. We dropped down the slope to Mudball Alley into the inkiest blackness imaginable; I thought Aflo had cut out but soon I could just see the bulb held at about a foot distance. On and down, where Aflo was now invisible at six inches and the roof and walls seemed to be closing in strangely. Soon the way narrowed and the line led my arm into a slot only a few inches square and there was no way on. For the moment I was perplexed, then annoyed; the line had slipped away and deserted us when we most needed its help. I reasoned the way on must be wide open somewhere nearby and tried to feel for it but to the left were just rocks and more rocks, and to the right I kept on bumping into Coase standing alongside. I handed him the line and pushed him forward hoping he would understand he was to try then after a few moments I signalled 'Up' and we returned to Nine. At the top of the mudbank he argued that, as he had more gas and sodalime than I, he should be the one to try again. He would signal 'down' if all was well and would come right back if he failed. He slipped into the blackness and disappeared. The twitching of the line ceased and I was left with my thoughts.

"With Aflo still burning brilliantly, the place was not unpleasant, and I reclined, cushioned by the oozing mud. The minutes passed by and I thought of quite a lot things but, although waiting was a strain it was also a chance for reflection. I thought of the episodes in my life which had finally led to this; the slow and steady spread of our diving from the crude beginnings in Swildon's Hole fourteen years before to this, my own greatest success, The Ninth Chamber and an open, though wet, way on. This incident might possibly have proved ugly and isolated us. If we could not clear the line quickly, our limited supplies would be spent and we would be trapped until a relief party could get to us. If we became trapped we were at least safe for a long while, but I thought of the immediate anxiety at the base and the most unpleasant task falling to Bill Mack if we did not get back right away and I thought of Mavis and her agony if we should be caught a longer time.

"But, surely enough, such fears were quite unfounded; some few minutes later there was a pull on the line; I responded, then received "Down!", three sharp pulls, one, two, pause then three."

Notebook No.30.

"Anxiety peaked between the second and third; two would mean failure, the third success. I replied 'Coming down'. Quickly doing my breathing drill, I picked up Aflo and struggled to free myself from the sucking grasp of the mud then shot down the slope to the bottom, sending another black wave before me. Coase was at the belay and, when I completely failed to find the onward line, he led me to it. It transpired later his own delay was in finding that bit of wire leading homewards for, at first, it was buried under the silt; after that to find the way on and free the trapped line was only a matter of moments.

"We blundered on in pitch blackness not recognising anything but the bends, then came to the iron ring - blessed iron ring! - one feels so safe when that is reached for it is 'only' at The Seventh and journey's end is assured. First Deep was welcome. The slope through Five seemed immensely long; it seemed scores of feet before my toes dug into the firm gravel which marks the entry to Four. Then through the archway to Three where we bumped into Bill Mack coming in to find us! We were overdue and the base had decided the 'search party' should set out; I think it was the 'search party' which had decided it for the base but, either way, it was a really brave act. Now Coase, in the lead, was truly mystified before he discovered it was Mack; he thought I had stolen a march on him and got ahead but could not figure how or where! Thus ended the first trip to The Ninth Chamber of Wookey Hole but, alas, that was not the end of the night's work, already so protracted that the gallant base team could no longer keep awake and were found to be alternately sleeping and recording entries. We had to recover the boats but, to cut a long story short, nearly everything imaginable went wrong in the recovery of V3 and finally, with only a whiff of gas left, I managed to tangle myself so effectively that I had to cut myself free and make a hurried exit to base. Believing Coase might also be short of gas, I clapped on another cylinder and, hoping my absorber would last, started down again. I found Coase happily carrying his boat and he indicated there was more waiting collection. I just managed to get it in spite of rapidly increasing depression and returned to base. Within five minutes of going to air, I was sick. That overworked sodalime was not everlasting.

"It was daylight as we came out and carrying out everything, bar the weights, and trundling it in barrows down the slope from the cave entrance reduced us to the extreme of fatigue. A press report completed the night's work save for the clearing up. After some food and a short rest we started again; slowly the mud was swept off down the river and the kit laid out or hung out to dry. We breakfasted in Wells, a welcome gesture from The Cave, and returned to pack and depart at the usual time."

This had been the finest achievement at Wookey so far but the way on was still a flooded passage. Thirteen years had passed since ambitiously we took our first dips at Wookey Hole; not thirteen consecutive years of effort, by any means, but, nevertheless, thirteen years out of my lifetime. Now, having gained a few hundred feet, we were faced with all the problems as before and more and, of course, no assurance of ever winning; the difficulties would ever increase as we pushed farther ahead. We knew nothing then of the insuperable difficulty of depth awaiting us oxygen-divers not much farther in; we could only hope with an ill-founded optimism. The Ninth Chamber was an excellent safe place for a staging depot; the first task would be to equip it with emergency supplies, food, heating and lighting facilities, spare equipment, gas, sodalime, tools, bedding, first aid, a telephone and anything else needed at a forward base or to cope with emergency. That alone was a big undertaking; equipment for carrying purposes capable of dry transport at depths down to 26 feet, including the effect of condensation, would have to be developed,. Then there would also be much work in getting an acceptably good survey of the regions we had just passed through; for example, how reprehensible would it not be to miss a high-level dry passage, if it should exist, by failing to gain the surface in Eight. By any calculation, progress up-river would be halted for some while and the effect of that on the party's interest and morale could hardly be foreseen. The entry to Nine had been effected by a couple of relatively old-stagers; the equipping of a forward base there would give scope for many less experienced divers and the very prospect of a trip to Nine could be a great incentive, thus broadening the Group's base for activities elsewhere. Such activities were already progressing, especially in the Derbyshire Section where their successes were soon to react in turn on the Wookey work, but of these other successes and failures these notes have little to say. Let the participants give their own record, if they have not already done so.

The current notebook is next occupied mainly with the equipment and technical problems of surveying and surfacing. It records an overwater survey using a modified Astrocompass as theodolite, to complement the underwater survey just finished between The First and The Third Chambers. Then the media are busy again, Pathé this time.

Notebook No.31.

This is similar in content; it finally arrives at Operation B6, with a preamble on a shopping expedition to Wells which can safely be omitted.

"OPERATION BUNG Six 25-9-48

"B6 started as a rather casual affair, something to get the divers tuned up for grimmer work. Harry Stanbury had not had a dip since an incident during M3, when his breathing apparatus suddenly deflated while he was well down in The Scullery. I, myself, had practically forgotten how to dive, for the whole summer had fleeted by while the visitors visited and our kit lay idle in Crooks' Rest...."

Notebook No.32.

"The number in gang had risen to nine... and kit transport to The Resurgence was soon under way; the motorcycles with panniers laden acted as mules, then all sorts of things were slung over them and over the riders, a curious and noisy turn-out which, by a hair's breadth, missed knocking down the owner of the mill on whose land we were working! The divers and dressers, also acting as mules, on returning with a second load brought stories of an irate mill owner who wanted to know what the commotion was about and who had said we could come on his land, for he had not been asked. Things looked bad for a while. Eventually I found Guy, the owner, but not before The Wingco had appeared and the two had had a bit of a barney. The Wingco had assumed responsibility for such arrangements and had forbidden me to communicate with The Mill. Wingco claimed to Guy that he had properly made arrangements with the Manager and it was deadlock. I told Guy our circumstances and how our hands were tied; he quickly calmed and we were allowed to continue.

The Wingco clearly had dropped a clanger but realised it and agreed I should keep Guy informed of our ops.

"As this was the first op. for a long time, we expected trouble; we got it. My own b.a. leaked. Then the skirt of my dress poured in water and had to be patched. Meantime Coase, the Leading Diver, had been down with Mack to take stock of the surroundings. Balch's barrel lay at the foot of the boulder ruckle and by it at one end was another second-century wine vessel, at the other end a skull. A further skull lay higher up the cave and sundry wreckage lay around.

"He brought out the vessel, after making a sketch, and reported to the Archeos; then one skull followed. Stanbury's dive was a great pleasure to him, for he had completely recovered his grip. The op. dawdled on until after dark and we eventually trundled our kit back again and made for The Belfry via The Hunters' Lodge. Mason joined us to chin over the job, especially its prospects, and urged us to complete the archeological work without undue delay; while we were agreed on the desirability of that, we were not prepared to commit ourselves just then. Ted and Dorian (Mason) left; we drew lots for bunks and turned in. There was an unusually good crop of low stories but eventually we dropped off to sleep."

"The sun rose once again to a lovely day; our run of luck for packing up has been extraordinary but we got up too late to do both the packing and the promised trip down Stoke Lane Swallet so just packed and went home.

"OPERATION BUNG Seven 2-20-48

"B7 was arranged, but only just and with many a hole through which we duly tumbled. Monday the program was drafted, Tuesday printed. It was okayed by Wingco but it was not yet cleared by The Mill. I had written to Guy, and Wingco was to have said 'please' for us but he could not (relations between the cousins were very strained) and fell ill with lumbago.... However, on Thursday we were given the O.K.... for two B-ops. Coase and Mack were advised but I had no time to advise Mason and Stanbury before rushing to catch the coach

to Canterbury (on a domestic outing). The coach called for a few moments at its garage and I siezed the chance to send a wire dictated to the girl in the coach office. Mavis called that I was holding up the bus; I bolted out, realised I had not paid, bolted back and found the girl and man looking first at the scribbled message, then at each other, then again at the message, puzzled and taken aback. I slapped a florin on the counter with 'Sorry' and bolted out again but heard the man say 'Ah, that's better!". Such was the tempo of the preparations. .....
Back at home I rapidly packed and made for the station, on six postulates: that we would be met at Wells, that the restaurant would be open, that Mrs. Andow would be at home (she provided our accommodation near the cave), that the Aflo batteries would have been charged, that there would be a team, and that the team would have some lights.

"We arrived at Wells at the appointed hour, if not the appointed minute, but no car. We rang Olive (Mrs. Wingco); none had been arranged, but she would fix it. We sat and waited, and waited, and waited until, realising waiting was useless, we hired one. Mrs. Andow was away, so we went on to the Belfry... next day the restaurant was open, but on its last weekend, a gang of six arrived and one hour behind schedule we were in the water. The diving was extraordinarily protracted; there were misunderstandings between divers and a general lack of coordination, that is, planning and control were poor, but slowly the second skull and a number of other bones were brought out. The area was closely searched for more but nothing new discovered. We sought and found the barrel stave that held The Bung, the mascot, as it were, of the operation. Coase had opened up the way down among the rocks of The Resurgence, just a little. I watched him start, but he made such a mess he was quickly lost to sight. I waited until surely he must have gone below, and started after him, only to land on his head a moment later. The way down the rubble slope is steep but quite nice now we are used to it; it has been enlarged, not only in imagination, but physically as well, still, when coming to it in the brown-out of the mud-clouds, previous experience of its passage is comforting. It goes down at about

45o to its full depth of 14 feet and administers a fair squeeze to the eardrums as you go. Until we got used to the place we used to leave a light at the top as a pilot for the return journey; it was distinctly comforting to see old Aflo's beam staring down between the mud patches. Not that the place is really terrifying, it is not; the roof is sound (we hope! one small piece did fall on me while I was playing with the barrel) and the slope is stable. Nevertheless, at each slight deviation from the grooved-out route, the diver touches back and front and has to manoeuvre to find the widest part. Just a gentle reminder of what it would be like if a rock moved and the diver were helplessly stuck between roof and floor.

"From the bottom the lights of the Witch's Kitchen could just be discerned as a huge but faint mouth at the top of the sandslope. To finish the day, three of us did the through route to First Chamber. One of us, George Lucy, was on his first cave dip; it must have been very impressive.... We were met in the First Chamber and George was dispatched by the tourist route to the entrance; we went back by the low-level route. A trainee was put down for a safe-water dip; that wound up the proceedings.... After a tangle of interest-serving, we reached The Belfry where Devenish, who had lifted us there, ran his beloved Jeep into Fair Lady ditch and truly bogged it down until the rest of the gang arrived.

"In the pub, (interest no.1), the cider was good; in the Wingco's drawing room, the Masons were putting the pressure on for an examination under the surface, not the air-water surface this time but in the river bed. They had many skulls, 13 or 14 now, but not many other bones or especially pottery or other datable objects, so they are anxious to redress the balance. Perhaps Mason would become a diver and see the job through for himself. For me to be his diver would have been goodbye to Nine and all that for a year or two; but for the SS the work would mean great opportunities for diving in less intimidating waters than the inner series.

"Sunday dawned fair; at least the low sun shone through the crinkles where the corrugated roof of The Belfry joined the walls and its light made the drops of condensation glisten brightly and the spiders' webs shone and trembled as occasional draughts of air touched them. That would be about eight o'clock: I had slept soundly all night, certainly I never heard the creaking of the bunks that makes the dreaming caver think his roof is coming in about his head. The usual kit attention next. Digger Harris called and lent a hand and a chin, too, for we had not met for years. I even had time to Dettol my breathing bag and brush down the floor, well, just a little. My travel kit was featherweight for a change, a passing van had picked up the heavy stuff, so I could get to Wells by bus after a final meal for the year at the restaurant and a quick look at the cave's washing down pump (for possible use on Operation Sandblast).

"So to Paddington once again; the train is passing through Savernake as I scribble, I am alone for the other two have gone to Stoke Lane Swallet. At Wookey we have cleared the surface layer of relics and we have linked The Resurgence with the First Chamber: B7 marks the end of another phase in the exploration of the cave."

Maybe that last comment was a little optimistic for the next op., one of those multiple hybrids, included an SB1 component, Sandblast, and another Bung, B8, this latter to collect any bits we might have missed. The other components were M7, some swimming practice in The Scullery, RG1 to place a ladder in Six-Two for security, J7 a look at the north end of Eight; SP1 to start stockpiling in Nine. Altogether much too ambitious.

"B8, J7, M7, RG1, SB1, SP1 23-10-48

Working steadily, but not too hard, in the interval I nearly had everything ready. There was no Aful, and if there were there would be no aquaplanes for it - a rather hypothetical system to assist a swimmer to adjust level, especially when loaded.... Stockpile was very doubtful still. The waterproofing qualilties of the various devices and their weighting were unknown factors and travelling on the Saturday left nc time for trials. On the Monday, Wally Gorham of Dunlops announced that a couple of bods from Admiralty Experimental Diving Unit would like to come to look and to dive with us, fortunately they would be bringing their own gear. (I heard much later they had been commissioned to spy on us for a security check).

"Bill Mack had a death in the family and had to cancel. Terry, my step-son, would be along to supplement the slave-gang. At Paddington we collected the trunk, no lightweight, and the innocent-looking satchel of lead weights. Terry could best tell how he and the Cloakroom Man collected the innocent-looking satchel! At Frome Coase had left a P-Party kit for us to pick up and had added a few oddments to the pack. Cloakroom man said 'It is where you left it, I said I wouldn't move it'. 'Now I wonder where I did leave it?' said I, then spotted it under the counter. It was my turn to be shaken and not to show it, but probably of no significance anyway. I picked it up and, with a little assistance, managed to get it on my back then reeled drunkenly as if my knees did not really belong to me. I subsided with it onto the weighing platform and got myself up leaving the dial still reading 95 lb.

"At Wells we were so intent on getting our lot out that we forgot the trunk which went on to Tucker Street. The Wingco was at Wells but so was his bitch Jessica and her pups, all off the same train, so there was no room for the trunk anyway. We made sure the trunk would be taken off for collection later.

"Tea for the guests and the London party was at 4:45 but Johnny Dwyer told us he had called at The Inn and tea would not be ready until 5:30. So I went for the trunk. On return, at 5:20, the landlord came over to us, 'Tea has been waiting since quarter to five!'. Explanations please, Johnny!... But where was Harry Stanbury, our last hope as a supporting diver? It seems his wife had had the last word and it was 'No'. Then came the rush of kit preparation, and no light. That had misfired from the Bristol end. It was dark long before we were ready; that afternoon train is a well-nigh impossible arrangement but along came Devenish with jeep and a lamp. No one had told him of the op;, he came on speculation and we were right grateful, both for lamp and the jeep, for the pile was exceptionally high and heavy. The next sad discovery was that the food box, specially prepared for wet transit, was missing. Add to that the unpreparedness of the frogsack gear (waterproof transit sacks), it seemed that SP1 would be scrubbed before it started.

"I was last as usual with my preparations so the boys nipped back to have one. In the cave we made a fairly orderly encampment, I was late again sorting my pile and the others were well ahead with their dressing by the time of the break for the final leak. Grosvenor, of AEDU, was ready prematurely, he was wearing a dress with no 'easy' position for the hood and I expect he took an even dimmer view of what followed. The swimmers, Coase and I, leapt in. My trim was fair, Don was light and could not control his depth; we soon had to return for adjustments and so stirred up the mud that B8 was wr tten off. I found great difficulty in levelling and we both porpoised badly during the fin op. We went through The Scullery hitting first bottom then roof and lost a lot of gas. Maybe fear of contacting bottom and stirring up mud may have been partly to blame. We had a mildly amusing incident; at the start we had been uncertain where to make exit so, down in the deep part, Don stopped to check but for some time could not find me until, looking upwards, he discovered me resting gently against the roof just above him!

"We chose the way to Three but made slow headway against the current. The simplest technique was to be just heavy, fending off from the bottom from time to time as required. (I had found no rational way of following an undulating passage; others did it, but I never discovered the knack.) One thing is certain; to follow an undulating passage and maintain zero buoyancy is much harder than swimming at constant depth in, say, the baths. There had been a lot of rain so the river was not at its best; it cleared quickly but visibility was distinctly poor.

"The under-five-hours divers then went in. Setterington and Lucy took the wash-down hose for SB1 and reported that it was quite O.K. for cutting sand and digging out rocks though, as expected, it did tend to wash the divers away rather easily. A good effect we had overlooked was the rapid local clearing owing to the large amount of clean water being pumped in.

Some control for the water jet is needed; the SS can work this out to their own satisfaction.

"Don and I then walked into Three with the AEDU boys and dived to Four where we parlayed. AEDU were a bit light, floated, and we had already run out of lead... Stan Shepperd was a relative novice, so was out of any trip to Six; I was not happy about Tom Grosvenor, probably because I was anxious about ourselves without having the burden of a passenger of unknown quality. Tom was not sticking his neck out to come so he too was left to watch the descent instead of taking part in it. It seemed a bit shabby but remembering the nasty mud in Six and the horrible sensations while finding a way from First Deep to Four, before one acquires a confidence born of experience that there is a way out if only the diver keeps calm and collected, it seemed the best course to take.

"We had already had a spot of bother with the ladder, nine feet of ponderous ironwork, it had fouled the Three-Four line and ripped it to bits so we started with some misgivings on our journey to erect it in Six. We staggered down to First Deep and, luckily, while I was on the mud climb to The Plain, Don was able to push and, while he was on the climb, I was able to pull; between us we got through. I heaved the head of the ladder round as The Gateway came into view but, as Don pointed out, my placing was at the wrong surface so round we went again but to erect it was beyond us. In retrospect it was folly to try. The way to the selected position was up a steep sandbank where there was little grip or manoeuvring room, but in any case the weight of the thing made a hoist impossible to a couple of nearly zero-buoyant divers so we returned sobered to Four. A new diving experience for me was that, when lifting a heavy load, the water shoots up between the wrist tendons at a rate of knots. Very unpleasant!

"Back in Four we consulted and confirmed the task to be abandoned then the four of us made for the base as the hour was striking midnight or something like that. In One we were undressed at an alarming speed, for Terry proved to be a master at debagging divers ...

"Next day... we sorted kit and nattered. We learned that our breathing is shallow and our breathing bags are under-inflated. Grosvenor and Shepperd seemed to have enjoyed their weekend and are keen to help through AEDU, presumably as a possible line of new thought on diving and as a testing ground for new equipment and techniques. They left us an Italian saboteur's two-piece rubber suit taken, I understand, by shooting some poor devil in the Med. and a Siebe-Gorman Amphibian Mark IV breathing set. We must take AEDU down Stoke or Swildon's for acclimatisation, then get them down to Wookey again."

Work on equipment and the like continued, including a lightweight ladder for Six, but the tasks of exploration had entered a rather uninteresting phase; the main objective seemed lost in a welter of detail. Operation Linlay 1, 13-1-48, was the start of laying a new and improved line system towards Seven, albeit for cost reasons or the mental outlook generated by perpetual shortage of funds, a grossly inadequate system. The work added little of note but gave Bill Weaver some valuable experience. L1 ended near The Second Deep. Its recording continued into Notebook No.33.

After L1 and more equipment problems came Operation Rearguard. It may well be we grossly overestimated the risks of travelling to and from Nine but we decided to establish an intermediate haven of refuge. In the event it was used but once and then was of no true avail. Stempels were wedged across Six-Two and boarded over then security chains added George Lucy took a prominent part in the work. Notebook No.34.

A development is hidden in the op. title "RG3,L2"; hitherto such composite ops. were basically serial affairs but RG3 and L2 ran simultaneously with two practically independent diving teams. RG3 made the platform a reality, with telephone, but further work on it remained to be done; L2 took the line through to Nine making Bill Mack the third diver to visit the new chamber but again there was work outstanding. RG3 has special interest inasmuch as here Bob Davies, of Derbyshire Section, entered the Wookey operations in which he was soon to have a crucial role. As an aside, divers also have their little private entertainments as I did while watching Davies struggling to get a plank into Six while the river insisted it should go the other way!

About the same time various carrying devices came into being, for example, the wonderful Trapped-Air Compensated Waterproof Apparatus Carrier, TACWAC, (to the gang 'Tick-Tack', or 'Tick-Toc'), which took the telephone to Six.

Diving also has its social or domestic problems; we had already lost one promising diver through wifely pressure but Tom Grosvenor got into a different kind of trouble. He had kindly booked a room for a friend, a double, and the acknowledgement arrived the day of his departure for Wookey. Ma-in-law took in the post and saw in it clear proof of those things she had always suspected. Aha! so this was the truth about these 'official' journeys away from home! By a stroke of luck, Tom was travelling in his caving togs. Such trifling contradictory evidence carried no weight with Ma-in-Law but Mrs.G. had better sense and knew the scarecrow that had just come down for breakfast was hardly planning a week-end with a Popsy!

L3, 15-1-49, carried the line-finishing work as far as the mud-slope; we were taping the line (already laid) at abrasion points while the platform slowly progressed as RG4. There were five divers at work. The L3 pair (Coase and I) were also supposed to do a much-postponed J7, a look round Eight, but merely gleaned scrappy impressions in passing. Also LP1, to explore the loopway at the foot of the mudslope; as its discoverer, I did that but it proved to be little more than another Balcombe's Folly. Stockpile, SP1, began at half past midnight, not very successfully, for the carrier bag shipped about a gallon of water, despite our gas-pressurising arrangement. On that op. we (still Coase and I) took the chance for a closer look at Nine.

The Mud of Nine

"... Once in Nine we could not resist the temptation to look with mouths agape at the tremendous walls and the high fissured roof in that splendid place. We wandered to the second surface and to the rift beyond. We properly noticed for the first time the astounding mud formations which stood in the bay where once the water lay but has now drained away; the mud has parted in places to form cliffs and gullies with serried pinnacles in ridges running aslant, the high ones by the cliff face growing smaller and smaller until they die out. Scenes such as one might expect to see from a plane flying high over Colerado. Then the drip and splash patterns in the mud are extraordinary. First, there are deep sockets where the drip from the high roof hits at scores of points in The Bay and bores to a depth of some inches; the sides of these craters are fluted rosettes; the angle of the crater eases at about half-depth and the fluting is lost as the diameter increases and the splash diminishes but their place is taken by another finer structure which in turn fades out or merges with the next system. On the edge of the pool, Nine-Two, there are steep-to banks of mud, sliced by major gullies and with a cliff or two complete with its pinnacles then we have yet another picture built up from the mosaic of splash from the surface of the pool, the whole overscored by horizontal markings incised into the mud, the contour lines of a host of levels the pool has attained and lost.

"Beyond the mud, it is fine sand really and quite firm to walk on, Coase wandered into the rift at the southerly end and started to climb. His Aflo picked out stalagmite incrustations and figures far finer than we had hitherto dreamed existed there. The colouring, with greens and greys predominant, is lovely indeed and the whole is thinly encrusted with sparkling crystals. A bishop, or rather an Orthodox Metropolitan, methinks, stands serenely near the back of the rift, some fifteen feet up just left of and below the opening which remains to be explored. ..."

Stay with that record a little longer.

"... Pulling ourselves together we suddenly realised how time had flown so hastened to pack, or re-pack, the stores we had brought. We left out the candles and the mask windows and returned the rest to the bag after wiping it down as best we could, leaving it to the kindly care, we hoped, of the silica gel. We feared, after close inspection of the carrier sack, that the fold-up seal would be unlikely to be much of a barrier to the damp but most of the things could stand exposure for some time; the more vulnerable, like the telephone, had their own internal containers. "With the telephone put away and the kit packed, we started the unpleasant part of the return - putting on the b.a., the transitory stage between the relative comfort of ordinary air existence and the delightfully restful buoyancy of life down under. Truly, the transitory stage is irritating in the extreme; every movement is hampered and difficult, sometimes dangerous. There was quite a measure of doubt about safely traversing from the niche or tiny bay, to which we first descend from the rocks above, round to the hand line. I felt happier when my feet were stuck well into the mud and I was on the right side of my breathing drill. A slip would have been unpleasant at the very best. I had not yet practised putting on my mask underwater and, in any case, I found I had managed already to lose my window. Even if all that were under control, a slip would mean a slide to the bottom down that steep slope. If you could put your mask on, or even grab the mouthpiece and fiddle for inaccessible gas taps while shooting down that lot, with ears wanking in and out, you would be a most exceptional diver!

"However, we passed safely round and soon slithered down the line under complete control to the bottom. Coase was leading and he seemed nearly vertically below me as I slid.... On the way back I called in for Mack at the platform. He was almost ready to come for base had given the alarm; SP-divers were overdue, it was three-quarters of an hour since they had signed off in Nine, would Mack investigate please? He must have been relieved for a rescue job is no picnic even for a fresh diver, let alone a dead-tired one. I was in quite bad sodalime trouble for my b.a. had sprung a leak and flooded the absorber and, while in Nine, it had got dead cold. I was just sufficiently clear in my thoughts to take comfort from the twitching of the line, which told that Mack was close behind.

"Base was really fed up; our comments about the soup over the phone (we had carried in a store of self-heating cans of soup) had led them to believe we were sitting in Nine enjoying a meal and they regarded that as not exactly clean play. It was after 3 a.m.; they were tired and quite rightly annoyed."

Shortly afterward came great news from Coase and the Derbyshire Section. They had broken through at Buxton Water (Peak Cavern) and at Speedwell; both gave new "dry" passages about 1,000 feet long with extensions possible. Cave Diving is really coming into its own.

Notebook No.35.

Gordon Marriot entered the scene of operations. Marriot was an ex-Royal Marine, one of the first Frogmen, hero of the D-Day beaches and now leading demonstrator in Butlin's displays. His name had previously come up at Wookey; Wingco was in favour, I was reluctant, being firmly of the opinion that a cave-diver should first and foremost be a caver and that no amount of diving skill can compensate for a lack of caving experience. The suggestion that he join us was dropped for very different reasons on Mrs.H.'s advice.

Stockpiling and Rearguard continued to completion; the lines were not quite completed and probably never will be, and we were ready as ever likely to be for the next push. That would be L4-A2.

"OPERATIONS L4,A2 26-2-49

"... Phoned from Westbury, the Wingco seemed at his best, sweet and affable, nothing too much trouble; he would meet the train and take us up to The Belfry. He did. We thought he knew best as he swept past the Rookham turning and up the main road to Bristol. He was a bit annoyed when he realised our destination was The Beeches, not Beechbarrow.... By half past five we were in the water. AEDU were absent. Marriott arrived, after a crash caving course, but had a cold and did not dive. The divers were Coase, Lucy and myself, so we scrubbed that part of L4 which was recovery of the old lighting cable to Six. Coase and Lucy went straight through to Nine; I followed slowly, taping. The water in their wake was fairly clear as far as First Deep thereafter the blackout was almost complete until I entered clear water beyond The Parcel belay (a much-wrapped rock near Nine). The taping was very slow, and it was impossible to fit a tape at every abrasion point... we may have to change to V.I.R. cable in the end... the mud was so thick I had to abandon the last two and awkward belays for another day. Looking ahead into the clear water, I saw a nasty-looking rift but no sign of the square-cut portal Coase had previously observed. The rift was at a wicked angle, about 70o, high right to low left, about 20 feet up and 10 down, with a useful-looking block in the middle but a horrid wedging waiting for the diver who slips down the slope to the bottom. I looked round but saw no other way on; I was hardly in a looking mood for I was cold from the long exposure; it had taken me an hour to this point and my thumbs were quite dead. I went up to Nine.

"At the Pinnacles, I loosened off and began to thaw again. Meantime Coase would look around below. He went down, his light flashed through the murky water and disappeared. It reappeared a few minutes later in clear water to illuminate the whole of Nine-One, then turned and disappeared again. We waited quite a long time and I began to get anxious and to pull my dress into diving order. I was just about to go in search when there was a splash behind the rocks which hid Nine-Two from view. He was out in the second surface; the bad lad had done the loopway, Second Loop, without warning us!

"We were relieved to see him and congratulations came easy. He had looked at the rift; it closed in but there were two bedding-plane inlets in the upper part, one being big enough to get through. He had, however, discovered another rift a few feet wide which led behind the wall of Nine, over a tumble of blocks to a place where he could see the surface of Ten and that of Nine-Two. He made for Nine-Two and got out with just a couple of turns left on his wire-drum.

"We held council and decided on a three-man visit to Ten. Coase led, Lucy followed for better vision and I was rear-marker. It was a fine slide down the mud then I crept slowly along the line they had left; it was almost black-out. The way was uphill... I felt gravel under my fingers at one place. like that in Five, then sand and silt again. I ran into Lucy who was stationed at the top of the sandbank but I could see nothing more. Coase was ahead and it appeared later that he had climbed a sharp ridge and just got his eyes out of the water. Ten's roof is flat and ten feet above the surface. I was signalled to return; I slid down pleasantly and went out to Nine-One. Coase had tried to locate a way on, seen on his Loop Two adventure, but the mud foiled him.

"We waited for the mud to clear then Coase and I had another go. I got a glimpse through the half-clear water of a fantastic ridge of rock rising high up towards the surface of Ten and seemingly a long way away. That was Coase's Arête.. We passed quickly into clear water and travelled over beautiful smooth sand, passing a great fallen block with an eyehole right through it, then downhill, like trudging over a snowfield, until suddenly we halted in our tracks. Below and to the right was deep water of the palest green, such very deep water it startled us. Coase was on the edge of a terrific drop and had halted just in time, in fact he reported later he had to hang on to the line to check his slide down the bank which finished a few feet farther on in fresh water! We stood, awestruck at this spectacle. The whole character of the cave had changed, in fact we had passed out of the conglomerate into the limestone. (Wookey Hole Cave lies in an ancient gorge in the Carboniferous Limestone infilled in Triassic days with Dolomitic Conglomerate.) The great trough at our feet ran down to the SE; we could see no surface; our own depth was 25 feet, and the roof would be about the level of the water-table. Ahead was a wide smooth black arch, below it the roof was indistinct but way down in the far corner was a gaping black hole where the river entered, maybe some 50 feet below us. We were staggered by this, it seemed so unreal, it could only be a cave-diver's dream. The sharp beams of our Aflos picked out the curves, ridges and slopes and the black holes below. It was more like a mountain scene than"

Notebook No.36.

"a river bed. At last we turned to go. Coase had tied off to a fallen slab and knocked off the tip as a souvenir - Into The Limestone! (but the slab happened to be conglomerate). We retraced our steps and for a long way the water was quite clear; the line ran straight ahead, cutting into the sand and leaving furry edges alongside our footmarks. Then the water became cloudy; we were still climbing and soon the big eye-hole block loomed up. It was knobbly and unlike either the limestone or conglomerate to which we were accustomed. We passed on into thick darkness... with a tingle of glee I rose up the steep slope to Nine and after a struggle landed on the hard rim of muddy sand. Coase quickly followed and we were once more mortals. ....

"For us as divers the depth is at once a joy and a blow. It is too deep to descend in oxygen kits but so lovely to look at. It raises an entirely new set of problems: of our breathing sets; of our own locomotion; of the efficacy of our kit transporting devices. A new world, new problems, a new approach. Time will tell.

"From Nine, after visiting Ten, we phoned the base; could Johnny (Ifold) get us some beer? Off shot Johnny to The Inn. No container? Then no beer. Undaunted Johnny went to see the Wingo; could Wingco please let us have a few empty beer bottles for a celebration? 'Will full ones do?' asked The Wingco.

"The train was on time for once and we nearly missed it. At Witham we noticed a middle-aged lady trying to get three large boxes onto the train which had pulled up almost out of the station. 'Could we assist?' we asked, 'Why, please!'. We did and noticed she was rummaging in her handbag. We politely declined the tip but she insisted and slid something into my tattered coat-pocket (I was in caving togs). At Westbury she apologised most tritely for the fourpence in my pocket and explained she had thought us Prisoners of War but the gentleman in her compartment had explained that we were 'famous people, the divers of Wookey Hole'!

Chapter 11

The CDG Coming of Age

In early 1949 The Cave Diving Group was in the throes of change. The Sections had been moving ahead, especially the Derbyshire Section which, with other caving groups, was making tremendous discoveries. At Wookey the change in the caving scene demanded change in technique. Until recently I personally had spear-headed the work there, but I was not changing. I was essentially a bottom-walking oxygen diver, I had not been able to master swimming adequately for cave work and its prospect did not thrill me. Likewise the change to mixture-breathing or air to cope with the depth of Eleven had no appeal, partly from conservatism, partly finance and the time the changeover would absorb. I was losing hope of finding any significant above-water extension of the cave and above all I was questioning if the tremendous efforts made, whether in running the CDG or the back-breaking struggles of transporting the kit, were worth their while. This undoubtedly was reflected in my diving and the change had not passed unnoticed for I find I had written amid the scribblings on mixture-breathing and fin practice that "Coase had already commented on my poor performance before the I-ops." (Ops. which followed the discovery of Eleven.) While I lacked the urge to meet the new requirements, there would be others only too keen to take the lead. Bob Davies was the first among these and he became our first fin exponent, followed quickly by Coase, but the change was not without the most serious setbacks.

Fins were used by Davies and Coase in reaching the surfaces of Eight and Ten. I had still failed to attain adequate competence in swimming and, after a final trial run in The Scullery, I withdrew from the swim-ops., S5-11 of 9-4-49.. On the same occasion, the two swimmers headed for Eleven and took a quite careful look at it noting, as is now to be expected, how the place had shrunk since its discovery. On the return journey from Forward Base tragedy struck. Mariott, also swimming, had made the visit to Nine in acordance with our policy of gradual acclimatisation; he ran out of oxygen on the way back and died. The accident was due to the use of fins as a secondary cause; the primary cause was that he dropped his spare oxygen cylinder when making a change, causing him to become buoyant and float off the line; in the blackout conditions prevailing, he stood no chance of finding it.

Corresponding with the great increase in diving activities, there was a need for organisational change; until recently the CDG organisation was centred on my own activities; the time had come to reshape it. As one member put it in commenting on my role, "any elected officer would have been slung out months ago". In practice, the slinging out was effected by other means; the stresses of the job had grown to such an extent that nature finally jibbed; I fell victim to eczema which persisted, with breaks, for a long time; that and domestic problems were more or less my final straw. My subsequent diving was progressively less enthusiastic; the dives themselves were mostly as a guest on Derbyshire Section or similar ops., until finally I found myself physically unable to keep up with the party returning from a late Wookey op. up the long pull to The Belfry. Came my fiftieth birthday, and I quit.

While the formal reorganisation of the CDG with an Executive Committee and its elected members, did not come into effect for some time yet my story of the Group's conception, childhood and youth is coming to an end. Conceived at Keld Head, born at Ffynnon Ddu, brought up at Wookey Hole it was now reaching manhood.

Chapter 12

Wookey Hole, Black Keld, Peak Cavern

Graham Balcombe with equipment outside Crook's Rest, 1949.

Although my own activities now have little or no organisational effect on the course of the CDG, there remain some further records in the notebooks of interest, primarily as "member's diving notes", which I wish to save from destruction, so I record them. They follow Avanti and the discovery of Eleven.

Notebook No.36 (cont.)

"30-3-49. Swimming at Baths. Considerable progress in level-keeping and manoeuvring but carbon-dioxide trouble again... Mack and Coase not so affected ..... "6-4-49. Swimming practice at Baths. Canister carefully packed using Siebe Gorman's recommended method... with Aful [Apparatus for underwater lighting]... 35 minutes almost continuously on the move; no serious symptoms and level control considerably improved but not assured, especially checking of upward movement... Results encouraging but not I1 standard... Second trip of 15 minutes, with Aful tied on to b.a. and hands used for level control, with much more satisfactory results. In fact I1 is now a fair bet as far as level control ability is concerned, that is, apart from mud, lighting and other problems. I reckon we will be on very thin ice on this op. but it should be a grand adventure even if it does not entirely succeed. Danger is probably not great; gas duration is likely to be the major unknown.

"OPERATION INNOMINATE One 9-4-49

"...Travelled with Marriott and family as far as Bristol whence his wife and 2½-year-old continued to Exeter.... Grosvenor was late and the promised sample of sodalime did not arrive. Coase and Davies already doing a B-op., nothing to report. Trouble with trim on going to Wookey underclothes; persistently nose-heavy and needed greater weighting to sink even on a minimum gas-bag. Eventually a fair trim. All this took a long time to determine and fix while splashing about in Three and Four, during which I lost the line and in the muddy water just could not recover it. It is all too easy to lose. Coase says it is immaterial if one's feet are light; maybe I am too pansy... sodalime seemed perfect. Delays in trimming put me out of the op. I1 was splendid, reported Davies and Coase. They swam out over the deep and into an aven which rose up to about -2 feet." That is,-2 ft if regarded as absolute level, which it was not, or +2 ft if a depth; anyhow it was 2 ft below water table.

"Marriott ran out of gas, an incredible happening for one so skilled." (Marriott was a swim-diver of very great experience; some 500 hours including war diving as a saboteur and on the D-day beaches.) "... Everybody was splendid." (The accident is the subject of Letter to Members No.14.) Notes on mixture diving follow, (among other things).

"20-5-49. Enquiry from Davies to know whether I will join next DS op. to which Mavis expressed her intention to reply. And she did." (His later comment was "My, she can give tongue!".)

"15-6-49. Weaver says very good idea to have a general meeting...."

22-9-49 Cave Diving for export. Equipment sent on loan to Delteil of Foix, Arriège, France.

23-9-49. Equipment improvements.

"BLACK KELD, WHARFEDALE 30-9-49

"A long and glorious summer had slipped away... eczema which attacked in April has gradually cleared" (only in remission it later proved) "... workshop improvements... arrears of CDG Letters... arrears of three years' photo prints. That brought it very close to the date for Black Keld and I decided to go. Just now I am in the train on the way there still wondering if it is all worth while.

"With only a week to go, an ill-defined pile of work awaited; much kit was at Wookey and irretrievable. A major item needed was the addition of a small reserve cylinder to a frogman b.a. and its design was a teaser. It is still much of a compromise, but will probably serve me,... the basic change is the clipping of a 1.8 cu.ft. Davis Submarine Escape Apparatus,

(DSEA), cylinder to the main cylinder... then sundry replacements, repairs and renovations; which wound up on the eve of departure with the emergency torch still useless and Aful still untouched.

"By nine p.m. I had a rucksack and a cabin trunk packed and started off for the station. I did not get beyond the first street corner, though. The kit was no heavier than a normal Wookey trip" (that would be about 100-lb trunk plus rucksack) "but I realised the folly of it all and declined to continue. I had intended to dump the load at St.Pancras and to take the rest next morning but this altered things. I stood pondering and the party nearly received a wire: 'Kit hopelessy heavy, attempt abandoned', then I returned to finish the rest of the packing; I would go by taxi despite the cost.

"I was up at six and, breakfast over, I was ready to go by half past seven but there was no reply from the cab-rank; half glad, half sorry, I went to the local station, and still half sorry, saw a cab pull in. The rest was an expensive but hardly justified 'luxury'; the cabby took his toll, getting the luggage to the train took porters in two relays and they took their whack. Not to mention the railway charges, even although they turned a semi-blind eye to the quantity and character of my luggage. Lucky indeed that DS were supplying the gas, for railways do not take kindly to that.

"The long toil of preparation, the hectic rushing about, the back-breaking loads, the high costs... all for an objective which would be made unattainable by a shower of rain and, as the last straw, experience shows that progress is almost invariably so relentlessly slow.... My diving ability had never been higher, my kit was at last behaving to satisfaction but there was that nagging thought which clouded my outlook - is it all worth while?

"The train rolled on, passing from a uniformly murky sky to one that had broken up into definite cloudbanks, then into a belt of drizzle, then further cloud which remained all day. At Skipton (2:30) I waited for the Kettlewell bus; the next would be 5:30. I paced... up and down the road... at last the bus came and, with not the slightest fuss over baggage, off we went to

Grassington. Half an hour's wait and the next bus took me to The Racehorses at Kettlewell. There I waited for the car which was to pick me up but none arrived. Finally, I left the trunk, the lead weights and Aful in the pub garage and humped the two rucksacks to Black Keld by dead reckoning, hit it plumb on the bow-stay and dropped down for the night.

"I scoffed some food and settled; the next I knew was that torches were shining in my face and Davies's dial was grinning down at me. At least one party had arrived so the meeting was not just one big hoax. Tents sprang up behind the wall, a primus buzzed its busy song and hot drinks appeared. So did the rest of the party... requested to collect my kit. They soon arrived without the kit; they had heard 'garage' but not 'Racehorses' and luckily the garage did not respond to their knocking - it was after 11 o'clock. So I spent an unpleasant night. The moon and stars had broken through; the half-moon hung low over Kilnsey Crag, while the ragged clouds moved slowly across her face; there was heavy dew and crisp cold air.

"After a long and vivid description of the Derbyshire Section's visit to France: how when you can no longer drive a bus down a French cave, 'c'est fin!'; how the French worthies with much 'Marchez!' and 'Tirez!' tried unsuccessfully to erect a 20-metre 'maypole' in a cave that lower down naturally had a 'resurgence de grande puissance'; or just how to drink the vin de pays from a goatskin bag. We laughed ourselves to sleep.

"We rose correspondingly late next morning... breakfast was at mid- morning, kit preparation lasted until lunchtime then we were free to dive. Davies and Coase went directly to the resurgence which did not look impressive but there seemed enough room to enter. They soon returned to report about 30 feet penetration into a roomy"

Notebook No,37

"passage about 10 feet wide and 6 feet high. Meantime I had been practising with fins in the water above the dam... my trials seemed eminently successful; the light, clipped to its new hook, seemed to be self-centring and satisfactory. We then got down to real business and as a trio slid into the resurgence and marched down the cave." (So not swimming.) "At about 100 feet the floor tilted up and there was was surface above; we climbed head and shoulders above water and inspected the small chamber. It was low-roofed, a break into a higher bed with an extension along the bedding plane back towards the entrance, through which, indeed, the party on the bank could hear us. At the little cliff-face, from under which the water rises as the resurgence, there is a low bedding plane opening, only an inch or so high; it is said that someone had blown a hunting horn down this and heard a distant echo. It is also said that otters were wont to go inside the entrance so presumably there was air-space behind. We had found such an air-space and a probable explanation of the echo.

"We could not find any way on for... we had disturbed mud and lost our chance. We retired and waited a while. Next time our pilot found the route, which turns hard left, and it led us slightly downwards for about 40 feet when the front diver suddenly halted and gesticulated. There at our feet was a great black hole in the floor! We could neither see across nor to the bottom, which meant at least 10 feet so, after admiring what we could see, we withdrew to consult. We agreed to give it best for the day and return to the attack in the morning so turned to the fleshpots and the Kettlewell pubs.

"During the morning we had some glorious hot sunshine but, alas! I left the photography until too late; clouds rolled up fast and obscured the sun and we saw it no more. While the sun lasted the dale looked beautiful; I do not think I have seen Wharfedale bathed in warm sunshine before. Next day, two of us collected the batteries and the milk then, at last, we turned to diving and were actually submerged by half past twelve. We were finning with the intention of crossing and examining the pot and Jack Thompson, who had had his first cave dip on the Saturday, was to come with us to the air chamber and observe what he could from that safe point. Bill Davis was to come to the pot, drop a weighted line and hold a guiding light for us. But he had trouble with his breathing bag and had to withdraw to have it fixed.

"We four carried on, three to the pot, leaving Jack in the chamber. Davies led, swimming out over the pot, but he found no way on then spiralled down to the bottom, trailing his wire line. The walls of the pot abound with ledges and projections, some perforated, and he inadvertantly swam through one of the holes; his line caught and he had to thread himself back again before continuing to the bottom. At the bottom the water comes in through a number of low bedding-plane slots (de grande puissance?) which are quite impenetrable to us so he returned. The marker light was quite invisible from the bottom so the line was a good precaution; we coiled down the rope and returned to base.

"My own swimming was very bad, just bumping and scraping from floor to ceiling and back again. The control achieved in the well-lit pond was lost in the murky water of the cave. Aful, in the open water, had been tied on tightly with string to its fixing ring and had behaved well and remained fore-and-aft most of the time; in the cave I had used an elastic binding and Aful looked anywhere but ahead. As third man I could see but little anyway, even when Aful did look ahead and, to boot, my other hand was occupied with the line and sinker. At the chamber I gave these to Coase with mumbled good wishes but did little better. It was most disappointing.

"Even so, the trips had been interesting and had had their moments of excitement, and the brief glimpses of the etched walls and roof added piquancy to a rather sombre whole. On exit we reported our conclusions and by then Bill Davis was back and the four of us made another trip, two pairs successively, quickly in and quickly back again. I escorted (?) Davis, then Coase escorted Thompson and 'a good time was had by all'. My level control was much better on this second trip: I quite enjoyed it.

"Meantime it was raining quite heavily and the onlookers and log-writers were having a poor time. Old friends had come to have a look and 'the Laird', (Holdsworth of Scar Ghyll), our host, who had made us so welcome and provided charging and drying facilities, had brought his wife down, and there was a complete hierarchy of stooges too. The start of the diving had been very ragged, but I think they were adequately entertained.

"So ended the Black Keld op. and, like its earlier number at Ffynnon Ddu, the conclusion was decisive, incontrovertible; our job was done and no others need waste their time in lowering the water or otherwise trying to gain entrance there. We could go home satisfied if not with a new discovery in the bag...."

That is followed by scrappy notes on workshop jobs: kit repairs and mods., duplicator repairs, and qhatting. (Qhatting is the soda-lime testing service for the CDG, "Quarter Hour Absortion Test", I had acquired half a hundredweight of the stuff). So on to Beta 12, a Derbyshire Section op. in the Peak Cavern series where such tremendous territorial gains had been achieved.

"OPERATION BETA Twelve 29-10-49

"I received sudden notice to attend a three-week management course at Stone in Staffordshire and the period would overlap the Beta 12 op. There was to have been a Sandblast Op. at Wookey that same weekend and I was to have been the Trainer Diver there but that was now impossible. It made Beta 12 possible and, after hurried missives to DS to warn them how little kit I would have, I hastily packed my stuff, plus some sodalime for DS, into six containers weighing 14 lb l5 oz each and posted them off." (The weight limit for parcels must have been 15 lb at that time.) "... On Saturday morning early enough I left with my bag of left-overs for Hope.... bus to Stone station, train to Stockport... where I had to change stations. A penny tram-ride, they said, so I took a penny tram asking conductor to see me off at Tiviot Dale Station: he forgot and I returned with the tram to reach the station just as the Sheffield train was about to depart. Porters shouted to hold it and directed me over the bridge; the guard hauled me aboard his van as the train steamed out.

"It steamed through Marple and New Mills, near my childhood's home, and brought back sharp memories. I had for company one very superior small boy, probably home from school for the weekend, and two fine little rough lads off for a weekend camp. One had a huge Bergen nearly as big as himself, the other a naval kitbag, certainly bigger than himself. They were going to camp in Edale said the one, or Hayfield said the other. The obviously more experienced traveller planned what meals they would cook on a camp fire to conserve their drop of methylated - if they had brought their stove! They got off at Edale, I at Hope, letting the superior one go on. Fish and chips made do for lunch then on to Revell's place where fine hospitalilty and all the latest news from Bagshaw Cavern awaited me. The Post Office was next door so avoiding the postal complications of the original Beta op.

"The next to arrive were Gordon Warwick and Lewis Railton of The Cave Research Group, to a renewal of reminiscences. Others began to arrive and soon we made for the divers' loft to prepare kit and fill cylinders for the fray. After an excellent tea, if somewhat dear, and a chinwag on the affairs and events of the group, we swung into action. On the back of eight we started in with the kit. There was quite a crowd of helpers but even more would have been welcome. In Derbyshire the divers are supposed to take things easily on the inward journey but they did not get off entirely free. Some time after nine we were ready and the Speedwell party had the siphons working." (The siphons turned an obstructing sump into a duck to ease the going especially for the transport team, the Sherpas.) "Four divers, Davies and Thompson, and Davis and Balcombe went in through Buxton Water. The water was muddy for me and I saw not a thing, I missed the Torricellian but found the squeeze and wriggled through; it certainly is a bit tight. In FH1 I was sent ahead." (The significance of "F.H." now eludes me; it might be Forward Halt, or perhaps Funk Hole.) "The Jaws, a hole between massive fallen blocks which obstruct the passage, should have been easy enough but a helmet I carried chose to get wedged and held up progress for some time during which Davis did not know what was happening and became uneasy about the stillness of the pair of feet still sticking out of his side of the hole. He pushed and pulled at them to see if the diver they belonged to was still conscious. The diver resented that a bit and kicked out. At last the obstruction gave way and I floated down into clear water, to the open passage, FH3 and land. On the way I lost that helmet and in seeking it smashed the Aful's unprotected bulb. Eventually a replacement bulb was fitted and I found my borrowed helmet but not by the aid of Aful.

"The Speedwell party soon arrived and relieved us of part of our kit. We marched on through that fine newly-found system, watching the almost circular tube change slowly to bedding-plane-and-rift, then halted a while at the foot of a ladder hanging down from the Speedwell Passage which joins our passage up near the roof. Passing Squaw's Junction with its two Moses-like streams, that is, seemingly flowing out of solid rock, but actually from a bedding plane, and a third, less mysterious in origin, we reached Lake Passage and, with a little difficulty, climbed into it and along to the chamber not far from the sump, maybe halfway between the main passage and the sump. The going in Lake Passage is not so easy; it would be no trouble if unencumbered but to a diver even the simple walk along the open cavern is a trial.

"We sat or reclined, the divers in comfortable puddles, the unequipped on the best rocks handy, and we waited while a large group of the party split off to visit the upstream passage of the main route. We waited maybe an hour, it seemed like two to three, and we grew chilly and uncomfortable. The other group at last became audible down the junction route then clattered past Lake Passage; the boom of flash powder told of their preoccupation and soon their footsteps receded downstream.

"The eight-way block of candles, which had welded itself together, was burning low. While someone fiddled with a refractory self-heat soup, I fiddled with the candles and at last succeeded in parting them. Still there was no sign of the rest of the party. There were two wet-clothed ones in our group who were getting very chilly until two noble-spirited divers disrobed and made over good dry sweaters to them while themselves donning the discarded wet ones 'to help dry them off'. At last we decided to wait no longer but to carry on with the dive. By now I, at least, had lost interest in the proceedings, but would be glad to get underwater if only for the comfortable support that water gives.

"So on with the kit; I mistakenly believed that the sump was just round the corner. It was a hundred feet or so farther on and the going was not the easiest. It proved better to do the transport in two trips. At the sump, not a roomy or impressive one, we soon made ready, but delayed a moment while Davies sought and recovered a lamp lost on the previous trip. Then he went through, followed by Thompson without any respirator, then myself and Davis. It was pleasant to dally underwater in comfort and compare the crossing in kit to the crossing without it; here at least divers score heavily. I thought of Swildon's and Stoke Lane and the effort needed there to make the plunge into the cold and repulsive holes; here to sink below the surface was an immeasurable relief.

"Soon reaching the other side, I quickly sobered again as we found ourselves faced with an unpleasant tight crawl among fallen slabs to the next sump. The going was the hardest yet, needing both hands for progress while wriggling along so that even the mask had to be put on. At last the sump awaited us. It was a curious hole, quite round and smooth, a contrast to the broken rock we had just passed. It looked its name, Ink Sump, the water was black and sinister by normal standards. Even so, to the diver it was a haven and refuge of comfort and after another irritating delay called Rest, we went in, Davies leading, I following and Davis standing by.

"Once under, it was as Davies had described it. Clean water, hardly a trace of mud anywhere and there was ample room. The passage zig-zagged easily along and Davies made a fast pace. We soon arrived at the belay, about 150 feet in, and tied on. A few feet farther and the roof and floor were close together. Davies was ahead, I was neatly wedged (not dangerously yet) between roof and fallen blocks; my b.a. had about two inches deeper draught than his. I shunted out and tried another spot. My reserve cylinder slid along a slot between rocks while the bag cover grated hard on the roof. It was a tight spot but probably no tighter than The Jaws.

"I lay awhile considering the implications. I might get through but might get wedged. I had not recharged the kit; we had agreed on a no-incident run. To my right there seemed to be a deeper trough at the other side of a large block. To go that away would mean dropping the line, and whatever way I took, there was the more serious problem of the return in the customary blindness. How would I fare in locating exactly the same spot on return, or if I left the line for the trough would I find either the trough or the line on return? I was still hesitating when Davies returned; he had twice tooted me on Aflohonk, 'Toot, are you O.K.?'. He had expected me to signal back by Aful for I had no Honk. But was I alright? I found it difficult to find a simple flashable answer anyway! It now appeared that Davies's sodalime had got wet and, all told, we agreed to return.

"Thus Beta 12 only added 5 feet to previous ground, at least, so said the report although Davies had been another 20 feet or so beyond the low part. From the farthest point we now started our trek back. The Ink Sump passage had remained remarkably clear; I need have had no fears of a blind return (always assuming we met no mud farther in), there was no need to hang on to the line; we hopped easily from boulder to boulder and very soon reached the sump. From the sump to the short trap had become no easier. Going through the trap I disdained to turn on the gas then, when truly under and breathing short breaths from a nearly empty bag, I suddenly realised my folly. I had done no breathing drill and just previously had been working hard; how did I know the bag mixture was safe? I grabbed hastily for the gas valve and it seemed ages before I got it open and effected a good blast on the by-pass!

"At the exit sump of this trap, the photographers had caught up with us and demanded a halt while they flashed away. I was feeling thoroughly fed up by now and showed it. Back at the little chamber we collected sundry oddments and, after yet further delay, made off. At Surprise View, the ladder pitch to Speedwell Passage, the first of the party was already starting up. A sideline parted and she slithered down tangled in the wreckage but supported by anxious hands from below. After a brief consultation, Railton went up hand-over-hand up the lifeline and from the top fixed the BSA ladder which had been lying by the pitch for, I think, two months; I also think I correctly record that the next man up did not use the lifeline.

"After waiting an age lying more or less comfortably in the water, then after the kit had been hoisted, it was my turn. I tied on firmly and called on the lifeline men to heave like b.....y, for I was in full kit including weights. They heaved, I slowly rose and at last reached the opening. Fortunately, from there it was only 15 feet of easy climbing. From there on the way got rather worse and I got more weary. It was a struggle to climb out of the groove and a struggle, when out, to keep out; the passage in most parts was not high enough for one to walk easily and my kit slopped from side to side and fore and aft. The rocky floor was not easy going though to any nimble unencumbered caver it would be no trouble at all. There were awkwardly sloping footholds, boulders and broken rock, sand, then deep mud-like sand. More than once I was forced to rest and by the time I had reached The Black Swan (Mucky Duck) I was about all in. We were a party of four divers with seven attendants and on return journeys divers help all they can. I think I had bitten off a bit more than I could chew.

"At B3" (lost again) "I had to discard my kit and to chain it along, dismantled; the kit was not prepared for manhandling through sandy muddy ducks and the muck must have got into many an unplugged orifice. Next time I shall be wiser. But the effect of taking off the kit was little short of miraculous! Soon I began to feel some life again, and excitement with it. It was a pleasure to move about; finally we wallowed through the long pools which guard the entrance to Speedwell Passage; life was joyous and gay once more and I was quite disappointed to find that the last of the kit had come through and there was no need to go back for more.

"The next hour (or so) was spent in laundry-work; being still half-kitted, I was pressed into rinsing out the party's muddy togs until finally I started out of the cave at nearly zero-hour for breakfast, after 13 hours underground and still in the trousers of my frogsuit. I grabbed a load and staggered with rapidly increasing weakness to the exit. The symptoms of fatigue had quickly returned and I was glad to find that on the second trip the load was much lighter, but by the time I reached daylight I was much more nearly done in and only just made it.

"At the entrance I changed; the others, bar one or two, had gone ahead and we had a great stack of kit waiting transportation. A party of YHA visitors arrived to see the cave. Where was the guide? He would be along very soon; would they meantime like to help us down with the kit? Whoosh! the kit disappeared down the pathway amid happy laughter and a clatter of boots. Wonderful.

"There followed a likewise wonderful breakfast at the pub and a leisurely rest and natter until midday opening time. (Breakfast was at 9:30 GMT. or 10:30 by our clocks for, during the night, the rest of Britain had put its clocks back.) At the loft we hurriedly packed and I was whisked away with Railton and Warwick to Newcastle where we called on Nellie Kirkham, also CRG, to guzzle her tea and scoff her cakes and to natter of mines and miners, lead, old style. Eventually Railton dropped me and my boxes right alongside my dormitory then slid off into the night."

There are some notes on how Coase and I cleared the fouled propellor of a motor cruiser in the Thames and how, in the process, Coase acquired a 20-lb slug of lead which must have been of some benefit to the CDG.

Notebook No.38.

There are notes here of trials with throat microphones and how they reacted to the pressures experienced in diving; of little interest now but one comment stands out.

"Practice at Granville Road Baths... for the first time diving was with kit unlimited and in ease and comfort; the Hillman took the strain ....."

Much too late, I had at last acquired a banger. There is also another different kind of tit-bit:

"10-12-50. Bad cold; Mavis easily persuaded me to stay abed for the morning (Sunday and raining). Sneaked out for a bath, taking a 75 atm. cylinder of gas...."

I3 was our first op. with the luxury of road transport. It was at Wookey Hole, sight-seeing and practice runs for recent divers, and we penetrated no farther than The Gateway. There is a note on the lines:

"The lines have been stripped clean everwhere and the braid-stripping algae itself stripped off, or died off, in turn. The lead markers are loose or more often missing; the white markers have also disappeared."

Notebook No.39.

There was another dilatory op. at Wookey Hole, I4, much the same as I3, doing a bit of tidying-up but achieving little. Beta 17, however, was rather better.

"OPERATION BETA Seventeen 8-3-52 & 9-3-52

"Since Beta 12, when I had declined to pass the low bit in Lake Passage (Ink Sump) on grounds that it would be too dangerous a place in muddy water, I had more than half expected, anyhow hoped, to be in on the next attempt and to vanquish that place. Had I known more about the place at the time, for the briefing was quite inadequate, I might have passed it there and then, recognising that discretion can be overworked.

"March 8th had been fixed for the next visit which was to include Far Sump as well. Three divers were scheduled; Davies, Davis and Thompson. For a long time now, Aflo had lain in pieces while the Cave Research Group book and domestic things claimed prior attention. With approaching zero-hour, having had to set aside Mavis's opposition, I had to set to with immoderate haste and only by departing two hours late on the day, and with a rather sketchy rig, did I manage the preparations. It happened that visits to Rugby and Humber Radio Stations were due about that time, which was financially helpful but contributed to the rush, for it entailed departure on the Friday. We loaded up the jallopy, started at 11:00 in tippling rain, broke down within the first five miles and after a bit of shuvving got a tow to a garage where the trouble cleared itself while localising.... the engine cut out twice during the journey then picked up again only to conk completely within sight of destination, Rugby. Petrol pump and jet were O.K. this time but a lorry driver, who had insisted on helping, found that the h.t. lead was loose, fixed it and that was the end of the trouble. After attending to the job at the Station we adjourned to the O'Neill's and later O'Neill and I met Sturgess, my boss, for the odd noggin at The Bell.

"On Saturday, O'Neill and I left our wives to spend the weekend together and headed northwards along the most direct route to Derby, Matlock and Bradwell. We were due at the loft at 17:00 but arrived early at Revell's place where we sat and nattered and played with his two sons. Thompson then arrived so we made for the loft and deposited a load of gear for DS use. Bill Davis arrived and kindly piloted us to The Nag's Head, a piloting we could well have dispensed with for Bill seems to be a mad driver, if that run were typical. At The Nag's Head we ate ham and eggs, later to discover how we would be stung for them, and the party of divers, local clubmen and the RAF Cadet team of twenty-odd helpers were briefed for the op. I was included in the diving team - cheers! or alas!, according to the emotions uppermost at the moment. The divers would dress at the cave entrance and according to practice would not carry any load except at Mucky Ducks. That was a practice quite foreign to our Somerset ops. and for the instant it left me feeling embarrassed.

"Understanding there was to be a barrow available, I had not unpacked my box of kit but there was no barrow so I had to look slippy and rearrange for porterage. During this, Thompson found he had... a connection leak. Allegedly hard-soldered, it was in fact soft... but the joint was temporarily repaired using a car soldering iron. About 20:00 we were off. Slowly the party crept forward; The Ducks were not siphoned, although a party had gone in earlier for this purpose. It seems the siphoning system is very sketchy in its operation and, whatever had been achieved before we arrived, there was now only an inch or two of airspace. Not that the divers minded but it must have been quite an ordeal for the Cadets on their first trip underground. The slime and muck beyond the ducks was unchanged but soon we were on hard ground again, in fact, queuing up at the ladder pitch.

"At last we reached the boulders and the upper sump, Sump 2. The water was clean and green; I looked forward to the dip, or, at least, the start of it, in spite of the tales of mud. Ready at last, the four divers submerged in succession without any noticeable hitch, what a change! I think I was third, the water was thickly muddied and the way on went sloping downwards, plunging into darkness despite my light, the roof only just keeping out of the way of the bottom. The passage was unpleasant and intimidating, in fact, it set me assuming all was as good as lost and cursing the idiocy of those creatures who seek such places for a pastime. At last the way on levelled then gradually rose again, reaching surface in an arc-roofed passage with a small strip of sandbank.

"On the bank sat Davies, and in the water stood Davis and Thompson; we were then a party of reduced morale. The first sump was pretty tough going for strangers and was in mud; we were in fact a little shaken. The bank was steep and we had to dig steps to get alongside it. It seemed to have been fixed that Thompson would lead and I should follow. We learned that the way was similar to the past sump, but more so, and the final way down was steep and muddy but we could let ourselves down on the line. But Thompson was not doing so well and we changed over. I made for the apparent way on, as judged from the overwater shape of the passage, for visibility underneath was only inches, and started down. It was like Sump 2, and I was not far down when called back with what I took to be emergency signals but was simply informed that I had gone the wrong way. Go to the left! they commanded; I did and found the roof firmly embedded in the sand. I followed to the right slowly downwards and soon found myself back on the same track I had previously begun, [with Thompson now in the lead?] I followed it downwards into the blackness, perhaps ten or twenty feet only, when Thompson, whose feet had been perpetually kicking me in the face, told me he had had enough. So had I but I was glad it was he who had called it off!

"With our tails between our legs we returned one by one to base. We crept slowly downstream, rather ashamed but nevertheless relieved. The party seemed set against any diving in Lake Passage, yet it seemed the greatest shame that we should be right on the spot and let the opportunity go by. For myself, I remember the, for me, extremely arduous passage, when fully kitted, between the two sumps of Lake Passage and hated the idea of it yet remembered the beautiful clear water of the far passage and the tinge of shame over the previous failure. We would not let this chance slip.

"I was first through the first sump and shepherded the others through to the other side. After the deep water came the dry-land crawl; it was hell; my lamp got torn off and, inch by inch, lagging far behind the others, I heaved, crawled, and wriggled onwards, reaching at last the beastly little hole and the slope. Wriggle, shift, heave and then, exhausted, relax for a moment, only to slide back to the starting point again. The others, already by the sump... , were laughing as I cursed and fumed along the slope. Then a short rest to pay off the oxygen debt and we were away; clear delightful water supporting us and making movement easy once again.

"The first few dozen feet seemed familiar, also the wide low place (just short of the place where I jammed last time) but I did not recognise the lowest and tightest place and had passed it unknowingly, maybe some minor kit mods. had made the difference. It seemed the whole place looked higher just ahead, always just ahead, while meantime bag and belly scraped roof and bottom; always tempting onwards and soon the place really did open up again. We passed the looped back-end of the Beta 12 line and continued, in an ever-growing passage of exquisite diving qualities, until at last it joined a bigger one at right angles to it. Our passage came in high up the side of the bigger one, like Speedwell into Buxton, and below us, reaching almost to the lip, was a fine bank of sand

and gravel in a huge cone to lead us down. We jumped from the lip and, turning left, saw a great expanse of cavern beyond and below. Part way down the slope we checked our depth. It seemed to me we had been descending fairly steeply most of the time yet occasional checks showed us to be only ten, then twelve, or fifteen feet (I can no longer clearly read the figures on my meter; it was my forty-fifth birthday we were celebrating); at this farthest point it seemed to read 20. Davies, however, said 28 and he had two meters. I tried to read his, but could not; he confirmed we were at the limit of depth, so I tied off and we returned; there was clear water all the way and no incident, save that at the low place I knocked my by-pass wide open. We had run out 290 feet of line and, believing we had finished the job to the limit of our oxygen equipment, returned happy and elated.

"It was not until days later Davies informed me he had misread his meters and we had only been 22 feet down. We had been under for 35 minutes, of which we had spent perhaps five waiting for my ears to clear and while belaying. The watching men on the shore were not sorry to see us back. Nor were the base party, or what was left of them. After we had traversed that crawl and plunged again through the sump that guards the place, and even lays the trap of a stepped roof to snare the weary diver on his way out, we were glad to pack up and stagger out; we did not see the main party again until reaching daylight at the entrance, at about 11 o'clock of the damp and dull Sunday morning. (On the way out, near Halfway House it interested me not a little to learn that Davies found it necessary to explain to a party working on the electrical installation that we had been cave-diving)."

(My notes do not make it clear but they had probably asked him anyway.)

"Peak Cavern has a handy stream where O'Neill and I washed out the gear and slung it to drip on the wall; we then adjourned for lunch, good but damnably dear, and a pint then packed up or collected our stuff from the loft and tootled back to Rugby where we sat and dozed, woke and dozed again until shoo'ed off to bed at nine o'clock. Such was Beta 17. Another hundred feet odd wrested from the cavern but the end not yet reached.

Chapter 13

Wookey Muddle, Swildon's Hole, New Divers, CDG Comes of Age, Swansong

Struan Robertson, Oliver Lloyd, Oliver Wells, Phil Davies, Graham Balcombe, Bob Davies & Derek Thorpe, outside the Belfry, 26/27 June 1954.

Notebook No.40

Derbyshire Section laid on an op. at Wookey but maybe had not coordinated too well with the local clubs for BEC were holding their AGM and Booze-Up. The op. was for line work and sightseeing only; there were five divers and no excitements. A somewhat similar op., at Dan-yr-Ogof, similarly calls for no special record. Yet another very belated op. did do something useful, photography in Nine, and the name of John Buxton appears. Buxton was shortly to be one of the mixture-breathing pioneers.

"L8,F2,FT2 27-6-53

"DS official ETA for assembly was 15:30... the Wingco-official time for entry to the cave was 20:30; we were late as usual and had the only too familiar hold-ups but at last divers actually entered the water at 23:34 .... At The Gateway the mud rose as usual and no way on could be seen. We were charged, on the previous op., to go into Eight by the bigger opening but now we had perforce to go the way we already knew by feel."

This reference to a bigger opening is still puzzling. I had had the impression there was such an alternative to The Giants Staircase, starting from just beyond Charybdis, where in fact I dropped Coase's Aflo when boating there, but in my time we never followed that possible lead.

"It was quite a feat getting the line through but we noted in passing that The Gateway is only 200 feet from Three. I was first down and went backwards, as I often do but this time of necessity because of the reel, else I might have seen something of the structure of the hole for the water was clear again below The Gateway. Below Nine-One we were pleased to find a neat secure block replacing the old 'parcel' belay then the fun began... digging our toes in as best we could .... I found the old hand-rope 10 feet down; I gave it a yank; it broke..... The forward-base telephone worked, but only just ... Buxton, Davies and Thompson soon arrived... the water was fairly clear and their lights could first be seen as a dim flashing under the far wall of Nine-One, soon becoming a continuous illumination. Later their beams became distinguishable, then the lights themselves, then the divers."

Notebook No.41.

"My tripod had not arrived, Coase's Retina II had packed up... with three cameras we took shots across the chamber to the rift at the S end, the mud terrace above Nine-Two... the mud craters near the rift; then back from the S end to The Depot... we estimated lengths and heights and took bearings.... Coase led back to base... and I was the rear-marker.... Slowly we slid to the bottom, hanging on hard to the cable,... I waited as the leading divers had halted. Soon it seemed something was amiss, Buxton was visible now and again but I could not even guess what was going on; I was beginning to get alarmed and tried to calm myself by thinking of the previous occasion when the line moved over but, thanks to Coase, everything ended happily. Buxton moved up into contact. He signalled Two Bells ('Up') so up I went, faster than the following divers which only increased my wait for them at the surface when each second seemed an age. Buxton then Coase arrived. What was the trouble? Coase had got into some bother and had had to abandon his baggage .... Buxton abandoned his in helping Coase .... Coase's problem was too few hands for his job; he needed four. The final mishap seemed to be that he had knocked open his by-pass .... We were back in Nine and the next move was to return under control; if we found the carrying-sacks so much the better but in any case we should return to base. We found no sacks but we returned, getting out of the water at 07:10.

"We had the choice of abandoning the luggage or letting the water clear then going in search. We partially undressed and adjourned for an hour or so .... Breakfast was rather half-hearted .... We formed a plan: swimmers Coase and Davies would fin in, one seeking high the other low .... Bottom-walkers Balcombe and Thompson were to be beacons at The Gateway ..... At 11:15 we went in, swimmers ahead... bottom-walkers stood flashing their lights... Ages seemed to pass, no returning swimmers appeared and, from my viewpoint, it seemed utterly impossible that any swimmer could find his way in that murk when suddenly Coase appeared along the line, stopped between us then hung, upsidedown and motionless, for quite a time... he was only trying to fish his Aflo out of a crack .... I escorted him to base and returned to my post..... The mud was worse .... Where was Davies? We moved down again into Eight, where he might be stranded, flashed our lights a while then returned to our post. I had hardly got through the low arch when to my immense relief I felt a hand grab my ankle... Davies signalled that bag or bags were tied to the line, so he went up and we went down... found one bag but no trace of the cameras... we had failed to interpret Bob Davies's complicated signals which, it transpired, meant cameras taken back to Nine. Neither of us was willing to believe the cameras were further on: presumably we did not wish to face the slope, though why I can now hardly guess for it can be quite delightful .... We decided to return with the one bag and enquire about the other. Thompson took the bag and we progressed with surprising speed as far as the Letter Box... but there we were halted. The stake belay had come adrift and the line led us up that nasty jumble of rocks under the low roof. Thompson gave the emergency signal but moved on; I grabbed the bag as he seemed to be moving well under his own power but I was prepared to drop it if needs be. There was no need; we went out together, slowly and steadily; he made no attempt to exit into Four. It transpired he had carbon-dioxide trouble but was quickly got out of his kit and recovered. Believe it or not the log only records an absence of 40 minutes. Davies and I re-charged our kits; the plan was for Balcombe without Aflo to go ahead, Davies to be rearguard and to wait at the bottom of the mud-slope. I would recover the bag, rejoin him then precede him back to base.

We left, outward bound, at 13:06, slowly and without any hitch; my ears were working to perfection and we soon reached the Nine-One slope where I went easily and delightfully up, unhooked the bag, coiled up the sling and went equally easily and delightfully to the bottom .... The camera-bag was weighted perfectly, just buoyant as the gas from the compensating system bubbled to waste, and it rode with little attention all the way back but with an occasional great roaring of escaping gas on the upslopes. We got out at 13:22 but Davies, it seems, had already begun to get anxious about the delay in Nine; it seemed quite satisfactory progress to me. Thus quarter of an hour can be taken as a standard time for a return trip to Nine.

"The story of Davies's exploit is yet to be told; daring, heroic, foolhardy or whatever it was, there is an epic behind the recovery of those two bags by a swimmer alone in Eight and Nine in water where the visibility must have been next to nil, no guide-line, no help from outside, an intrepid frogman pitting his skill, determination and the reliability of his kit against the grim intricacies and the mud of the route to Nine. After searching high and low in Eight and Nine, he had found the cameras tucked up in a crevice between the two chambers, floating hard against the roof.

"At half-past one we started to clear out of the cave... Devenish's jeep flew to and fro and by three o'clock we were respectable enough to accept a kind invitation from Mrs. Wingco to take luncheon at The Restaurant, despite that the hour was so abnormal. We lunched, enjoyed it, and each received a bill for six shillings! Methinks they are guessing their cave has had its diving chips."

I find it dificult to choose suitable comment to close the record of this operation but I suppose it must be admitted that it did succeed in laying the new line (L8), that it did acquire some meagre low-grade survey information (F2, "Footrule Two") and that some photographs were taken (FT2, Flashlight 2, though only Davies' camera made any worthwhile contribution). My impression was that the title "Disgrace Abounding" had been given to the wrong op.

SWILDON'S HOLE

Discoveries of new passages in Swildon's Hole had sharpened interest in the possibilities beyond The Great Bell. (I had taken a brief look, at the time of the discovery of Swildon's II, at the high-level features beyond Sump I but then thought the passage would not "go", anyway, there were more important things to think about). DS now turned its attentions to a fresh look at the lower end; Sump II must presumably lead to Sump III which would be the next challenge. Davies and I were to be the challengers; just as well that Davies would be Leading Diver for my enthusiasm for the project was not high, it meant work and more work of preparation, for the task of getting the kit down to Sump II in usable condition was more formidable than anything we had hitherto attempted. As usual the time required was badly miscalculated, leaving car servicing and the like to the final mad rush. The op. was in two stages, first, the kit went in.

Undated but after 19-6-54.

"The miscalculation of the time needed to prepare is evident from what goes before," (pages of sketches of fitted carrying boxes, gen on boiler suits, rebuild of Aflo, wire-marking, so on and so on) "resulting in the usual high-pressure panicking before the start.

"Nunwick arrived 08:30, collected car and serviced it. At 10:50 we were off... and arrived there at 15:10-ish. Lloyd's organisation" (Dr. Oliver C. Lloyd, Controller of Operations) "was quite plastic and not upset by our late arrival and, fairly obviously, he and his Sherpas were not yet aware of quite what they had let themselves in for at Dr. Robert E. Davies's request of a stranger; they were not even put out at my apologetic announcement that I had not been able to conform exactly to specification for packages, namely no larger than a rucksack, no heavier than 15 lb, although they would probably meet the bump test requirement. After some measure of planning and some grub, we moved off....

"Trouble soon came; Aflotop" (presumably I had split Aflo into two packages)

"would not go along the top part of the cave by about quarter of an inch but one bright lad took it round the Wet Way, rejoining at Jacob's Ladder. We had fourteen parcels and there were seven of us. I was the old man of the party, Lloyd was perhaps 35-40 (Doctor-medical,- or was he Doctor-scientific? I forget - botanist, lepidopterist) the rest were extremely youthful. The next catch was at the keyhole above the 40-foot pitch but Aflo just went through the upper storey. Lloyd's party were using that lovely new nylon line and karabiner; they are keen and capable. Swildon's looked strange in places; memory is none too reliable. At Sump I, three of us were to go through and FGB was 'privileged' to go first. Warming up at the lower side was enormously helped by 'cuddling up'. The packages came through like clockwork. At the upper side they were handled from the submerged block ('our' block); at the lower side we soon found we could sit in comfort on Aflotop and Sesal," (my breathing kit) "nice smooth boxes, and when wading attention was needed, the middleman, the warmest, was driven into the pool and another took his place, like penguins in a blizzard. Ten or eleven packages came through and we left them on the sandbank. Nunwick did not join us, he was cold and Lloyd discouraged him.

"It was the warmest and most pleasant session ever in Swildon's II, and the most interesting, calm and serene passage of the smooth-bottomed sump. We went on to look at Duck II then up to the mucky sump, a miserable little thing approached over a long bank of amusing mud with the return journey terminating in a grand bear-slide into the main streamway.

"Then back through Sump I, a pause for some chocolate, and back up the long passages to the surface; our little group went up the Wet Way (little to lose, we thought) but it was a mistake, it is not quicker than the usual route and we found the sporting going at the end of that trip to be trying. We came out to the gentle light of the moon hanging low over the trees, and to the smell of hayfields, after about eight hours below.

"We changed in the barn, spent the night at Hillgrove, and arrived back in London about three o'clock of another day of glorious weather.

"NO SWILDON'S III 26-6-54

"... Mavis and I arrived at Taunton about 10:30. I did not stay long and returned to Mendip, passing through Wells as the clocks struck midnight. There were about four people in their bunks; I quietly dumped my kit and crept into my sleeping bag.

"We got up at about nine and the time slipped quickly by as we sorted out our bits and pieces and nattered of the plan of attack. To me the most immediate problem was how much clothing I could pile on as a compromise between being able to get down the cave" (we would be wearing our diving attire) "and not getting too cold underwater.... We slipped into Wells for a quick lunch but got back a few minutes late for Hillgrove Zero but, no matter, the party was not yet complete. About 15 hr we moved on to Priddy to change and at 16:10 started down the cave. The party was quite lightly loaded; Davies's Aflo was the major package, but in diving dress it was heavy going. For me, the tightest bit was the keyhole, I only just made it because of bad footwork in clumsy boots." (Why, I wonder, did I not duck under?)

"At Sump I, I was again pushed through as No.1. This time, in dress and mask the problem would be to sink. Davies said no weighting really necessary but I much preferred a bit of lead and tied it amidships. Davies was probably right for the lead trailed on the deck as a dragline while I floated hard up against the roof and I had to heave quite hard on the line to make any progress. We gathered at The Bend (our diving base), seven all told, and began preparation. All 23 packages had survived the journey splendidly, nothing damaged and nothing vital got wet. The boxes, for example, while having had their waterproof wrappings holed at the corners had only shipped a few drops which were absorbed by the inner wrappings leaving the contents quite dry.

"It was about 19 hours when we arrived and 21:50 when three toots signalled 'divers descending',"

Notebook No.42.

"what time the Tiger Sherpas settled down to reading their science fiction, or to nattering, or just shivering and dozing with the prospect of up to six hours expected (feared, hoped for?) delay, with the alarm set to go off in eight hours time. They had taken through some dry clothes, had a primus going as needed, and they huddled together for warmth.

"The Bend as a base was fair enough but it was a little rough getting thence to the sump with weights and Aflo; we did it in two trips. A benzedrene taken about 19:30 was probably working well for I felt in no way dozy - none of that pre-op. escapist somnalism! We planned to go first into the Big (or

Great) Bell by keeping right, whither the route should be easy. While thus planning, I lolled back on a rock which proved to be Davies's Aflo and I bent it; after all that care in getting it down a diver nearly did it in! The water was very, very muddy and our hopes were (1) a short muddy run to open passages or, (2) if the volume of water increased considerably we could expect it to be clearer or, (3) if the cross section was restricted then maybe we could wait for the mud to clear. Hardly expecting the second or third, we agreed to go not more than 50 feet for a start and subject to the line holding promise of safe return.

Don Coase & Graham Balcombe, Swildon's Hole, 26 June 1954 (Phil Davies).

"In 1936 I had gone straight ahead on entering the sump, about 20 feet to Little Bell, then under the right hand end of it up a muddy squeeze into Great Bell; the rope had pulled over after me and on return it led me straight back through a copious passage to base. The line had been hand-held and presumably about mid-stream at the point where the depth suddenly increases. Hence the proposal to go direct to Big Bell.

Bob went down and I followed closely behind; visibility was nil; Aflo could be seen as just a brown haze, if held not too far away, but disappeared in billowing fog when put down. The line was anchored to a stalactite about 40 feet upstream and lay along the W wall. Instead of breaking straight through to Big Bell, I found myself following the line which ran under a low roof and seemed to double back. Whether the line had pulled over to a narrower place or whether my b.a., which is a bit thicker than Bob's, was holding me or whether it was just cool feet I could not say but, although he was through and I could hear him splashing about, I could not make it. Of this I am sure; I could not get through at the point in question or within reach to the left, without tunnelling through the mud. To the right I feared to let the line run loose lest it should fox us. I was certain there is a righthand way in open stream which would lead us to destination. I lay in the muck a while, pondering on correct action then signalled 'up'. The next I knew was that the line doubled back leaving me on a bight; I slowly moved back and regained the stream passage. I cannot recollect now whether Bob reached base before or after I did .... It appeared that Bob had entered a small chamber with a mudbank above water, tallying roughly with the description of Little Bell, so dived under its right wall and came into a big stream passage, only to find the stream flowing towards him, in fact, from the base....

"Mystified, we had another go and repeated exactly the same performance. He got through but I could not then he went direct to base. Next we tried following the gravel this time we reached Little Bell. It seemed rather larger than my memory of it, (10 x 5 x 8 feet high), so I left identification as uncertain, but we went down under the right wall, direction roughly SW; Little Bell runs NS like the base passage. Bob went through but again I stuck. This time it seemed exactly like the 1936 dive from Little to Big Bell but now I had bulkier apparatus. I moved about an inch at a time while Bob was splashing about at a surface .... I heaved and shoved with bag scraping on the roof; the mud parted as when a yacht touches ground and I sailed up the slope into the chamber. Again it did not quite tally with Big Bell but was similar, if rather smaller than my impression, and again the line pulled straight back to the N end of the chamber, itself a NS rift. This seemed to clinch it. We could expect a clear run back to base in due course. Here again everything was thick mud and, as the water was only three feet deep, we sank down deeply.

"We patrolled the W wall, finding no holes, and passed on to the S end where the way on was even more apparent than in 1936. Only the SE end was not closely examined. At the S end it proved to be a short duck, passed mask on, gas off, to another chamber. I had decided the previous chamber, 30 x 10 x 12 feet high, must be Big Bell; the new one is 25 x 15 x 30 max. height and developed in the NS direction again; we had entered in its E wall near the N end, with little to show where... so we arrowed the route. At the N end and S end were mud banks. I explored the N end but found no way on. Bob got out onto the S bank and marked an arrow to assure the way home. High pockets in the roof were blind. Everywhere was thick mud again, except from NE to W wall, where pebbles and gravel were mixed with it - the stream bed again? I cannot clearly recollect anything of the bottom at the duck; I do not remember mud there.

"The W wall contains an alcove and the gravel-mud leads in its general direction. I followed round from the S bank to the alcove and found a smallish gap below the wall, continuing all the way. Leading Diver went down and was forced from N end towards the S by the rock wall." (I now find this last sentence quite unintelligible.) "He thinks he got in about 25 feet and there was no way on big enough to pass, the direction was generally SW. Nothing was actually measured; meters could not be seen let alone read, just general impressions and guesswork. I tried and reached about 15 feet on the same basis then I was not too displeased to feel that, for a change, it was Bob who gave me the two pulls. That was the end. We slowly made our way back, leaving the line belayed at the entrance to the new chamber. The way back was not, repeat was not, the expected easy open passage. It was low and unpleasant, but it led back nevertheless..... On return to the sump, we lolled in the water and discussed results then toured the E wall to Little Bell and confirmed no way out exists there. Checking over what we had done, we decided that beyond reasonable doubt we had followed round the whole sump and no way on existed other than the impassable hole in the far chamber and we concluded (erroneously, as it was later to be proved) that no purpose would be served by further diving either now on our part, or by any future diving party. So we gave two toots on the horn, which passed unheard, and staggered back to the dressing base after not the worst dive ever but a dive in the worst conditions ever (for me, that is), for Sump II is an evil place. Did I have to name the op., I think Operation Elsan would be fitting.....

"Then came the reporting, the soup and miscellaneous fodder, glucose, biscuits and some cheese, Cheddar, much prized by Lloyd, but to my taste not impressive. His eulogies made me think of that magnificent piece of Lancashire we once happed upon in Preston, or even the Cheshire in the dish at home, so I was disappointed. Then the dismantling and re-packing took a mighty time but at last we were on the move.... By 05:30 all the party was through Sump I, my lead was left to assist any future party and to relieve our own.... A gas cylinder had also been abandoned.... We each took one package... as it happened (perhaps that was just me) I chose a rather weighty one and made rather heavy weather of the journey but was relieved betimes by Struan Robertson who was a veritable tiger and many a time caused me to reflect on my passing years.... Nine o'clock it was when we got out... We later called on old Balch to tell him the outcome. He had no idea where we had been and was more concerned to think that Mason was seemingly claiming credit for starting diving in Mendip, that Professor Palmer would be making changes in The Museum and so on, than in our news which did not quite register with him. Ah well, 85 is a good old age.... A tackle party went down to recover left-overs and ladders while we breakfasted and had a snooze... the last of the baggage was out at about four o'clock - stout fellows! It was Aflotop that had given most trouble, especially just above the 40-foot, where letting it down was one thing, getting it up quite another.... "

The rest was routine surface-stuff: tea at the hut, then to Taunton arriving about nine, calling on sister Jessie and her bloke, eating again then off to my parents' place at Buckland St.Mary, where the old man was still up and glad to see us, and so to roost. Next day the kit dried a bit before a trip to Wells Cathedral. On the Tuesday we packed up and got away, reaching home at five.

"OPERATION AVERNUS

Operation Avernus by DS on 25-9-54 was an attempt to penetrate further into the flooded parts of Clapham Cave, from Giant's Hall and beyond Leakey's Chamber. It was of no great significance however.

Another op. was Buxton's Choice at Wookey Hole. Its purpose was to introduce O.C.Wells to the diving there; Wells was to be one of the mixture-men in due course.

Notebook No.43.

"OPERATION BUXTON'S CHOICE   1-10-55

"... I travelled down with Nunwick; the journey was very cautious and steady for, as Nunwick explained, it was his own car.... At Wookey there was quite a crowd of divers, helpers and maybe others, for it was an 'open meet'. Coase, a daddy of a few days' standing, came to look for a moment; he had been threatened with the job of nappy-washing and was rushing out to buy a washing-machine. Reports have it these machines are also useful for doing caving togs, but the emptying-pipe clogs rather easily.... Wingco was away but Olive and her two new and noisy Alsatians were ready to cope.... We laid about the kit and were ready for transport a mere quarter hour after the Program Zero of six o'clock.... Luke Devenish was diving and, after being inserted into his dress, he was totally incapable of getting into the driving seat of his van so Controller Hasell did the driving... For once, I was first ready for the water.... First

Wookey Muddle, …, Swansong

trip, I took Wells and Buxton on a brief trip to Four and Five.... Second trip, with same divers was a bit of line clearance in Five. ....Third trip, same divers, was sightseeing in Five.... On the next trip, to Six and near Seven, Buxton sprang a dress leak and had to withdraw.... Meantime Devenish had been splashing around on a rope in Three.... Then gas checks and Wells did his second trip to Seven in preparation for a trip to Nine.... The formal purpose of the op. having been achieved, we packed up in time for a pint at The Inn. For myself, I found various deficiencies calling for attention; leaking bag-valve, need for better ear venting, need for audible signalling, etcetera. No electrifying advances but Buxton and Wells were to make big contributions to the CDG's future.

THE CAVE DIVING GROUP

A meeting of CDG members was held on 17-10-55, under the auspices of The Derbyshire Section, to liquidate the old CDG and give birth to a new. The CDG was to be re-organised as a normal club with President, Chairman, Secretaries and Committee Members. This ratified the de facto drift that had been occurring as the old "headquarters" lost the keen edge of interest and the Sections, especially the highly successful Derbyshire Section, had become increasingly autonomous.

Now The Cave Diving Group has truly come of age.

"OPERATION SWANSONG 29-6-57

"A job at Somerton Radio Station offered a good opportunity to... join The Wookey Hole Divers in their cave.... On the Saturday I arrived at Wookey Hole at 17:00... and the nattering began. In the cave by 19:00? Don't be so silly, that is merely what the op. orders stated! Eventually we did get in, Buxton, Davies and I as divers with a helper or two. First, patrol One to Three for The Archeos. Rather uncomfortable trip, ear trouble attributed to poor equalisation, bad face-mask leakage and poor visibility. No bones found. After a long delay in Three we made off to Nine, Buxton's first Nine-trip. For me it was a pretty miserable trip and for the reasons as above. The relief was that the mudhole in Eight was clear and the view from the Nine mudslope belay was especially good. One of the tasks was to drop algae-traps (bricks with bits of D3 wire attached; the outer covering of the Army D3 is a waxed braiding and the algae of the region seem to love it). Davies placed his in Six... I was to place mine in the Bear Pit, below Nine-One, but the place was so steep it seemed quite impracticable, probably because of mask and general discomforture rather than real difficulty, and I was glad to heave it up into Nine.

"Davies was not bubbling with enthusiasm; it seems he is a variable diver and this could hardly have been an encouraging trip so, after about half-an-hour doing nothing much, we followed the indefatiguable Buxton back to base, not sorry to get back and call it a day.

"On Sunday it took more or less all day to pack up, hand in my kit, and natter, feed and natter again. For this was my last dive; my fiftieth birthday had passed a little while ago and I could not go any longer at the prodigious pace of the younger men; I was a handicap to them. When I look around and note the magnificent achievements of cave-divers and, in particular, of The Cave Diving Group, I shall be ever proud to have been in from the beginning with such splendid companions.

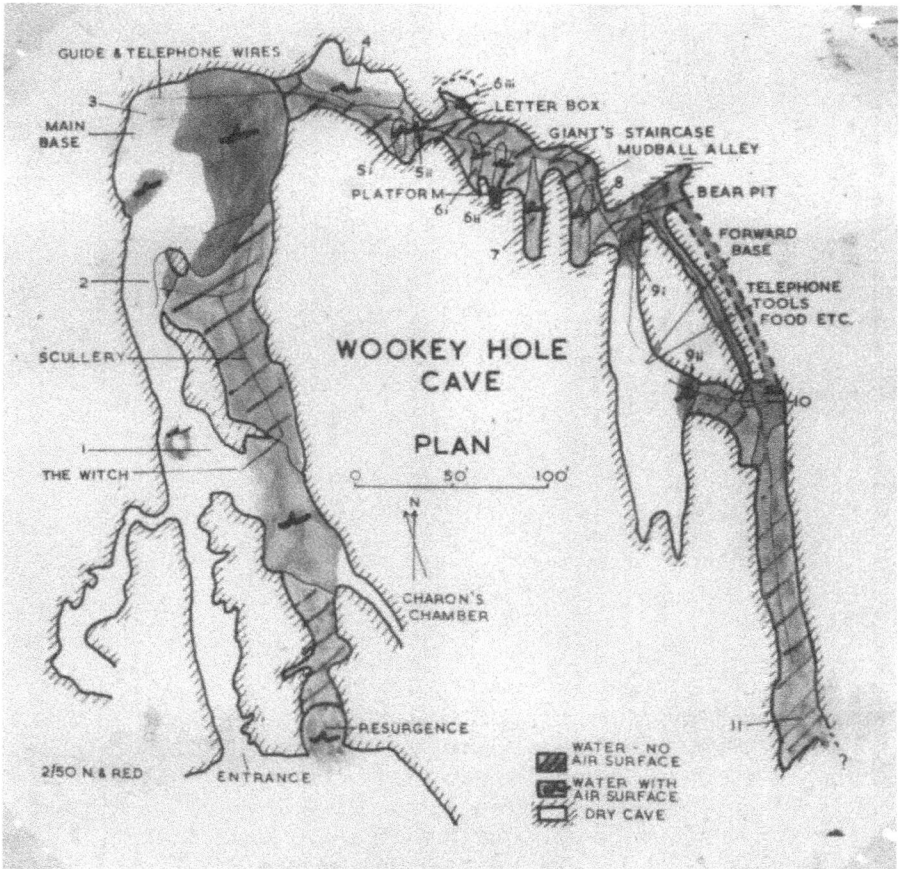

WOOKEY HOLE
CAVE

PLAN

Plan of Wookey Hole Cave, February 1950 (Bob Davies).

Postscript[5]

Maire Trendell (née Urwin), Phil Collett, Bob Cork, Jack Sheppard, Dany Bradshaw, Rob Parker, Dan Hasell, Julian Walker, Ian Rolland, Graham Balcombe, James Cobbett, Rob Palmer, John Parker, Dave Morris, Brian Woodward, Trevor Hughes, Dave Savage, Tim Reynolds, Phil Davies, Mike Wooding, Ken Dawe, Pete Eckford & Steve Wynne Roberts, Wookey Hole, 4 October 1985 (Chris Howes).

It was the Dive 99 show at the NEC. I was sitting with Graham on the Historical Diving Society stand. It was his day and he loved every moment. Nearby a video of the Wookey Hole Divers 50th Anniversary was playing in a continuous loop. Rob Palmer was providing a commentary whilst Rob Parker, amongst others, paraded old bits of equipment; quite literally ghosts in the machine.

---

[5] reproduced from CDG Newsletter 136:2 (July 2000)

During a quiet interlude, a young woman watched the video in fascination; she glanced at Graham then returned her attention to the screen. Slowly comprehension transformed her face. She turned then gave Graham a warm smile of recognition. Graham's charm didn't falter as he took the young woman's hand and kissed it.

After we sat, without words, each with his own thoughts. There was something about her that prompted a stream of consciousness, fragments of memory running through the mind's eye like an old film.

Perhaps we were both back at the Mineries Pool, different epochs, different lovers but the cave divers radio was on an open channel when he said, "She wanted me to marry her...I was too ambitious". He was referring to Mossy. I considered an answer. I considered the man a passionate atheist who had embraced communism to fill the spiritual void after he had rejected his strict catholic education and upbringing. The only remnant was the guilt and it's dogged pursuit.

Graham's eyes would light up when he talked of Jack Sheppard. "I showed him what was on the other side of The Wall". Then remorse when he found he couldn't go through the service after agreeing to be Jack's best man. Emotion following emotion like cloud shadows on the landscape of a bright day.

He spoke of how, after Marriott's death, the pleasure of the diving ebbed away. That in some way he felt responsible but equally he knew such feelings were irrational.

There were brighter moments, when after a visit to Siebe Gorman he declared, "That mucky little pool at the bottom of Swildons Hole was on hold!"

We talked of many things that afternoon but the thing that stood out the most was that at the he wanted no mourners, apart from not being able to cope with the "mumbo jumbo", there was the other part of him. The fact that some of those who would follow on would have neither grave - nor any mourners; how in all conscience could he?

He peered about him. "So much I could not of dreamt".

He looked at me. "Would it have been different?"

"No" I answered, "Kings have abdicated for less."

His epitaph is that he helped to create a Group that will outlive his beliefs and that he lived to see that which he loved so much was to be so successful.

Mike "Fish" Jeanmaire, CDG Chairman (1987-2007).

Index

www.ingramcontent.com/pod-product-compliance
Lightning Source LLC
Chambersburg PA
CBHW030915090426
42737CB00007B/203